Workshop on Humans and Computer-Assisted Translation

(HaCaT 2014)

Held at the 14th Conference of the European Chapter of the Association for Computational Linguistics

Gothenburg, Sweden
26 April 2014

ISBN: 978-1-63266-398-6

Printed from e-media with permission by:

Curran Associates, Inc.
57 Morehouse Lane
Red Hook, NY 12571

CURRAN ASSOCIATES INC.
proceedings
.com

Some format issues inherent in the e-media version may also appear in this print version.

Printed by Curran Associates, Inc. (2014)

For permission requests, please contact the Association for Computational Linguistics
at the address below.

Association for Computational Linguistics
209 N. Eighth Street
Stroudsburg, Pennsylvania 18360

Phone: 1-570-476-8006
Fax: 1-570-476-0860

acl@aclweb.org

Additional copies of this publication are available from:

Curran Associates, Inc.
57 Morehouse Lane
Red Hook, NY 12571 USA
Phone: 845-758-0400
Fax: 845-758-2634
Email: curran@proceedings.com
Web: www.proceedings.com

Introduction

The quality of automatic translation of human languages has improved tremendously over the past decade or so. While they still do not achieve publication-quality performance in most cases, state-of-the-art machine translation systems can now deliver a level of quality that make the post-editing of raw machine output by human translators a viable and cost-effective alternative to translation from scratch. Moreover, computerized workflow management can improve consistency in translation, in particular with respect to terminology, and can give translators easy access to dictionaries, glossaries and databases of past translations.

Much research in the machine translation community in the past has focused on improving fully automatic MT, but interest in integrating information technology — and specifically machine translation technology — into the translator's workflow is growing in many areas of research: in machine translation research as to how best to provide useful information to the human translator, in translation tool development as to how to make the best use of this information, and in translation process studies in understanding the cognitive and physical processes that take place when humans post-edit or interact with computer-produced translations.

This workshop brings together researchers investigating issues in human-computer interaction in the context of translation from a variety of research angles. We have been able to assemble a wonderful roster of talks, posters and system demonstrations that nicely illustrate the current state of research, and we look forward to a productive day of learning and fruitful discussions.

Enjoy!

Ulrich Germann
Michael Carl
Philipp Koehn
Germán Sanchis-Trilles
Francisco Casacuberta
Robin Hill
Sharon O'Brien

Workshop Organisers

Ulrich Germann, University of Edinburgh (UK)
Michael Carl, Copenhagen Business School (Denmark)
Philipp Koehn, Johns Hopkins University (USA)
Germán Sanchis-Trilles, Universitat Politècnica de València (Spain)
Francisco Casacuberta, Universitat Politècnica de València (Spain)
Robin Hill, University of Edinburgh (UK)
Sharon O'Brien, Dublin City University (Ireland)

Programme Committee

Fabio Alves
Srinivas Bangalore
Nicola Bertoldi
Pierrette Bouillon
Christian Buck
Michael Carl
Francisco Casacuberta
George Foster
Robert Frederking
Johanna Gerlach
Ulrich Germann
Barry Haddow
Robin Hill
Fred Hollowood
Pierre Isabelle
Philipp Koehn
Roland Kuhn
Philippe Langlais
Guy Lapalme
Pascual Martínes-Gómez
Cettolo Mauro
Bertolomé Mesa-Lao
Matteo Negri
Sharon O'Brien
Manny Rayner
Germán Sanchis-Trilles
Violeta Seretan
Christophe Servan
Michel Simard
Lucia Specia
Sara Stymne
Marco Turchi
Bonnie Webber

This workshop was supported by the European Union 7th Framework Programme (FP7/2007-2013) under the CASMACAT project (grant agreement N° 287576).

Table of Contents

Conference Program

Saturday, 26 April 2014

8:50–9:00	Opening Remarks
	Session 1: Oral Presentations
9:00–9:30	*Word Confidence Estimation for SMT N-best List Re-ranking* Ngoc Quang Luong, Laurent Besacier and Benjamin Lecouteux
9:30–9:50	*Proofreading Human Translations with an E-pen* Vicent Alabau and Luis A. Leiva
9:50–10:10	*Estimating Grammar Correctness for a Priori Estimation of Machine Translation Post-Editing Effort* Nicholas H. Kirk, Guchun Zhang and Georg Groh
10:10–10:30	*On-The-Fly Translator Assistant (Readability and Terminology Handling)* Svetlana Sheremetyeva
10:30-11:00	Coffee Break
	Invited Talk
11:00–12:00	*Translators in the Loop: Understanding How they Work with CAT Tools* Maureen Ehrensberger-Dow
12:-13:30	Lunch Break
	Session 2: Oral Presentations
13:30–14:00	*Measuring the Cognitive Effort of Literal Translation Processes* Moritz Schaeffer and Michael Carl
14:00–14:30	*The Impact of Machine Translation Quality on Human Post-Editing* Philipp Koehn and Ulrich Germann
14:30–15:00	*Beyond Linguistic Equivalence. An Empirical Study of Translation Evaluation in a Translation Learner Corpus* Mihaela Vela, Anne-Kathrin Schumann and Andrea Wurm
15:00–15:30	*Black-box integration of heterogeneous bilingual resources into an interactive translation system* Juan Antonio Pérez-Ortiz, Daniel Torregrosa and Mikel Forcada
15:30-16:00	Coffee Break

Saturday, 26 April 2014 (continued)

System Demos

16:00-18:00 *The ACCEPT Portal: An Online Framework for the Pre-editing and Post-editing of User-Generated Content*
Violeta Seretan, Johann Roturier, David Silva and Pierrette Bouillon

16:00-18:00 *Real Time Adaptive Machine Translation for Post-Editing with cdec and TransCenter*
Michael Denkowski, Alon Lavie, Isabel Lacruz and Chris Dyer

Poster Session

16:00-18:00 *Confidence-based Active Learning Methods for Machine Translation*
Varvara Logacheva and Lucia Specia

16:00-18:00 *Online Word Alignment for Online Adaptive Machine Translation*
M. Amin Farajian, Nicola Bertoldi and Marcello Federico

16:00-18:00 *Quantifying the Influence of MT Output in the Translators' Performance: A Case Study in Technical Translation*
Marcos Zampieri and Mihaela Vela

16:00-18:00 *Speech-Enabled Computer-Aided Translation: A Satisfaction Survey with Post-Editor Trainees*
Bartolomé Mesa-Lao

Word Confidence Estimation for SMT *N*-best List Re-ranking

Ngoc-Quang Luong **Laurent Besacier** **Benjamin Lecouteux**
LIG, Campus de Grenoble
41, Rue des Mathématiques,
UJF - BP53, F-38041 Grenoble Cedex 9, France
{ngoc-quang.luong,laurent.besacier,benjamin.lecouteux}@imag.fr

Abstract

This paper proposes to use Word Confidence Estimation (WCE) information to improve MT outputs via *N*-best list reranking. From the confidence label assigned for each word in the MT hypothesis, we add six scores to the baseline log-linear model in order to re-rank the *N*-best list. Firstly, the correlation between the WCE-based sentence-level scores and the conventional evaluation scores (BLEU, TER, TERp-A) is investigated. Then, the *N*-best list re-ranking is evaluated over different WCE system performance levels: from our real and efficient WCE system (ranked 1st during last WMT 2013 *Quality Estimation* Task) to an oracle WCE (which simulates an interactive scenario where a user simply validates words of a MT hypothesis and the new output will be automatically re-generated). The results suggest that our real WCE system slightly (but significantly) improves the baseline while the oracle one extremely boosts it; and better WCE leads to better MT quality.

1 Introduction

A number of methods to improve MT hypotheses after decoding have been proposed in the past, such as: post-editing, re-ranking or re-decoding. Post-editing (Parton et al., 2012) is a human-inspired task where the machine post edits translations in a second automatic pass. In re-ranking (Zhang et al., 2006; Duh and Kirchhoff, 2008; Bach et al., 2011), more features are used along with the multiple model scores for re-determining the 1-best among *N*-best list. Meanwhile, re-decoding process (Venugopal et al., 2007) intervenes directly into the decoder's search graph (e.g. adds more reward or penalty scores), driving it to another better path.

This work aims at re-ranking the *N*-best list to improve MT quality. Generally, during the translation task, the decoder traverses through paths in its search space, computes the objective function values for them and outputs the one with highest score as the best hypothesis. Besides, those with lower scores can also be generated in a so-called *N*-best list. The decoder's function consists of parameters from different models, such as translation, distortion, word penalties, reordering, language models, etc. In the *N*-best list, although the current 1-best beats the remains in terms of model score, it might not be exactly the closest to the human reference. Therefore, adding more decoder independent features would be expected to raise up a better candidate. In this work, we build six additional features based on the labels predicted by our Word Confidence Estimation (WCE) system, then integrate them with the existing decoder scores for re-ranking hypotheses in the *N*-best list. More precisely, ***in the second pass***, our reranker aggregates over decoder and WCE-based weighted scores and utilizes the obtained sum to sort out the best candidate. The novelty of this paper lies on the following contributions: the correlation between WCE-based sentence-level scores and conventional evaluation scores (BLEU, TER, TERp-A) is first investigated. Then, we conduct the *N*-best list re-ranking over different WCE system performance levels: starting by a real WCE, passing through several gradually improved (simulated) systems and finally the "oracle" one. From these in-depth experiments, the role of WCE in improving MT quality via re-ranking *N*-best list is confirmed and reinforced.

The remaining parts of this article are organized as follows: in section 2 we summarize some outstanding approaches in *N*-best list re-ranking as well as in WCE. Section 3 describes our WCE system construction, followed by proposed features.

The experiments along with results and in-depth analysis of WCE scores' contribution (as WCE system gets better) are presented in Section 4 and Section 5. The last section concludes the paper and points out some ongoing work.

2 Related Work

2.1 *N*-best List Re-ranking

Walking through various related work concerning this issue, we observe some prominent ideas. The first attempt focuses on proposing additional Language Models. Kirchhoff and Yang (2005) train one word-based 4-gram model (with modified Kneser-Ney smoothing) and one factored trigram one, then combine them with seven decoder scores for re-ranking *N*-best lists of several SMT systems. Their proposed LMs increase the translation quality of the baselines (measured by BLEU score) from 21.6 to 22.0 (Finnish - English), or from 30.5 to 31.0 (Spanish - English). Meanwhile, Zhang et al. (2006) experiment a distributed LM where each server, among the total of 150, hosts a portion of the data and responses its client, allowing them to exploit an extremely large corpus (2.7 billion word English Gigaword) for estimating N-gram probability. The quality of their Chinese - English hypotheses after the re-scoring process by using this LM is improved 4.8% (from BLEU 31.44 to 32.64, oracle score = 37.48).
In one other direction, several authors propose to replace the current linear scoring function used by the decoder by more efficient functions. Sokolov et al. (2012) learn their non-linear scoring function in a learning-to-rank paradigm, applying Boosting algorithm. Their gains on the WMT'{10, 11, 12} are shown modest yet consistent and higher than those based on linear scoring functions. Duh and Kirchhoff (2008) use Minimum Error Rate Training (MERT) (Och, 2003) as a weak learner and build their own solution, BoostedMERT, a highly-expressive re-ranker created by voting among multiple MERT ones. Their proposed model dramatically beats the decoder's log-linear model (43.7 vs. 42.0 BLEU) in IWSLT 2007 Arabic - English task. Applying solely *goodness* (the sentence confidence) scores, Bach et al. (2011) obtain very consistent TER reductions (0.7 and 0.6 on the dev and test set) after a 5-list re-ranking for their Arabic - English SMT hypotheses. This latter work is the one that is the most related to our paper. However, the major differences are: (1) our proposed sentence scores *are computed based on word confidence labels*; and (2) we perform an in-depth study of the use of WCE for N-best reranking and assess its usefulness in a simulated interactive scenario.

2.2 Word Confidence Estimation

Confidence Estimation (CE) is the task of identifying the correct parts and detecting the translation errors in MT output. If the error is predicted for each word, this becomes WCE. The interesting uses of WCE include: pointing out the words that need to be corrected by the post-editor, telling readers about the reliability of a specific portion, and selecting the best segments among options from multiple translation systems for combination.
Dealing with this problem, various approaches have been proposed: Blatz et al. (2003) combine several features using neural network and naive Bayes learning algorithms. One of the most effective feature combinations is the Word Posterior Probability (WPP) as suggested by Ueffing et al. (2003) associated with IBM-model based features (Blatz et al., 2004). Ueffing and Ney (2005) propose an approach for phrase-based translation models: a phrase is a sequence of contiguous words and is extracted from the word-aligned bilingual training corpus. The confidence value of each word is then computed by summing over all phrase pairs in which the target part contains this word. Xiong et al. (2010) integrate target word's Part-Of-Speech (POS) and train them by Maximum Entropy Model, allowing significative gains in comparison to WPP features. The novel features from source side, alignment context, and dependency structure (Bach et al., 2011) help to augment marginally in F-score as well as the Pearson correlation with human judgment. Other approaches are based on external features (Soricut and Echihabi, 2010; Felice and Specia, 2012) allowing to cope with various MT systems (e.g. statistical, rule based etc.). Among the numerous WCE applications, we consider its contribution in a specific step of SMT pipeline: *N*-best list re-ranking. Our WCE system and the proposed re-ranking features are presented in the next section.

3 Our Approach

Our approach can be expressed in three steps: investigate the potential of using word-level score in *N*-best list re-ranking, build the WCE system and extract additional features to integrate with the existing log-linear model.

3.1 Investigating the correlation between "word quality" scores and other metrics

Firstly, we investigate the correlation between sentence-level scores (obtained from WCE labels) and conventional evaluation scores (BLEU (Papineni et al., 2002), TER and TERp-A (Snover et al., 2008)). For each sentence, a word quality score (WQS) is calculated by:

$$WQS = \frac{\#''G''(good)\ words}{\#words} \quad (1)$$

In other words, we are trying to answer the following question: can the high percentage of *"G"* (good) words (predicted by WCE system) in a MT output ensure its possibility of having a better BLEU and low TER (TERp-A) value ? This investigation is a strong prerequisite for further experiments in order to check that WCE scores do not bring additional "noise" to the re-ranking process. In this experiment, we compute WQS over our entire French - English data set (total of 10,881 1-best translations) for which WCE **oracle labels** are available (see Section 3.2 to see how they were obtained). The results are plotted in Figure 1, where the *y* axis shows the *"G"* (good) word percentage, and the *x* axis shows BLEU (1a), TER (1b) or TERp-A (1c) scores. It can be seen from Figure 1 that the major parts of points (the densest areas) in all three cases conform the common tendency: In Figure 1a, the higher "G" percentage, the higher BLEU is; on the contrary, in Figure 1b (Figure 1c), the higher "G" percentage, the lower TER (TERp-A) is. We notice some outliers, i.e. sentences with most or almost words labeled "good", yet still have low BLEU or high TER (TERp-A) scores. This phenomenon is to be expected when many (unknown) source words are not translated or when the (unique) reference is simply too far from the hypothesis. Nevertheless, the information extracted from oracle WCE labels seems useful to build an efficient re-ranker.

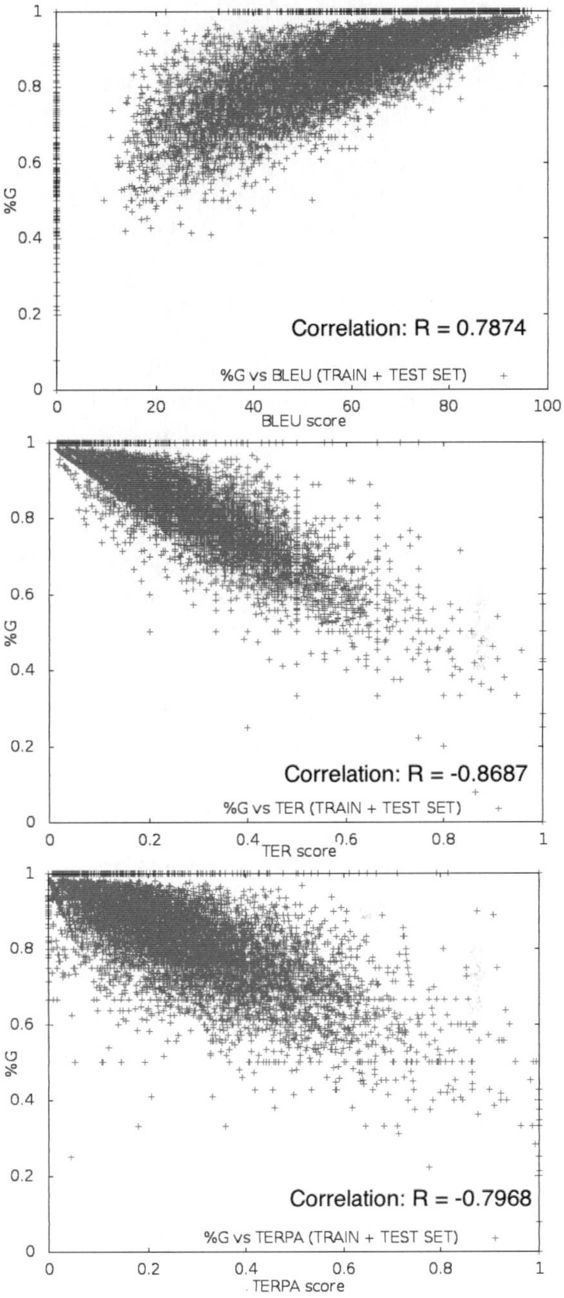

Figure 1: The correlation between WQS in a sentence and its overall quality measured by : (a) BLEU, (b) TER and (c) TERp-A metrics

3.2 WCE System Preparation

Essentially, a WCE system construction consists of two pivotal elements: the features (the SMT system dependent or independent information extracted for each word to represent its characteristics) and the machine learning method (to train the prediction model). Motivated by the idea of addressing WCE problem as a sequence labeling process, we employ the Conditional Random Fields (CRFs) for our model training, with WAPITI toolkit (Lavergne et al., 2010). Basically, CRF computes the probability of the output sequence $Y = (y_1, y_2, ..., y_N)$ given the input sequence $X = (x_1, x_2, ..., x_N)$ by:

$$p_\theta(Y|X) = \frac{1}{Z_\theta(X)} exp\left\{\sum_{k=1}^{K} \theta_k F_k(X,Y)\right\} \quad (2)$$

where $F_k(X,Y) = \sum_{t=1}^{T} f_k(y_{t-1}, y_t, x_t)$; $\{f_k\}$ $(k = \overline{1,K})$ is a set of feature functions; $\{\theta_k\}$ $(k = \overline{1,K})$ are the associated parameter values; and $Z_\theta(x)$ is the normalization function.

In terms of features, a number of knowledge sources are employed for extracting them, resulting in the major types listed below. We briefly summarize them in this work, further details about total of 25 features can be referred in (Luong et al., 2013a).

- Target Side: target word; bigram (trigram) backward sequences; number of occurrences
- Source Side: source word(s) aligned to the target word
- Alignment Context: the combinations of the target (source) word and all aligned source (target) words in the window ± 2
- Word posterior probability
- Pseudo-reference (Google Translate): whether the current word appears in the pseudo reference or not[1]?
- Graph topology: number of alternative paths in the confusion set, maximum and minimum values of posterior probability distribution
- Language model (LM) based: length of the longest sequence of the current word and its previous ones in the target (resp. source) LM. For example, with the target word w_i: if the sequence $w_{i-2}w_{i-1}w_i$ appears in the target LM but the sequence $w_{i-3}w_{i-2}w_{i-1}w_i$ does not, the n-gram value for w_i will be 3.
- Lexical Features: word's Part-Of-Speech (POS); sequence of POS of all its aligned source words; POS bigram (trigram) backward sequences; punctuation; proper name; numerical
- Syntactic Features: Null link; constituent label; depth in the constituent tree
- Semantic Features: number of word senses in WordNet.

Interestingly, this feature set was also used in our English - Spanish WCE system which got the first rank in WMT 2013 Quality Estimation Shared Task (Luong et al., 2013b).

For building the WCE training and test sets, we use a dataset of 10,881 French sentences (Potet et al., 2012) , and apply a baseline SMT system to generate hypotheses (1000-best list). Our baseline SMT system (presented for WMT 2010 evaluation) keeps the Moses's default setting (Koehn et al., 2007): log-linear model with 14 weighted feature functions. The translation model is trained on the Europarl and News parallel corpora of WMT10[2] evaluation campaign (1,638,440 sentences). The target language model is trained by the SRI language modeling toolkit (Stolcke, 2002) on the news monolingual corpus (48,653,884 sentences).

Translators were then invited to correct MT outputs, giving us the same amount of post editions (Potet et al., 2012). The set of triples (source, hypothesis, post edition) is then divided into the training set (10000 first triples) and test set (881 remaining). To train the WCE model, we extract all above features for words of the **1-best hypotheses** of the training set. For the test set, the features are built **for all 1000 best translations** of each source sentence. Another essential element is the word's confidence labels (or so-called WCE oracle labels) used to train the prediction model as well as to judge the WCE results. They are set by using TERp-A toolkit (Snover et al., 2008) in one of the following classes: "I' (insertions), "S" (substitutions), "T" (stem matches), "Y" (synonym matches), "P" (phrasal substitutions), "E" (exact matches) and then simplified into binary class: *"G"* (good word) or *"B"* (bad word) (Luong et al., 2013a).

Once having the prediction model built with all features, we apply it on the test set (881 x 1000 best = 881000 sentences) and get needed WCE labels. Figure 2 shows an example about the classification results for one sentence. Comparing with the reference labels, we can point out easily the correct classifications for *"G"* words (e.g. in case of *operation*, *added*) and for *"B"* words (e.g. *is*, *have*), as well as classification errors (e.g. *a*, *combat*). According to the Precision (Pr), Recall (Rc) and F-score (F) shown in Table 1, our WCE system reaches very promising performance in predicting *"G"* label, and acceptable for *"B"* label. These labels will be used to calculate our proposed

[1]This is our first-time experimented feature and does not appear in (Luong et al., 2013a)

[2]http://www.statmt.org/wmt10/

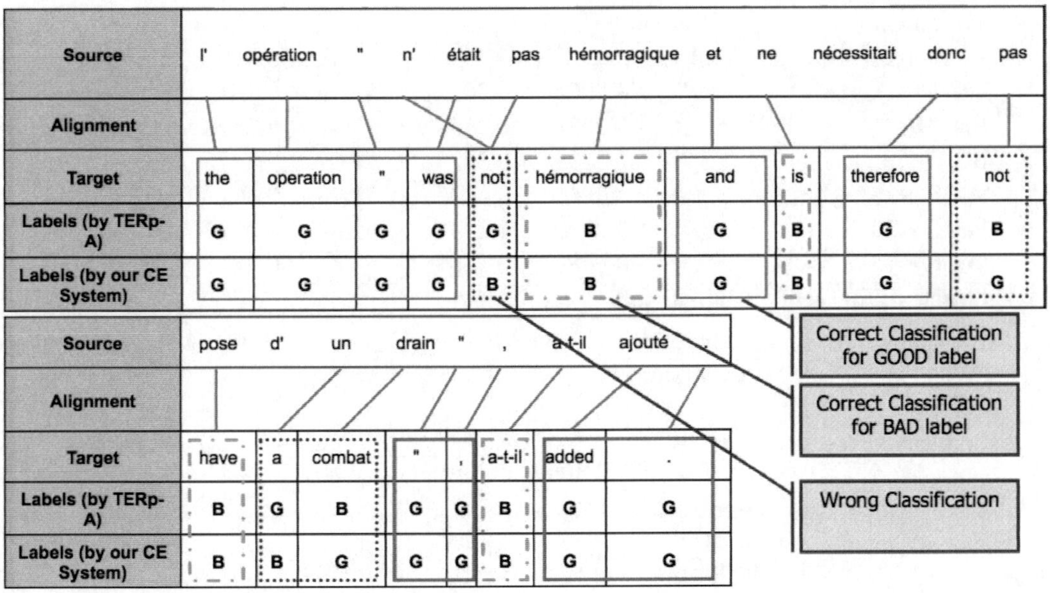

Figure 2: Example of our WCE classification results for one MT hypothesis

features (section 3.3).

Label	Pr(%)	Rc(%)	F(%)
Good (G)	84.36	91.22	**87.65**
Bad (B)	51.34	35.95	**42.29**

Table 1: Pr, Rc and F for "G" and "B" labels of our WCE system

3.3 Proposed Features

Since the scores resulted from the WCE system are for words, we have to synthesize them in sentence level scores for integrating with the 14 decoder scores. Six proposed scores involve:

- The ratio of number of good words to total number of words. (1 score)
- The ratio of number of good nouns (verbs) to total number of nouns (verbs)[3]. (2 scores)
- The ratio of number of n consecutive good word sequences to the total number of consecutive word sequences ; n=2, n=3 and n=4. (3 scores)

For instance, in case of the hypothesis in Figure 2: among the total of 18 words, we have 12 labeled as *"G"*; and 7 out of 17 word pairs (bigram) are labeled as *"GG"*, etc. Hence, some of the above scores can be written as:

$$\begin{aligned} \frac{\#good\ words}{\#words} &= \frac{12}{18} = 0.667 \\ \frac{\#good\ bigrams}{\#bigrams} &= \frac{7}{17} = 0.4118 \\ \frac{\#good\ trigrams}{\#trigrams} &= \frac{3}{16} = 0.1875 \end{aligned} \quad (3)$$

With the features simply derived from WCE labels and not from CRF model scores (i.e. the probability $p(G)$, $p(B)$) , we expect to spread out the evaluation up to the "oracle" setting, where the users validate a word as "G" or "B" without providing any confidence score.

4 Experiments

4.1 Experimental Settings

As described in Section 3.2, our SMT system generates 1000-best list for each source sentence, and among them, the best hypothesis was determined by using the objective function based on 14 decoder scores, including: 7 reordering scores, 1 language model score, 5 translation model scores and 1 word penalty score. Initially, all six additional WCE-based scores are weighted as 1.0. Then, two optimization methods: MERT and Margin Infused Relaxed Algorithm (MIRA) (Watanabe et al., 2007) are applied to optimize the weights of all 20 scores of the re-ranker. In both methods, we carry out a **2-fold cross validation** on the N-best

[3] We decide not to experiment with adjectives, adverbs and conjunctions since their number can be 0 in many cases.

Systems	MERT			MIRA		
	BLEU	**TER**	**TERp-A**	**BLEU**	**TER**	**TERp-A**
BL	52.31	0.2905	0.3058	50.69	0.3087	0.3036
BL+OR	**58.10**	**0.2551**	**0.2544**	**55.41**	**0.2778**	**0.2682**
BL+WCE	52.77	0.2891	0.3025	51.01	0.3055	0.3012
WCE + 25%	53.45	0.2866	0.2903	51.33	0.3010	0.2987
WCE + 50%	55.77	0.2730	0.2745	53.63	0.2933	0.2903
WCE + 75%	56.40	0.2687	0.2669	54.35	0.2848	0.2822
Oracle BLEU score	**BLEU=60.48**					

Table 2: Translation quality of the baseline system (only decoder scores) and that with additional scores from real "WCE" or "oracle" WCE system

System	MERT		
	Better	Equivalent	Worse
BL+WCE	159	601	121
BL+OR	**517**	261	153
WCE+25%	253	436	192
WCE+50%	320	449	112
WCE+75%	461	243	177

Table 3: Quality comparison (measured by TER) between the baseline and two integrated systems in details (How many sentences are improved, kept equivalent or degraded, out of 881 test sentences?

test set. In other words, we split our *N*-best test set into two equivalent subsets: S1 and S2. Playing the role of a development set, S1 will be used to optimize the 20 weights for re-ranking S2 (and vice versa). Finally two result subsets (new 1-best after re-ranking process) are merged for evaluation. To better acknowledge the impact of the proposed scores, we calculate them not only using our real WCE system, but also using an oracle WCE (further called "WCE scores" and "oracle scores", respectively). To summarize, we experiment with the three following systems:

- **BL**: Baseline SMT system with 14 above decoder scores
- **BL+WCE**: Baseline + 6 real WCE scores
- **BL+OR**: Baseline + 6 oracle WCE scores (simulating an interactive scenario).

4.2 Results and Analysis

The translation quality of **BL**, **BL+WCE** and **BL+OR**, optimized by MERT and MIRA method are reported in Table 2. Meanwhile, Table 3 depicts in details the number of sentences in the two integrated systems which outperform, remain equivalent or degrade the baseline hypothesis (when match against the references, measured by TER). It can be observed from Table 2 that the integration of **oracle scores** significantly boosts the MT output quality, measured by all three metrics and optimized by both methods employed. We gained 5.79 and 4.72 points in BLEU score, by MERT and MIRA (respectively). With TER, **BL+OR** helps to gain 0.03 point in both two methods. Meanwhile, in case of TERp-A, the improvement is 0.05 point for MERT and 0.03 point for MIRA. It is worthy to mention that the possibility of obtaining such oracle labels is definitely doable through a human-interaction scenario (which could be built from a tool like PET (Post-Editing Tool) (Aziz et al., 2012) for instance). In such an environment, ***once having the hypothesis produced by the first pass (translation task)***, the human editor could simply click on words considered as bad (B), the other words being implicitly considered as correct (G).

Breaking down the analysis into sentence level, as described on Table 3, **BL+OR** (MERT) yields nearly 59% (517 over 881) better outputs than the baseline and only 17% of worse ones. Furthermore, Table 2 shows that in case of our test set, optimizing by MERT is pretty more beneficial than MIRA (we do not have a clear explanation of this yet).

For more insightful understanding about WCE scores' acuteness, we make a comparison with

the most possible optimal BLEU score that could be obtained from the N-best list. Applying the sentence-level BLEU+1 (Nakov et al., 2012) metric over candidates in the list, we are able to select the one with highest score and aggregate all of them in an oracle-best translation; the resulting performance obtained is **60.48**. This score accounts for a fact that the simulated interactive scenario (**BL+OR**) lacks only 2.38 points (in case of MERT) to be optimal and clearly overpass the baseline (8.17 points below the best score).
The contribution of a real WCE system seems more modest: **BL+WCE** marginally increases BLEU scores of **BL** (0.46 gain in case of optimizing by MERT and 0.32 by MIRA). For both TER and TERp-A metric, the progressions are also negligible. To verify the significance of this result, we estimate the p-value between BLEU of **BL+WCE** system and BLEU of baseline **BL** relying on Approximate Randomization (AR) method (Clark et al., 2011) which indicates if the improvement yielded by the optimized system is likely to be generated again by some random processes (randomized optimizers). After various optimizer runs, we selected randomly *5* optimizer outputs, perform the AR test and obtain a p-value of **0.01**. This result reveals that the improvement yielded by **BL+WCE** is significative although small, originated from the contribution of WCE score, not by any optimizer variance. This modest but positive change in BLEU score using WCE features, encourages us to investigate and analyze further about WCE scores' impact, supposing WCE performance is getting better. More in-depth analysis is presented in the next section.

5 Further Understanding of WCE scores role in N-best Re-ranking via Improvement Simulation

We think it would be very interesting and useful to answer the following question: do WCE scores really effectively help to increase MT output quality when the WCE system is getting better and better? To do this, our proposition is as follows: firstly, by using the oracle labels, we filter out all wrongly classified words in the test set and push them into a temporary set, called **T**. Then, we correct randomly a percentage (25%, 50%, or 75%) of labels in **T**. Finally, the altered **T** will be integrated back with the correctly predicted part (by the WCE system) in order to form a new "simulated" result set. This strategy results in three "virtual" WCE systems called **"WCE+N%"** (N=25, 50 or 75), which use 14 decoder scores and 6 "simulated" WCE scores. Table 4 shows the performance of these systems in term of F score (%). From each of the above systems, the whole exper-

System	F("G")	F("B")	Overall F
WCE+25%	89.87	58.84	63.51
WCE+50%	93.21	73.09	76.11
WCE+75%	96.58	86.87	88.33
Oracle labels	100	100	100

Table 4: The performances (Fscore) of simulated WCE systems

imental setting is identical to what we did with the original WCE and oracle systems: six scores are built and combined with existing 14 system scores for each hypothesis in the N-best list. After that, MERT and MIRA methods are invoked to optimize their weights, and finally the reordering is performed thanks to these scores and appropriate optimal weights. The translation quality measured by BLEU, TER and TERp-A after re-ranking using **"WCE+N%"** (N=25,50,75) can be seen also in Table 2. The number of translations which outperform, keep intact and decline in comparison to the baseline are shown in Table 3 for MERT optimization.
We note that all obtained scores fit our guess and expectation: the better performance WCE system reaches, the clearer its role in improving MT output quality. Diminishing 25% of the wrongly predicted words leads to a gain 0.68 point (by MERT) and 0.32 (by MIRA) in BLEU score. More significant increases of BLEU 3.00 and BLEU 3.63 (MERT) can be achieved when prediction errors are cut off up to 50% and 75%. Figure 3 presents an overview of the results obtained and helps us to predict the MT improvements expected if the WCE system improves in the future. Table 5 shows several examples where WCE scores drive SMT system to better reference-correlated hypothesis. In the first example, the baseline generates the hypothesis in which the source phrase *"pour sa part"* remains untranslated. On the contrary, **WCE+50%** overcomes this drawback by resulting in a correct translation phrase: *"for his part"*. The latter translation needs only one edit operation (shift for *"Bettencourt-Meyers"*) to become its reference. In example 2, **BL+OR** selects the

Example 1 (from WCE+50%)	
Source	Pour sa part , l' avocat de Françoise Bettencourt-Meyers , Olivier Metzner , s' est félicité de la décision du tribunal .
Hypothesis (Baseline SMT)	The lawyer of *Bettencourt-Meyers* Françoise , Olivier Metzner , welcomed the court 's decision .
Hypothesis (SMT+WCE scores)	*For his part ,* the lawyer of *Bettencourt-Meyers* Françoise , Olivier Metzner , welcomed the court 's decision .
Post-edition	*For his part ,* the lawyer of Françoise Bettencourt-Meyers , Olivier Metzner , welcomed the court 's decision .
Example 2 (from BL+OR)	
Source	Pour l' otre , l' accord risque " de creuser la tombe d' un très grand nombre de pme du secteur dans les 12 prochains mois " .
Hypothesis (Baseline MT)	For the otre the agreement is likely to *deepen the grave* of a very large number of *smes in the sector* in the next 12 months " .
Hypothesis (SMT+WCE scores)	For the otre agreement , the risk " *digging the grave* of a very large number of *medium-sized businesses* in the next 12 months " .
Post-edition	For the otre , the agreement risks " *digging the grave* of a very large number of *small- and medium-sized businesses* in the next 12 months " .

Table 5: Examples of MT hypothesis before and after reranking using the additional scores from WCE+50% (Example 1) and BL+OR (Example 2) system

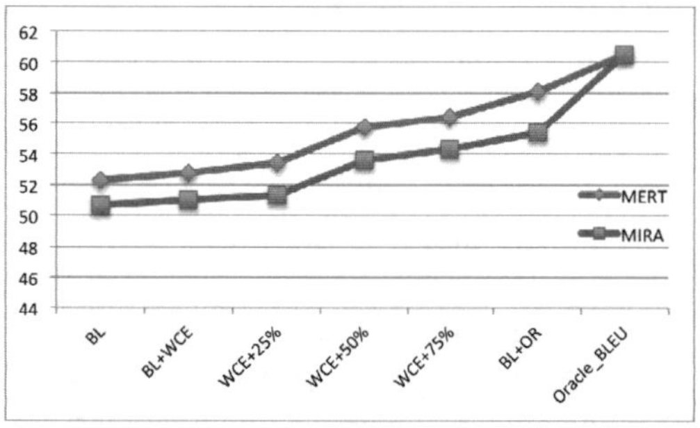

Figure 3: Comparison of the performance of various systems: the integrations of WCE features, which the quality increases gradually, lead to the linear improvement of translation outputs.

better hypothesis, in which the phrases *"creuser la tombe"* and *''pme du secteur"* are translated into *"digging the grave"* and *"medium-sized businesses"*, respectively, better than those of the baseline (*"deepen the grave"* and *"smes in the sector"*).

6 Conclusions And Perspectives

So far, the word confidence scores have been exploited in several applications, e.g. post-editing, sentence quality assessment or multiple MT-system combination, yet very few studies (except Bach et al. (2011)) propose to investigate them for boosting MT quality. Thus, this paper proposed several features extracted from a WCE system and combined them with existing decoder scores for re-ranking *N*-best lists. Our WCE model is built using CRFs, on a variety of types of features for the French - English SMT task. Due to its limitations in predicting translation errors ("B" label), WCE scores ensure only a modest improvement in translation quality over the baseline SMT. Nevertheless, further experiments about the simulation of WCE performance suggest that such types of score contribute dramatically if they are built from an accurate WCE system. They also show that with the help of an "ideal" WCE, the MT system reaches quite close to its most optimal possible quality. These scores are totally independent from the decoder, they can be seen as a way to introduce lexical, syntactic and semantic information (used for WCE) in a SMT pipeline.

As future work, we plan to focus on augmenting our WCE performance using more linguistic features as well as advanced techniques (feature selection, Boosting method...). In the same time, we would like to integrate the WCE scores in the decoder's search graph to redirect the decoding process (preliminary experiments, not reported here yet, have shown that this is a very promising avenue of research).

References

Wilker Aziz, Sheila C. M. de Sousa, and Lucia Specia. Pet: a tool for post-editing and assessing machine translation. In *Proceedings of the Eight International Conference on Language Resources and Evaluation (LREC'12)*, Istanbul, Turkey, May 23-25 2012.

Nguyen Bach, Fei Huang, and Yaser Al-Onaizan. Goodness: A method for measuring machine translation confidence. In *Proceedings of the 49th Annual Meeting of the Association for Computational Linguistics*, pages 211–219, Portland, Oregon, June 19-24 2011.

John Blatz, Erin Fitzgerald, George Foster, Simona Gandrabur, Cyril Goutte, Alex Kulesza, Alberto Sanchis, and Nicola Ueffing. Confidence estimation for machine translation. Technical report, JHU/CLSP Summer Workshop, 2003.

John Blatz, Erin Fitzgerald, George Foster, Simona Gandrabur, Cyril Goutte, Alex Kulesza, Alberto Sanchis, and Nicola Ueffing. Confidence estimation for machine translation. In *Proceedings of COLING 2004*, pages 315–321, Geneva, April 2004.

Jonathan Clark, Chris Dyer, Alon Lavie, and Noah Smith. Better hypothesis testing for statistical machine translation: Controlling for optimizer instability. In *Proceedings of the Association for Computational Lingustics*, 2011.

Kevin Duh and Katrin Kirchhoff. Beyond log-linear models: Boosted minimum error rate training for n-best re-ranking. In *Proc. of ACL, Short Papers*, 2008.

Mariano Felice and Lucia Specia. Linguistic features for quality estimation. In *Proceedings of the 7th Workshop on Statistical Machine Translation*, pages 96–103, Montreal, Canada, June 7-8 2012.

Katrin Kirchhoff and Mei Yang. Improved language modeling for statistical machine translation. In *Proceedings of the ACL Workshop on Building and Using Parallel Texts*, pages 125–128, Ann Arbor, Michigan, June 2005.

Philipp Koehn, Hieu Hoang, Alexandra Birch, Chris Callison-Burch, Marcello Federico, Nicola Bertoldi, Brooke Cowan, Wade Shen, Christine Moran, Richard Zens, Chris Dyer, Ondrej Bojar, Alexandra Constantin, and Evan Herbst. Moses: Open source toolkit for statistical machine translation. In *Proceedings of the 45th Annual Meeting of the Association for Computational Linguistics*, pages 177–180, Prague, Czech Republic, June 2007.

Thomas Lavergne, Olivier Cappé, and François Yvon. Practical very large scale crfs. In *Proceedings of the 48th Annual Meeting of the Association for Computational Linguistics*, pages 504–513, 2010.

Ngoc Quang Luong, Laurent Besacier, and Benjamin Lecouteux. Word confidence estimation and its integration in sentence quality estimation for machine translation. In *Proceedings of The Fifth International Conference on Knowledge and Systems Engineering (KSE 2013)*, Hanoi, Vietnam, October 17-19 2013a.

Ngoc Quang Luong, Benjamin Lecouteux, and Laurent Besacier. LIG system for WMT13 QE task: Investigating the usefulness of features in word confidence estimation for MT. In *Proceedings of the Eighth Workshop on Statistical Machine Translation*, pages 396–391, Sofia, Bulgaria, August 2013b. Association for Computational Linguistics.

Preslav Nakov, Francisco Guzman, and Stephan Vogel. Optimizing for sentence-level bleu+1 yields short translations. In *Proceedings of COLING 2012*, pages 1979–1994, Mumbai, India, December 8 -15 2012.

Franz Josef Och. Minimum error rate training in statistical machine translation. In *Proceedings of the 41st Annual Meeting of the Association for Computational Linguistics*, pages 160–167, July 2003.

Kishore Papineni, Salim Roukos, Todd Ard, and Wei-Jing Zhu. Bleu: a method for automatic evaluation of machine translation. In *Proceedings of the 40th Annual Meeting of the Association for Computational Linguistics*, 2002.

Kristen Parton, Nizar Habash, Kathleen McKeown, Gonzalo Iglesias, and Adrià de Gispert. Can automatic post-editing make mt more meaningful? In *Proceedings of the 16th EAMT*, pages 111–118, Trento, Italy, 28-30 May 2012.

M Potet, R Emmanuelle E, L Besacier, and H Blanchon. Collection of a large database of french-english smt output corrections. In *Proceedings of the eighth international conference on Language Resources and Evaluation (LREC)*, Istanbul, Turkey, May 2012.

Matthew Snover, Nitin Madnani, Bonnie Dorr, and Richard Schwartz. Terp system description. In *MetricsMATR workshop at AMTA*, 2008.

Artem Sokolov, Guillaume Wisniewski, and Francois Yvon. Non-linear n-best list reranking with few features. In *Proceedings of AMTA*, 2012.

Radu Soricut and Abdessamad Echihabi. Trustrank: Inducing trust in automatic translations via ranking. In *Proceedings of the 48th ACL (Association for Computational Linguistics)*, pages 612–621, Uppsala, Sweden, July 2010.

Andreas Stolcke. Srilm - an extensible language modeling toolkit. In *Seventh International Conference on Spoken Language Processing*, pages 901–904, Denver, USA, 2002.

Nicola Ueffing and Hermann Ney. Word-level confidence estimation for machine translation using phrased-based translation models. In *Proceedings of Human Language Technology Conference and Conference on Empirical Methods in Natural Language Processing*, pages 763–770, Vancouver, 2005.

Nicola Ueffing, Klaus Macherey, and Hermann Ney. Confidence measures for statistical machine translation. In *Proceedings of the MT Summit IX*, pages 394–401, New Orleans, LA, September 2003.

Ashish Venugopal, Andreas Zollmann, and Stephan Vogel. An efficient two-pass approach to synchronous-cfg driven statistical mt. In *Proceedings of Human Language Technologies 2007: The Conference of the North American Chapter of the Association for Computational Linguistics*, April 2007.

Taro Watanabe, Jun Suzuki, Hajime Tsukada, and Hideki Isozaki. Online large-margin training for statistical machine translation. In *Proceedings of the 2007 Joint Conference on Empirical Methods in Natural Language Processing and Computational Natural Language Learning*, pages 64–773,, Prague, Czech Republic, June 2007.

Deyi Xiong, Min Zhang, and Haizhou Li. Error detection for statistical machine translation using linguistic features. In *Proceedings of the 48th Association for Computational Linguistics*, pages 604–611, Uppsala, Sweden, July 2010.

Ying Zhang, Almut Silja Hildebrand, and Stephan Vogel. Distributed language modeling for n-best list re-ranking. In *Proceedings of the 2006 Conference on Empirical Methods in Natural Language Processing (EMNLP 2006)*, pages 216–223, Sydney, July 2006.

Proofreading Human Translations with an E-pen

Vicent Alabau and **Luis A. Leiva**
PRHLT Research Center
Universitat Politècnica de València
{valabau,luileito}@prhlt.upv.es

Abstract

Proofreading translated text is a task aimed at checking for correctness, consistency, and appropriate writing style. While this has been typically done with a keyboard and a mouse, pen-based devices set an opportunity for making such corrections in a comfortable way, as if proofreading on physical paper. Arguably, this way of interacting with a computer is very appropriate when a small number of modifications are required to achieve high-quality standards. In this paper, we propose a taxonomy of pen gestures that is tailored to machine translation review tasks, after human translator intervention. In addition, we evaluate the recognition accuracy of these gestures using a couple of popular gesture recognizers. Finally, we comment on open challenges and limitations, and discuss possible avenues for future work.

1 Introduction

Currently, the workflow of many translation agencies include a final reviewing or proofreading process[1] where the translators' work is checked for correctness, consistency and appropriate writing style. If the translation quality is good enough, only a small amount of changes would be necessary to reach a high-quality result. However, the required corrections are often spread sparingly and unequally among the screen, which renders mouse/keyboard interaction both inefficient and unappealing.

As a result of the popularization of touchscreen and pen-based devices, text-editing applications can be operated today in a similar way people interact with pen and paper. This way of reviewing is arguably more natural and efficient than a keyboard or a mouse, since the e-pen can be used both to locate and correct an erroneous word, all at once. Additionally, the expressiveness of e-pen interaction provides an opportunity to integrate useful gestures that are able correct other common mistakes, such as word reordering or capitalization.

2 Related Work

The first attempt that we are aware of to post-edit text with an e-pen interface dates back to the early seventies of the past century (Coleman, 1969). In that work, Coleman proposed a set of unistroke gestures for post-editing. Later on, the same corpus was used by (Rubine, 1991) in his seminal work about gesture recognition with excellent recognition results. However, the gesture set is too simplistic to be used in a real translation task today.

Most of the modern applications to generate and edit textual content using "digital ink" are based on *ad-hoc* interaction protocols[2] and often do not ship handwriting recognition software. To our knowledge, *MyScript Notes Mobile*[3] is the closest system to provide a natural onscreen paper-like interaction style, including some text-editing gestures and a powerful handwriting recognition software. However, this application relies on spatial relations of the ink strokes to perform handwriting recog-

[1]The reviewing process can be seen as a detailed proofreading process where the target sentence is also compared against the source sentence for errors such as mistranslations, etc. However, for the purpose of this paper, we can use the terms reviewing and proofreading indistinguishably.

[2]`http://appadvice.com/appguides/show/handwriting-apps-for-ipad`

[3]`http://www.visionobjects.com`

nition. For instance, to insert a new word in the middle of a sentence the user needs to make room for space explicitly (i.e., if the word has N characters, the user needs to perform an *Insert Space* gesture N times). Moreover, the produced text does not flow on the UI, i.e., it is fixed to the position of the ink, which makes it difficult to modify. As a result, this system does not seem suitable for reviewing translations. Other comparable work is MinGestures (Leiva et al., 2013), which proposes a simplified set of gestures for interactive text post-editing. Although MinGestures is very efficient and accurate, it is also very limited in expressiveness. Only basic edition capabilities are allowed (insertion, deletion, and substitution). Thus, advanced e-pen gestures cannot be used to improve the efficiency of the reviewer.

On the other hand, there are applications for post-editing text where user interactions are leveraged to propagate text corrections to the rest of the sentence. CueTIP (Shilman et al., 2006), CATTI (Romero et al., 2009) and IMT (Alabau et al., 2014) are the most advanced representatives of this kind of applications. These systems allow the user to correct text either in the form of unconstrained cursive handwriting or (limited) pen gestures. Then, the corrections are leveraged by the system to provide smart auto-completion capabilities. This way, user interaction is not only taken into account to amend the proposed correction but other mistakes in the surrounding text are automatically amended as well. However, user interaction is limited in these cases. In CueTIP, only one handwritten character can be submitted at a time and only 4 gestures can be performed (join, split, delete, and substitution). In CATTI, the user can handwrite text freely but is still limited to perform 4 gestures as well (substitute, insert, delete, and reject). Finally, IMT does not support gestures other than substitution. Although the auto-completion capability is a very interesting and promising topic, it should not be considered for reviewing: given the locality of the small amount of changes that are probably needed, auto-completion can make more harm than good.

Thus, in light of the current limitations of state-of-the-art approaches, in this work we present an exploratory research of how paper-like interaction should be approached to allow proofreading translated texts.

3 A Taxonomy of Proofreading Gestures

Indicating text modifications on a sheet of paper can be made in many different ways. However, the lack of a consensus may lead to misinterpretations. Fortunately, a series of authoritative proofreading and copy-editing symbols have been proposed (AMA, 2007; CMO, 2010), even leading to an eventual standardization (BS, 2005; ISO, 1983).

We have studied the aforementioned authoritative sources and have found that there is a huge overlap in the proposed symbols, with only minor variations. Moreover, such symbols are meant to ease human-human communication and therefore we need to adapt them to ease human-computer communication. This way, we will focus on those symbols that could be used to review using stroke-based gestures. As such, we will study gestures that allow to change the *content* and not the *formatting* of the text. We can define the following high-level operations; see Figure 1:

Word change: change text's written form.
Letter case: change word/character casing.
Punctuation: insert punctuation symbols.
Word combination: separate or join words.
Selection: select words or characters.
Text displacement: move text around.

It is worth noting that punctuation symbols are represented explicitly in the literature, probably because of their importance in copy-editing tasks. In addition, dot and hyphen symbols are represented differently from other insertion symbols. The purpose of this convention is to reduce visual ambiguity in human recognition. Finally, the selection operation is often devoted to spell out numbers or abbreviations.

4 Preliminary Evaluation

The initial taxonomy (Figure 1) aims to be a complete set of symbols for proofreading and copy-editing onscreen. Nonetheless, the success of these gestures will depend on the accu-

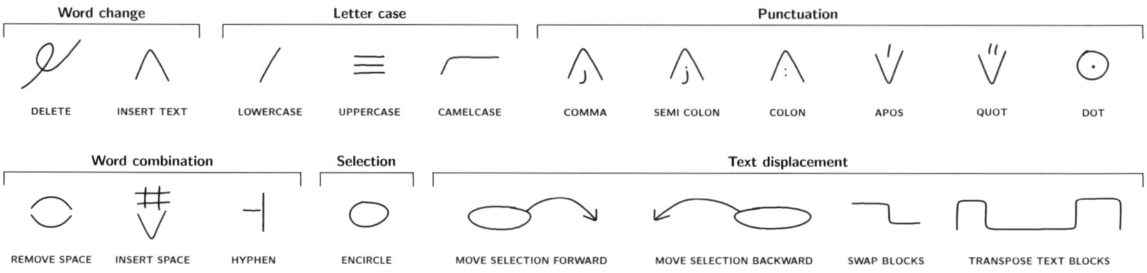

Figure 1: Initial taxonomy, based on *de facto* proofreading symbols.

racy of gesture recognizers, to correctly translate gestures into commands.

As a first approach, we wanted to evaluate these symbols with state-of-the-art gesture recognizers. The initial taxonomy differs significantly from other gesture sets in the literature (Anthony and Wobbrock, 2012; Vatavu et al., 2012), in the sense that the symbols we are researching are not expected to be drawn in isolation. Instead, reviewers will issue a gesture in a very specific context, and so a proofreading symbol may change its meaning. This is specially true for symbols involving multiple spans of text or block displacements: depending of the size of the span or the length of the displacement, the aspect ratio and proportions among the different parts of the gesture strokes may vary. Thus, the final shape of the gesture can be significantly different. An example is given in Figure 2.

(a) MOVE FORWARD with 1 selected word and 2 word displacement.

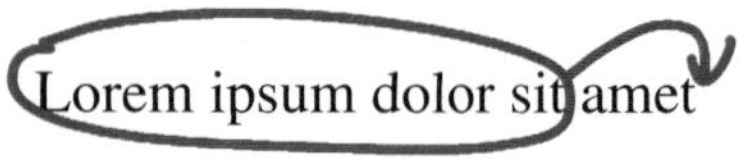

(b) MOVE FORWARD with 4 selected words and 1 word displacement.

Figure 2: Examples of the same gesture executed with different proportions. As a result, the shapes of both gestures significantly diverge from each other.

4.1 Gesture Samples Acquisition

We carried out a controlled study in a real-world setup. We developed an application that requested a set of random challenges to the users (Figure 3). Then, we asked the users if they would prefer to do the acquisition on a digitizer tablet or on a tablet computer. On a 1 to 5 point scale, with 1 meaning 'I prefer writing with a digitizer pen' and 5 'I prefer writing with a pen-capable tablet', users indicated that they would prefer a tablet computer (M=4.6, SD=0.8). Consequently, we deployed the application into a Lenovo ThinkPad tablet, which had to be operated with an e-pen. To make the paper-like experience more realistic, the touchscreen functionality was disabled, so that users could rest their hands on the screen. Eventually, 12 users aged 24–36 submitted 5 times each gesture following the aforementioned random challenges.

Figure 3: Acquisition application.

4.2 The Family of \$ Recognizers

In HCI, there is a popular "dollar series" of template-matching gesture recognizers, using a nearest-neighbor classifier with scoring functions based on Euclidean distance. The \$ recognizers present several advantages over other classifiers based on more complex pattern recognition algorithms. First, \$ recognizers are easily understandable and fast to integrate or re-implement in different programming languages. Second, they do not depend on large amounts of training data to achieve high accuracy, just on a small number of predefined templates.

In particular, \$N (Anthony and Wobbrock, 2012) and \$P (Vatavu et al., 2012) can be used to recognize multi-stroke gestures, so they were the only suitable candidates to recognize our initial gesture taxonomy. On the one hand, \$N deals with multiple strokes by recombining in every possible way the strokes of the templates in order to generate new instances of unistroke templates, and then apply either the \$1 recognizer (Wobbrock et al., 2007) or Protractor (Li, 2010). On the other hand, \$P considers gesture strokes as a cloud of points, removing thus information about stroke sequentiality. Then, the best match is found using an approximation of the Hungarian algorithm, which pairs points from the template with points of the query gesture.

4.3 Results

We evaluated three fundamental aspects of the recognition process: accuracy, recognition time and memory requirements to store the whole set of templates. Aiming for a portable recognizer that could work on most everyday devices, we decided to use a JavaScript (rotation invariant) version of the \$ family recognizers. Experiments were executed as a `nodejs` program on a Ubuntu Linux computer with a 2.83 GHz Intel QuadCore™ and 4 GB of RAM. We followed a leaving-one-out (LOO) setup, i.e., each user's set of gestures was used as templates and tested against the rest of the user's gestures. All the values show the average of the different LOO runs.

Table 1 summarizes the experimental results. For the \$N recognizer we found that, by resampling to 32 points and 5 templates, we can achieve very good recognition times ($0.7ms$ in average) but high recognition error rate (23.6%). On the other hand, the \$P recognizer behaves even worse, with 27.1% error rate. Memory requirements are marginal but recognition times increase more than one order of magnitude.

It must be noted that the space needed by \$N to store just one template of n strokes is $n! \times 2^n$ times the space for the original template (Vatavu et al., 2012). This is actually a huge waste of resources. For instance, one template of the INSERT SPACE gesture requires

Recognizer	Error	Time	Mem. usage
\$N	23.6%	0.7 ms	102 MB
\$P	27.1%	45 ms	1.8 MB

Table 1: Results for \$N and \$P recognizers, with gestures resampled to 32 points and using 5 templates per gesture.

3840 times the original size, assuming that the user has introduced the minimum strokes required. With a resampling 8 points, \$N needs almost 33MB of RAM to store 5 templates per gesture.

4.4 Error analysis

Surprised by the high error rates we decided to delve into the results of the most accurate setup so we could find the source of errors. We observed that the most difficult gesture to recognize was REMOVE SPACE, which represented 12% of the total number of errors; being confused with COMMA and SEMI COLON more than 50% of the time, probably because they are formed by two arcs. It was also confused, though less frequently, with MOVE SELECTION FORWARD/BACKWARD. These gestures, excepting the circle part, are also composed by two arcs.

On the other hand, punctuation symbols accounted for 37% of the errors, being mostly confused with each other, as they have very similar shapes. Finally, some errors are harder to dissect. For instance, UPPERCASE was confused mainly with both MOVE SELECTION (4.4% of the errors), and punctuation and displacement operations were also confused with each other at some time, despite their very different visual shapes and sizes. We suspect it is because of the internal normalization procedures of the \$ recognizers.

5 Discussion

Our results suggest that the \$ family of gesture recognizers, although popular, are not appropriate for proofreading translated texts. Our assumption is that the normalization procedures of these recognizers—mainly scaling and resampling— are not appropriate to gestures for which the proportions of its constituent parts may vary according to the context. For

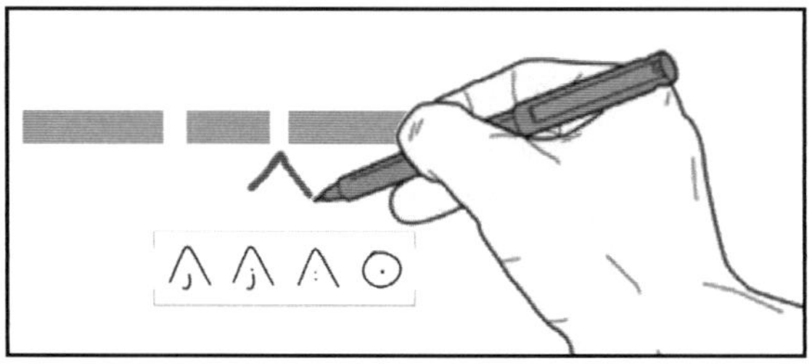

Figure 4: One proposal for gesture set simplification. A Pop-up menu could assist the user to disambiguate among perceptually similar gestures.

example, after resizing a MOVE SELECTION FORWARD that selects a small word and has a long arrow, the final shape would be primarily that of the arrow (Figure 2).

In the light of this analysis, several actions can be taken for future work. Firstly, other gesture recognizers should be explored that can deal with stroke sequences without resampling (Myers and Rabiner, 1981; Sezgin and Davis, 2005; Álvaro et al., 2013). However, it must be remarked that response time is crucial to ensure an adequate user experience. Therefore, the underlying algorithms should be implementable on thin clients, such as mobile devices, with reasonable recognition times.

Secondly, it would be also necessary to reduce the set of gestures, but not at the expense of reducing also expressiveness as Leiva et al. (2013) did. For instance, taking advantage of the interaction that computers can provide, we can group punctuation operations, SPACE, and INSERT HYPHEN all into INSERT ABOVE and BELOW gestures. Both gestures would pop-up a menu where the user could select deterministically the symbol to insert; see Figure 4. In the same manner, letter casing operations could be grouped into a single SELECTION category, which would also provide a contextual menu to trigger the right command. The resulting set of gestures should be, in principle, much easier to recognize.

Additionally, the current set of proofreading gestures present further challenges. For instance, we would need to identify the *semantics* of the gestures, i.e., which elements in the text are affected by the gesture and how the system should proceed to accomplish the task.

6 Conclusions

In this work we have defined a set of gestures that is suitable for the reviewing process of human-translated text. We have performed an evaluation on gestures generated by real users that show that popular recognizers are not able to achieve a satisfactory accuracy. In consequence, we have identified a series of areas for improvement that could make e-pen devices realizable in the near future.

7 Acknowledgments

This work is supported by the 7th Framework Program of European Commission under grant agreements 287576 (CasMaCat) and 600707 (tranScriptorium).

References

V. Alabau, A. Sanchis, and F. Casacuberta. 2014. Improving on-line handwritten recognition in interactive machine translation. *Pattern Recognition*, 47(3):1217–1228.

2007. AMA manual of style: A guide for authors and editors. 10th ed. Oxford University Press.

L. Anthony and J. O. Wobbrock. 2012. $N-protractor: a fast and accurate multistroke recognizer. In *Proc. GI*, pages 117–120.

2005. BS 5261-2:2005. Copy preparation and proof correction.

2010. The Chicago manual of style. 16th ed. University Of Chicago Press.

M. L. Coleman. 1969. Text editing on a graphic display device using hand-drawn proofreader's symbols. In *Pertinent Concepts in Computer Graphics, Proc. 2nd Univ. Illinois Conf. on Computer Graphics*, pages 283–290.

1983. ISO 5776:1983. Symbols for text correction.

L. A. Leiva, V. Alabau, and E. Vidal. 2013. Error-proof, high-performance, and context-aware gestures for interactive text edition. In *Proc. CHI EA*, pages 1227–1232.

Y. Li. 2010. Protractor: a fast and accurate gesture recognizer. In *Proc. CHI*, pages 2169–2172.

C. S. Myers and L. R. Rabiner. 1981. A comparative study of several dynamic time-warping algorithms for connected-word. *Bell System Technical Journal*.

V. Romero, L. A. Leiva, A. H. Toselli, and E. Vidal. 2009. Interactive multimodal transcription of text images using a web-based demo system. In *Proc. IUI*, pages 477–478.

D. Rubine. 1991. Specifying gestures by example. In *Proc. SIGGRAPH*, pages 329–337.

T. M. Sezgin and R. Davis. 2005. HMM-based efficient sketch recognition. In *Proc. IUI*, pages 281–283.

M. Shilman, D. S. Tan, and P. Simard. 2006. CueTIP: a mixed-initiative interface for correcting handwriting errors. In *Proc. UIST*, pages 323–332.

R. D. Vatavu, L. Anthony, and J. O. Wobbrock. 2012. Gestures as point clouds: A $P recognizer for user interface prototypes. In *Proc. ICMI*, pages 273–280.

J. O. Wobbrock, A. D. Wilson, and Y. Li. 2007. Gestures without libraries, toolkits or training: A $1 recognizer for user interface prototypes. In *Proc. UIST*, pages 159–168.

F. Álvaro, J.-A. Sánchez, and J.-M. Benedí. 2013. Classification of on-line mathematical symbols with hybrid features and recurrent neural networks. In *Proc. ICDAR*, pages 1012–1016.

Estimating Grammar Correctness for a Priori Estimation of Machine Translation Post-Editing Effort

Nicholas H. Kirk, Guchun Zhang
Alpha Calligraphic Research Cambridge Ltd.
St Andrew's House, St Andrew's Road,
Cambridge CB4 1DL, UK
{nkirk,gzhang}@alphacrc.com

Georg Groh
Fakultat für Informatik
Technische Universität München,
Germany
grohg@in.tum.de

Abstract

We present a supervised learning pilot application for estimating Machine Translation (MT) output reusability, in view of supporting a human post-editor of MT content. We train our model on typed dependencies (labeled grammar relationships) extracted from human reference and raw MT data, to then predict grammar relationship correctness values that we aggregate to provide a binary segment-level evaluation. In view of scaling up to larger data, we provide implemented Naïve Bayes and Stochastic Gradient Descent with Support Vector Machine loss function approaches and their evaluation, and verify the correlation of predicted values with human judgement.

1 Introduction

Currently the Machine Translation (MT) research community attempts to seamlessly integrate both humans and MT-instances in the workflow of textual translation. Efforts towards this integration focus, for instance, on automating a posteriori processes such as post-editing (Simard et al., 2007), or other format coherence maintenance (e.g. date, spelling). Our contribution addresses cases when a post-editor has to start a segment from scratch, because the MT raw output turns out to be a hindrance rather than an aid, and the corresponding evaluation time between editing and manually re-translating a sequence is wasted a posteriori. Reasons for unusable MT output in this context could potentially be a combination of the following or more factors, with reference to the target segment:

- the word order, or grammar, are such that the sentence structure is unintelligible
- the lexical semantics of the words do not convey the meaning of the source segment

These lexical or structural factors can be present to various extents and their threshold of identification can be subjective for each post-editor, but hypothetically any intervention on the latter points is quantifiable in terms of post-editing time, being this the most observable aspect of post-editing effort (Krings, 2001). This paper proposes a supervised learning approach to discriminate typed grammar relation instances that compose a human-written sentence from any other form, in order to identify segments that can potentially lead to time loss on the basis of its incorrect grammar or word adjacency and delete them before post-editing. The remainder presents the project's assumptions and the nature of the adopted learning features (Section 2), the high-level algorithmic approach and the theory behind the adopted prediction models (Section 3). We then provide our implementation outline and the evaluation approaches (Section 4). In conclusion we present current limitations (Section 5), related and future work (Section 6), and the conclusions (Section 7).

2 Concept

We will now provide some background and a series of assertions as regards creating a classification method to estimate MT output grammar correctness, which mainly aims to support the post-editor in assessing which segments will take longer to post-edit than to translate from scratch. We assume the following post-editing behavioral phases:

1. Read source and/or target to various extents, in order to:
   - check grammatical consistency of target
   - check whether semantics have been conveyed between source and target
2. Insert or delete text accordingly

Given the lack of robust adequacy understanding methods (i.e. verifying meaning conveyance), we will perform analysis at a grammar and word order level, and for this we will seek a grammar-related formalism that is informative, scalable and robust to multiple, potentially unseen grammar instance variants. We therefore exploit typed dependencies (De Marneffe and Manning, 2008), a labeled, directed grammar relationship among pairs of words, which provides information on the order of arguments and their relationship type. Figure 1 shows words of a segment instance, and for each of these the unary and binary predicates of Part-Of-Speech tagging and typed dependency, respectively.

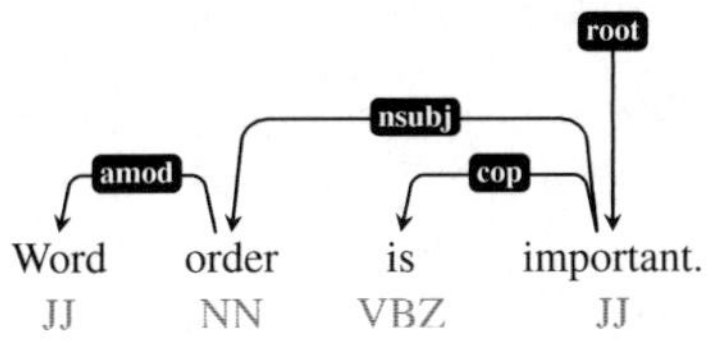

Figure 1: Example of words that compose a segment instance, their typed dependencies (illustrated as labeled directed edges), and the Part-Of-Speech (POS) tags.

3 Algorithm

Having discussed our aim and the required informativeness, we present a pipeline for both training a hypothesis model and the prediction itself (Figure 2). The process comprises a typed dependency extraction module (M1) that, given a set of sentences from a `test` or `training` text, provides instances of grammar relationships in the form of two word arguments ($arg1$, $arg2$) and a type label ($deptype$), which we will adopt as features. In the training phase, a training module (M2) labels the feature data obtained from $\{trainHuman\}$ instances as 1, and from $\{trainHuman \setminus trainMT\}$ as 0, where $\setminus$ is the set difference operator. We therefore consider any typed dependency instance that does not appear in the human reference text as 'bad'. This assumption holds when training on large datasets that comprise different grammar variants. From such labeled dataset, M2 then formulates a hypothesis model. More details on generating the hypothesis are provided in the next paragraph. During a test phase, various instances of a prediction module (M3) exploit such hypothesis model

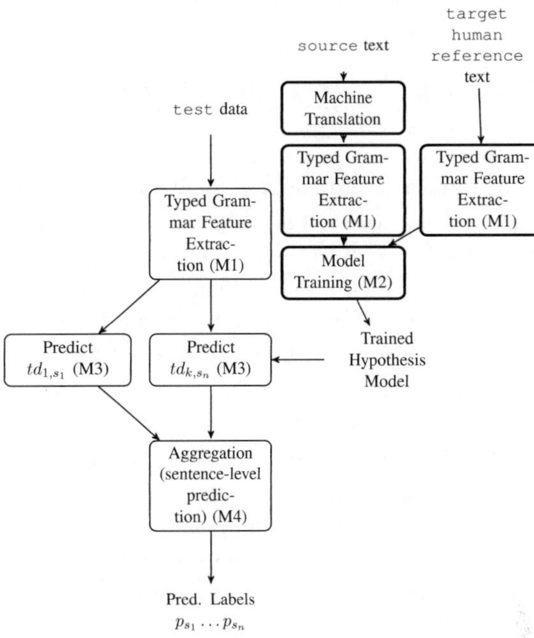

Figure 2: Abstract implementation pipeline for training the hypothesis model (in bold), and for the prediction itself of a typed dependency-based segment reusability estimator.

to predict the grammar relationship goodness values of $td_{1,s_i} \dots td_{k,s_i}$ for a sentence s_i and its typed dependencies $td_1 \dots td_k$, for all sentences $s_i \in \{s_1 \dots s_n\}$. A final phase (M4) aggregates the output predictions of grammar relationships for each sentence, in order to construct segment-level estimations (Equation 1).

$$P_{s_i} = \frac{1}{k} \sum_{j=1}^{k} P_{td_{j,s_i}} \quad (1)$$

Hypothesis Model Given our aim to achieve method robustness and breadth of applicability, and that context abstraction is potentially achievable since correctness of a grammar relationship is not dependent on neighbouring dependencies, we train on a high number of diverse training instances. In order to obtain a reduction in time and space complexity, we approximate our hypothesis by making sample independence assumptions, such as the Naïve Bayes (NB) approach (Good, 1965). NB is a model that assumes feature independence, i.e. the 'naiveness' implies that every feature F_i is conditionally independent of every other feature F_j for $j \neq i$ given the class C. Equation 2 describes the core of all current NB variants.

$$p(C|F_1 \dots F_n) \propto p(C) \prod_{i=1}^{n} p(F_i|C) \quad (2)$$

Such generative model is efficient and requires just one linear iteration for training, hence its suitability for large input scaling. Unfortunately, the modeling assumptions that enable efficient computability come at the expense of accuracy. More precisely, NB-based methods maximize likelihood conditioned only over the class label C, and not over the set of all other remaining features, and as a result its effectiveness is often outperformed by discriminative classifiers such as Support Vector Machines (SVM) (Crammer and Singer, 2002; Puurula, 2012). However, given its high efficiency and scalability, we will use NB as our primary model and compare it with an algorithm that has deeper modeling assumptions, but exploits inference approximation to reduce complexity, namely SVM with Stochastic Gradient Descent for parameter finding. Approximated inference is often achieved via traditional gradient descent methods (see Equation 3 for linear classification or regression approaches) that are largely used, first-order, stepwise optimization algorithms that seek minima of a problem with large dimensionality and unknown convexity status.

$$w_{t+1} = w_t - \gamma_t \frac{1}{n} \sum_{i=1}^{n} \nabla_w Q(z_t, w_t) \quad (3)$$

where our objective is to iteratively minimize, given an initial parameterization (starting point w_0, number of iterations, step length γ_0), and a function $Q(w)$, or more specifically when within the machine learning context, an *empirical risk* $E_n(f)$, defined as:

$$Q(w) = E_n(f) = \frac{1}{n} \sum_{i=1}^{n} l\left(f\left(x_i\right), y_i\right) \quad (4)$$

where in turn $l(\hat{y}, y)$ is a *loss function* that quantifies the cost of predicting $\hat{y}$ when the actual answer is y. One advantage is computational efficiency, while the disadvantages include the inability to provide certainty of termination or result determinism. Recent literature partially circumvents these problems (Hager and Zhang, 2005), and the use of such family of algorithms has been rediscovered for large scale data learning, whose applications prefer approximate over exact inference, by using a stochastic variant (Equation 5) of the traditional method (Zhang, 2004; Bottou, 2010), which samples a subset of the training data.

$$w_{t+1} = w_t - \gamma_t \nabla_w Q(z_t, w_t) \quad (5)$$

We adopt a *hinge loss* function for Support Vector Machine (SVM) classification, a method which has proven to be reliable for elaborating high scale, sparsely distributed instance vector applications that have dense concept vectors (Joachims, 1998; Rosasco et al., 2004).

4 Implementation & Evaluation

As a proof-of-concept and means of evaluation, we constructed a Java prototype that implements the pipeline in Figure 2, by making use of the Moses process (Koehn et al., 2007) for machine translation, the Stanford Parser (De Marneffe and Manning, 2008) for typed dependency extraction, the API of the general-purpose machine learning analysis platform Weka (Hall et al., 2009) for training and prediction, and ad-hoc implementations of the remaining specified modules. Typed dependency extraction is possible by feeding a pre-trained language-specific Probabilistic Context-Free Grammar (PCFG) into the parser, which is a model that defines probabilistic grammar production rules for such language. Such a model is trained beforehand on a large, syntactically annotated text corpus (i.e. a treebank) (Jelinek et al., 1992).

4.1 Experiment

We used our prototype on a subset of the Europarl test data (Koehn, 2005), extracting 536404 instances from 11270 human reference lines, and from 11270 machine-translated lines that share the same source. Our Naive Bayes algorithm (using word frequencies, no pruning) required 1.08 seconds to formulate a hypothesis model, versus the 28613.64 seconds required for the construction of a Stochastic Gradient Descent model (hinge loss function for SVM, step length 0.01, 500 steps, no pruning). A 10-fold cross validation on the training set provided a correct instance classification of 67.0168% for NB model, versus the 66.0118% of the SGD model. Table 1 provides further statistics of the latter evaluations.

		Precision	Recall	F-1
NB	'good'	0.665	0.839	0.742
	'bad'	0.683	0.451	0.543
SGD	'good'	0.646	0.883	0.746
	'bad'	0.709	0.370	0.487

Table 1: Precision and recall values of the 10-fold cross validation for both NB and SGD methods

4.2 Correlation with Human Judgement

We organized a survey among post-editors to gather human judgement values on a small set of 80 segments, for independent analysis and for comparison with machine predicted labels. Four translators with different experience level (in terms of years, 10+,5,1+, 1) evaluated a questionnaire of 80 Europarl-domain segments. Half of these were official human reference Europarl segments, while the other half were MT processed $FR \rightarrow EN$ segments. The process first involved a binary labeling task $\{\texttt{aid|hindrance}\}$ (two instances of results are in Figure 3), and the second a phase assigning a mark $\{\texttt{0...10}\}$ to define its level of usefulness. Together with the $lineNumber$, we will consider these three features and their data as the human judgement dataset. By aggregating the human binary evaluations with a majority vote and comparing these with the sentence-level prediction of our system, *NB correctly classified 82.5% of the segments, while SGD classified 83.75%.*

Preliminary clustering analysis on the latter confirmed the intuitive idea of the subjectivity of this kind of reusability evaluation for each translator. An unsupervised categorization was performed using an Expectation Maximization (EM) of Gaussian mixtures on the human judgement survey dataset, to understand distributional properties and use this as a basis to evaluate how the prototype results correlate with human judgement. Starting with a human-only dataset and no initial prior, the EM algorithm estimated by cross-validation only one homogeneous cluster. By then providing the number of clusters (i.e. the number of human translators, 4), the cluster evaluation assignments were not aligned with the number of instances present for each translator, which implies post-editor behavior indistinguishability via this method. Once machine predicted samples are added to the evaluation set, a further step is to verify whether the cluster assignments are within an acceptable neighborhood of the previous cluster assignment values. As shown in Table 2, cluster assignment percentages of NB predicted labels are closer to the original cluster assignments from the training set than SGD value-based cluster assignments. The clustering approach described will be used as a preliminary method for effectiveness evaluation, i.e. by evaluating the extent to which machine predicted values are a mixture of human behavior data based on the cluster assignment value distance from the generating model values.

label	eval.: human		eval.: NB		eval.: SGD	
0	179	(56%)	52	(65%)	58	(73%)
1	24	(8%)	3	(4%)	2	(3%)
2	52	(16%)	7	(9%)	2	(3%)
3	65	(20%)	18	(23%)	18	(23%)

Table 2: Evaluation data obtained with the cluster model generated from the human judgement dataset, with the number of clusters defined as 4.

```
1) on the issue of Jerusalem , they
have shown in a spirit of openness
and a capacity for listening hopeless .

2) that is completely disproportionate
and it does no favours for the
peace process .
```

Figure 3: Examples of segments classified as 'bad' (1) and 'good' (2) by all the post-editors of the experiment described in Section 4.2.

5 Limitations

Method robustness would imply that the grammar relationships under test are known, or that the prediction algorithm reacts well to unseen data. Figure 4 presents an example that shows how typed dependencies of two related sentences (namely reference and MT output of the same source) and the word usage itself can be scarcely related, or not overlap. This highlights that we cannot assume training coverage of the typed dependencies in the test segment, even if the contained words are present in the training set in multiple grammatical contexts. This stresses the importance of the scaling requirement and the complexity reduction measures stated in Section 3, in order to train diverse grammatical instance variants. A further aspect to consider with the Naïve Bayes formulation is that the model defines a likelihood for each entry conditioned on an unconditional class probability, which is correlated to the ratio of 'bad' and 'good' grammar relationships present in the training set. This information usage decreases robustness, as the model captures quality information of the MT instance, which can be subject to variability (e.g. the language pair, MT instance setup).

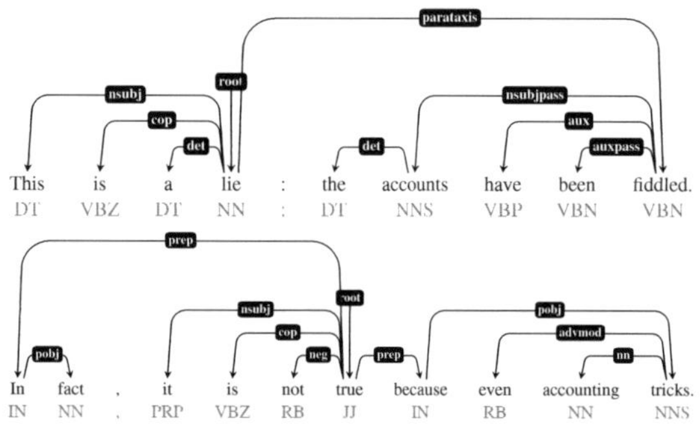

Figure 4: Human reference and raw MT output derived from the test subset of Europarl FR-EN corpus, which show typed dependency relationships, the words, and related part-of-speech tags that highlight possible word usage variance

6 Related & Future Work

In order to estimate MT output quality, literature in the past has traditionally compared an automatically translated sentence to one or more human text references (Papineni et al., 2002), while other work has exploited unlabeled dependencies in order to take into account legitimate grammatical or lexical choice variations (Liu and Gildea, 2005). Other work improves the classification effectiveness of the latter by considering typed dependencies (Owczarzak et al., 2007). Some data-driven, referenceless evaluation approaches to learning human judgement have been introduced (Corston-Oliver et al., 2001), which exploit syntactic features and linguistic indicators (Gamon et al., 2005), but have also been combined with typed dependency features (He and Way, 2009). Estimation of post-editing effort is a growing concern addressed by Confidence Estimation (CE) (Specia, 2011), but so far, to the best of our knowledge, work within the domain performs supervised learning of statistical linguistic features (Felice and Specia, 2012), but not of dependency features, i.e. the main focus of this contribution. Previous quality estimation methods differ in nature from the presented view, given that they attempt to predict a discrete level of post-editing effort (Bojar et al., 2013), more subject to annotation subjectivity, or to perform binary classification (Hardmeier, 2011), but do not focus on segment reusability estimation. Future work will focus on testing the hypothesis modeling and feature extraction for scalability on larger context-abstract data, and verifying the distinguishability of predicted values from more human-annotated judgements using the method stated in Section 4.2. Time gain values have not yet been acquired given the unusability of the time productivity metrics currently favored, which do not exhibit direct correlation with real PE time, and are also focus of future investigations. Futhermore, evaluation on the WMT Quality Estimation Shared Task datasets will be performed, for comparisons with state of the art methods of post-editing effort quantification (Bojar et al., 2013).

7 Conclusions

The presented pilot study proposes a grammar-based analysis for categorizing MT output in terms of whether it is an aid or a hindrance to the post-editor. Our contributions are mainly the (i) use of typed dependency learning for binary evaluation of confidence estimation and (ii) the analysis of adequate algorithmic solutions to achieve its scalability and context abstraction. Preliminary results show that aggregation of predictions operated at a typed dependency level provide an evaluation that resembles the segment-level judgement displayed by post-editors. Futhermore, for the hypothesis models created on the dataset tested, Naïve Bayes outperformed Stochastic Gradient Descent with hinge loss for Support Vector Machine in terms of training efficiency, and is on a par regarding classification effectiveness. We have showed the preliminary advantages of typed dependency-based estimation in terms of context abstraction, which provides a novel type of assistance to human post-editors and correlates with post-editing cost rather than commonly analyzed linguistic metrics.

References

Ondřej Bojar, Christian Buck, Chris Callison-Burch, Christian Federmann, Barry Haddow, Philipp Koehn, Christof Monz, Matt Post, Radu Soricut, and Lucia Specia. 2013. Findings of the 2013 Workshop on Statistical Machine Translation. In *Proceedings of the Eighth Workshop on Statistical Machine Translation*, pages 1–44, Sofia, Bulgaria, August. Association for Computational Linguistics.

Léon Bottou. 2010. Large-scale machine learning with stochastic gradient descent. In *Proceedings of COMPSTAT'2010*, pages 177–186. Springer.

Simon Corston-Oliver, Michael Gamon, and Chris Brockett. 2001. A machine learning approach to the automatic evaluation of machine translation. In *Proceedings of the 39th Annual Meeting on Association for Computational Linguistics*, pages 148–155. Association for Computational Linguistics.

Koby Crammer and Yoram Singer. 2002. On the learnability and design of output codes for multiclass problems. *Machine Learning*, 47(2-3):201–233.

Marie-Catherine De Marneffe and Christopher D Manning. 2008. The stanford typed dependencies representation. In *Coling 2008: Proceedings of the workshop on Cross-Framework and Cross-Domain Parser Evaluation*, pages 1–8. Association for Computational Linguistics.

Mariano Felice and Lucia Specia. 2012. Linguistic features for quality estimation. In *Proceedings of the Seventh Workshop on Statistical Machine Translation*, pages 96–103. Association for Computational Linguistics.

Michael Gamon, Anthony Aue, and Martine Smets. 2005. Sentence-level mt evaluation without reference translations: Beyond language modeling. In *Proceedings of EAMT*, pages 103–111.

Irving John Good. 1965. *The estimation of probabilities: An essay on modern Bayesian methods*, volume 30. MIT press Cambridge, MA.

William W Hager and Hongchao Zhang. 2005. A new conjugate gradient method with guaranteed descent and an efficient line search. *SIAM Journal on Optimization*, 16(1):170–192.

Mark Hall, Eibe Frank, Geoffrey Holmes, Bernhard Pfahringer, Peter Reutemann, and Ian H Witten. 2009. The weka data mining software: an update. *ACM SIGKDD Explorations Newsletter*, 11(1):10–18.

Christian Hardmeier. 2011. Improving machine translation quality prediction with syntactic tree kernels. In *Proceedings of the 15th conference of the European Association for Machine Translation (EAMT 2011)*, pages 233–240.

Yifan He and Andy Way. 2009. Learning labelled dependencies in machine translation evaluation.

Frederick Jelinek, John D Lafferty, and Robert L Mercer. 1992. *Basic methods of probabilistic context free grammars*. Springer.

Thorsten Joachims. 1998. *Text categorization with support vector machines: Learning with many relevant features*. Springer.

Philipp Koehn, Hieu Hoang, Alexandra Birch, Chris Callison-Burch, Marcello Federico, Nicola Bertoldi, Brooke Cowan, Wade Shen, Christine Moran, Richard Zens, et al. 2007. Moses: Open source toolkit for statistical machine translation. In *Proceedings of the 45th Annual Meeting of the ACL on Interactive Poster and Demonstration Sessions*, pages 177–180. Association for Computational Linguistics.

Philipp Koehn. 2005. Europarl: A parallel corpus for statistical machine translation. In *MT summit*, volume 5.

Hans P Krings. 2001. *Repairing texts: empirical investigations of machine translation post-editing processes*, volume 5. Kent State University Press.

Ding Liu and Daniel Gildea. 2005. Syntactic features for evaluation of machine translation. In *Proceedings of the ACL Workshop on Intrinsic and Extrinsic Evaluation Measures for Machine Translation and/or Summarization*, pages 25–32.

Karolina Owczarzak, Josef Van Genabith, and Andy Way. 2007. Dependency-based automatic evaluation for machine translation. In *Proceedings of the NAACL-HLT 2007/AMTA Workshop on Syntax and Structure in Statistical Translation*, pages 80–87. Association for Computational Linguistics.

Kishore Papineni, Salim Roukos, Todd Ward, and Wei-Jing Zhu. 2002. Bleu: a method for automatic evaluation of machine translation. In *Proceedings of the 40th annual meeting on association for computational linguistics*, pages 311–318. Association for Computational Linguistics.

Antti Puurula. 2012. Combining modifications to multinomial naive bayes for text classification. In *Information Retrieval Technology*, pages 114–125. Springer.

Lorenzo Rosasco, Ernesto De Vito, Andrea Caponnetto, Michele Piana, and Alessandro Verri. 2004. Are loss functions all the same? *Neural Computation*, 16(5):1063–1076.

Michel Simard, Cyril Goutte, and Pierre Isabelle. 2007. Statistical phrase-based post-editing.

Lucia Specia. 2011. Exploiting objective annotations for measuring translation post-editing effort. In *Proceedings of the 15th Conference of the European Association for Machine Translation*, pages 73–80.

Tong Zhang. 2004. Solving large scale linear prediction problems using stochastic gradient descent algorithms. In *Proceedings of the twenty-first international conference on Machine learning*, page 116. ACM.

On-The-Fly Translator Assistant (Readability and Terminology Handling)

Svetlana Sheremetyeva
National Research South Ural State University / pr.Lenina 74, 454080 Chelyabinsk, Russia
LanA Consulting ApS/ Moellekrog 4, Vejby, 3210, Copenhagen, Denmark
lanaconsult@mail.dk

Abstract

This paper describes a new methodology for developing CAT tools that assist translators of technical and scientific texts by (i) on-the-fly highlight of nominal and verbal terminology in a source language (SL) document that lifts possible syntactic ambiguity and thus essentially raises the document readability and (ii) simultaneous translation of all SL document one- and multi-component lexical units. The methodology is based on a language-independent hybrid extraction technique used for document analysis, and language-dependent shallow linguistic knowledge. It is targeted at intelligent output and computationally attractive properties. The approach is illustrated by its implementation into a CAT tool for the Russian-English language pair. Such tools can also be integrated into full MT systems.

1 Introduction

Exploding volume of professional publications demand operative international exchange of scientific and technical information and thus put in focus operativeness and quality of translation services. In spite of the great progress of MT that saves translation time, required translation quality so far cannot be achieved without human judgment (Koehn, 2009). Therefore in great demand are CAT tools designed to support and facilitate human translation.

CAT tools are developed to automate postediting and often involve controlled language. The most popular tools are translation memory (TM) tools whose function is to save the translation units in a database so that they can be re-used through special "fuzzy search" features. The efficiency of TM (as well as translation quality as such) is directly related to the problem of the comprehensiveness of multilingual lexicons. A translator who, as a rule, does not possess enough of expert knowledge in a scientific or technological domain spends about 75% of time for translating terminology, which do not guarantee the correctness of translation equivalents she/he uses. The percentage of mistakes in translating professional terminology reaches 40% (Kudashev, 2007). It is therefore essential to develop methodologies that could help human translators solve this problem, the huge resource being the Internet, if properly used. In this paper we suggest one of the possible ways to do so.

We would like to address the importance of text readability in the human translation performance. Readability relates to (though does not coincide with) the notion of translatability in MT research. Readability in human translation is associated with the level of clarity of a SL text for human understanding. Every translator knows how difficult it can be to understand professional texts, not only because of the abundance of terminology but also due to complex syntax and syntactic ambiguity. The ultimate example of a low readability text is the patent claim (Shinmori et al., 2003) that is written in the form of one nominal sentence with extremely complex “inhuman” syntactic structure that can run for a page or more. Low readability is often the case with scientific and technical papers as well.

In this paper we describe our effort to develop a portable between domains and languages CAT tool that can on-the-fly improve the readability of professional texts and provide for reliable terminology translation.

We paid special attention to multiword noun terminology, the most frequent and important terminological unit in special texts that can rarely be found in full in existing lexicons. When translated properly, multicomponent NPs do not only provide for the correct understanding of the corresponding target language (TL) term but in many cases lift syntactic ambiguity.

The tool can find a broad application, e.g., it can be useful for any non-SL speaker for a quick document digest. The settings of the tool allow the extraction of keyword translation pairs in case it is needed, e.g., for search purposes. It can also be integrated into a full MT system.

We implemented our methodology into a fully functional tool for the Russian-English language pair and conducted experiments for other domains and language pairs. In selecting Russian as a first SL we were motivated by two major considerations. Firstly, Russia has a huge pool of scientific and technical papers which are unavailable for non-Russian speakers without turning to expensive translation services. Secondly, our scientific challenge was to develop a hybrid methodology applicable to inflecting languages. Popular SMT and hybrid techniques working well on configurational and morphologically poor languages, such as English, fail on non-configurational languages with rich morphology (Sharoff, 2004). Russian is an ultimate example of such a language. It has a free word order; a typical Russian word has from 9 (for nouns) up to 50 forms (for verbs). In what follows we first present the tool and then describe the underlying methodology.

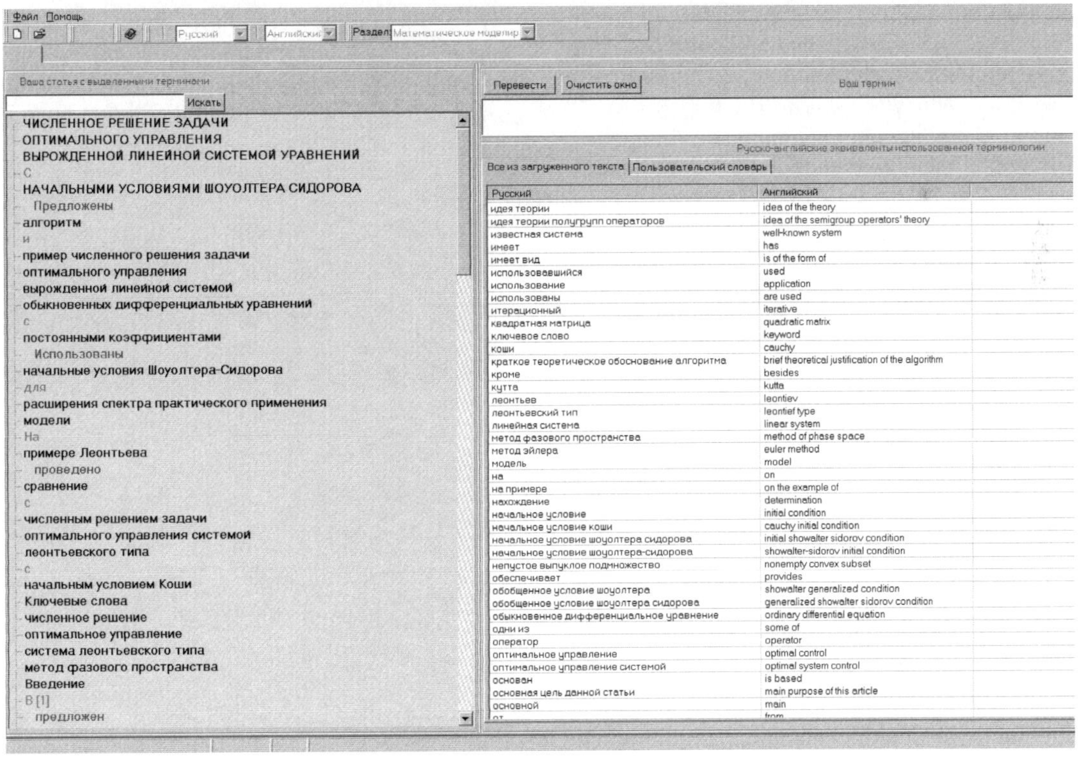

Figure 1. A screenshot of the Russian-to-English CAT tool user interface at the bookmark "show all". The left pane displays a SL interactive text of a scientific paper in mathematical modelling with explicitly marked (bold faced) nominal terminology and verbs (in blue). The left pane contains the alphabetically ordered list of all 1-4 component Russian terms with their English equivalents. On the top of the right pane there is a type-in area which permits searching for the translations of terms longer than 4 words in the tool knowledge base. The second bookmark on the top of the Ru-En equivalent area allows opening a user dictionary for the user to collect terms she/he might need in the future.

2 The Tool

The tool takes a SL text an as input and on the fly produces output at two levels:

- a marked-up interactive SL text with highlighted multi-component nominal and verbal terminology (NPs and VPs);
- a list of all single- and multi-component SL-TL units found in the input text.

Text mark-up improves input readability and helps translator quicker and better understand the syntactic structure of the input. This feature combined with on-the-fly translation of *all* 1-4 component SL text lexical units reduces translation time and effort and raises translation quality. The tool can be used as an e-dictionary where terms are searched through a type-in area in the user interface.

Translation equivalents are normalized as follows. SL NPs are outputted in nominative singular, while VPs are presented in a finite form keeping the SL voice, tense and number features. For example, in the Russian-to-English tool the Russian VP wordform "*смонтированные*"_*past participle, perfective, plural* (literally *"done")* will be outputted as "*смонтированы*"_ *finite, past, plural = "were mounted"*.

The tool user interface has a lot of effort-saving functionalities. A click on a unit in the marked up input text in the left pane highlights its TL equivalent in the alphabetically sorted list of translations on the right pane. It is possible to create user dictionaries accumulating terminology from different texts, saving these dictionaries and projects, etc. A screenshot of the user interface in shown in Figure 1.

3 Methodology and Development Issues

3.1 Architecture

The overall architecture of the tool is shown in Figure 2. The tool engine consists of a shallow analyzer including three fully automatic modules, - a SL hybrid NP extractor, shallow parser and imbedded machine translation module meant to translate terminology. The knowledge base contains shallow linguistic knowledge, - lexicons and rules.

The NP extractor is a hybrid stand-alone tool pipelined to the system. We built it following the methodology of NP extraction for the English language as described in (Sheremetyeva, 2009) and ported it to the Russian language.

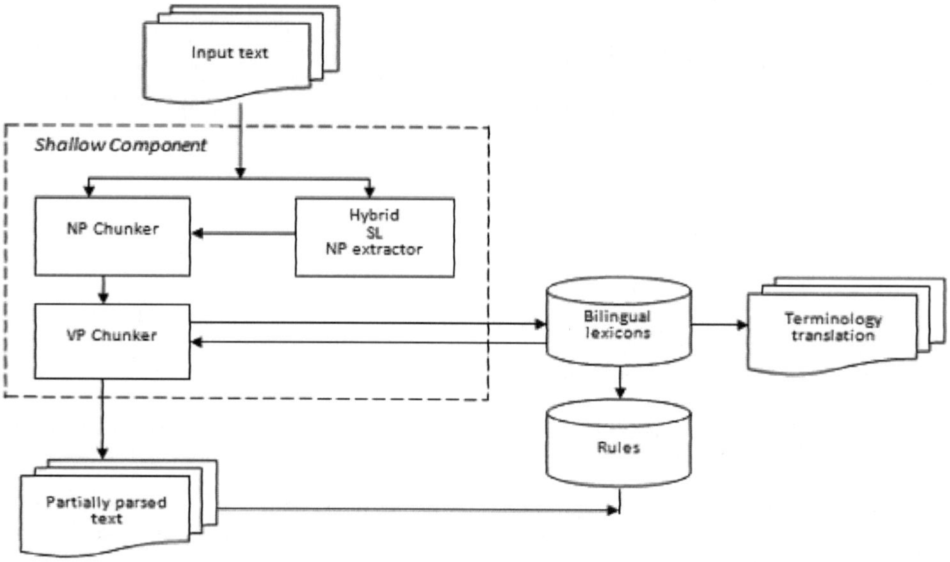

Figure 2. The architecture of the CAT tool.

The extraction methodology combines statistical techniques, heuristics and very shallow linguistic knowledge. The knowledge base consists of a number of unilingual lexicons, - sort of extended lists of stop words forbidden in particular (first, middle or last) positions in a typed lexical unit (Russian NP in our case).

NP extraction procedure starts with n-gram calculation and then removes n-grams, which cannot be NPs by successive matching components of calculated n-grams against the stop lexicons. The extraction itself thus neither requires such demanding NLP procedures, as tagging, morphological normalization, POS pattern match, etc., nor does it rely on statistical counts (statistical counts are only used to sort out keywords). The latter makes this extraction methodology suitable for inflecting languages (Russian in our case) where frequencies of n-grams are low.

Porting the NP extractor from English to Russian consisted in substituting English stop lexicons of the tool with the Russian equivalents. We did this by translating each of the English stop lists into Russian using a free online system PROMT (http://www.translate.ru) followed by manual brush-up.

The NP extractor does not rely on a preconstructed corpus, works on small texts, does not miss low frequency units and can reliably extract *all* NPs from an input text. We excluded a lemmatizer from the original extraction algorithm and kept all extracted Russian NPs in their textual forms. The noun phrases thus extracted are of 1 to 4 components due to the limitations of the extractor that uses a 4-gram model. The extractor was also used for lexicon acquisition.

The shallow parser consists of an NP chunker, VP chunker and tagger. The first users the knowledge dynamically produced by the NP extractor (lists of all NPs of an input text in their text form). The VP chunker and tagger turn to the Russian entries of the tool bilingual lexicon. The tagger is actually a supertagger as it assigns supertags coding all morphological features, such as part-of-speech, number, gender, tense, etc.

The machine translation module translates text chunks into English using simple transfer and generation rules working over the space of supertags as found in the CAT tool bilingual lexicon.

3.2 Bilingual lexicon

To ensure correct terminology translation the bilingual lexicon of the tool should necessarily be tuned to a specific domain for which it is to be used. The lexicon is organized as a set of shallow cross-referenced monolingual entries of lexical units listed with their part-of-speech class and explicit paradigms of domain-relevant wordforms. This is the type of resource that, once build for some other purpose, can be simply fed into the system. Acquisition of this type of knowledge for every new pair of languages is what existing SMT tools can provide either in advance or on the fly, as reported in (2012 et al.,). In our work striving for correctness we combined automatic techniques with manual check and manual acquisition.

The Russian vocabulary was created in two steps. First, an initial corpus of Russian scientific papers on mathematical modelling of approximately 80 000 wordforms was acquired on Internet. We then ported the NP extractor described above to other Russian parts-of-speech and automatically extracted domain specific typed lexical units (NPs, VPs, ADJs, etc) consisting of 1 up to 4 components from the corpus. These automatically extracted lists of lexemes were further checked by human acquirers and 14 000 of them were used as a seed Russian vocabulary.

The seed vocabulary was then used to acquire longer Russian lexemes both from the initial corpus, and the Internet, which is in fact an unlimited corpus. The following methodology was applied. The seed lexical units were used as keywords in the Internet search engines. New Russian terminological units including seed terms highlighted in the two first pages of the search results were included in the lexicon. For example, for the seed (key) term *«псевдообращение»* the following multi-component terms popped-up on the Internet: *«псевдообращение сопряженной системы», «псевдообращение матриц с вырожденными весами», «псевдообращение Мура-Пенроуза»*, etc. As a result, the seed Russian vocabulary was extended to 60 000 single- and multi-component units up to seven-eight words long.

Lexical acquisition of English equivalents was done based on existing domain lexicons, parallel/comparable corpora and raw Internet resources. The last needs to be explained. In case neither existing lexicons, nor parallel/comparable corpora could provide for a reliable English equivalent, which was mostly the case with long terms, translation hypotheses were made based on different combinations of translation variants of component words. Every translation hypothesis was then checked in the Internet search engine. If an engine (we used Google) showed a translation version in the search results, the hypothesis was considered confirmed and the English equivalent was included in the tool lexicon. For example, the Russian term *«роевое представление частицы»* could not be found in any of existing lexicons, the following English equivalents of the Russian term components were found:

рой – swarm; представление - conception, expression, representation, performance, configuration; частица – bit, fraction, particle, shard, corpuscle.

If you create a translation hypothesis by using the first translation variant for every component of the Russian term you will get: *«swarm conception of a bit» or «bit swarm conception».* Used as key words in Google, the search results do not contain these words combined in a term. This translation hypothesis was rejected. Another hypothesis *«particle swarm representation»* used as key words in Google gives the English term *«Particle Swarm Optimization and Priority Representation»* from the paper on mathematical modelling by Philip Brooks, a native English speaker. «Particle swarm representation» is accepted as a correct English translation of the Russian term *«роевое представление частицы»*. Though tedious, this methodology allowed careful detection of the up-to-date highly reliable translation that could hardly be achieved otherwise.

3.3 Workflow

The raw SL document first goes to the automatic NP extractor, which produces a list of one- to four component noun phrases. The dynamically created NP list is then used as knowledge for the NP chunker, which by matching the extracted list against the input text chunks (brackets) noun phrases in the document. The morphological tagger completes morphological analysis of these chunks by looking them up in the NP entries of the tool lexicon. The text strings between chunked NPs is then supplied to the VP chunker that matches this input against verb wordforms, as listed in the morphological zones of verb entries. In case of a match the text string is chunked as VP and a corresponding supertag from the lexicon is assigned. The text strings which were left between NP and VP chunks are then looked up in the rest of the entries of the lexicon and tagged. The fact that in every chunking/tagging pass only the type-relevant lexicon entries are searched practically lifts the ambiguity problem in morphological analysis.

Finally, based on classified chunk borders, the document is turned into an interactive ("clickable") text with NP and VP phrases highlighted in different colours.

The output of the shallow analysis stage (fully (super) tagged lexical units) is passed to the machine translation module that following simple rules generates SL-TL lexical pairs for all the lexica of the text (See Figure 1).

4 Status and Conclusions

The viability of the methodology we have described was proved by its implementation in a Russian-English CAT tool for the domain of scientific papers on mathematical modelling. The tool is fully developed. The domain bilingual static knowledge sources have been carefully crafted based on corpora analysis and internet resources. The programming shell of the tool is language independent and provides for knowledge administration in all the tool modules to improve their performance.

The extractor of Russian nominal terminology currently performs with 98, 4 % of recall and 96, 1% precision. The shallow clunker based on the extraction results and lexicon shows even higher accuracy. This is explained, on the one hand, by the high performance of the NP extractor, and, on the other hand, by the nature of inflecting languages. Rich morphology turns out to be an advantage in our approach. Great variety of morphological forms lowers ambiguity between NP components and verb paradigms.

We could not yet find any publications describing research meant for similar output. This leaves the comparison between other methodologies/tools and ours as a future work. In general user evaluation results show a reasonably small number of failures that are being improved by brushing up the bilingual lexicon.

We intend to a) improve the quality of the tool by updating the tool knowledge based on the user feedback; b) integrate the tool into a full MT system and c) develop a search facility on the basis of the our extraction strategy.

References

Enache Ramona, Cristina Espana-Bonet, Aarne Ranta, Lluıs Marquez. 2012. A Hybrid System for Patent Translation. *Proceedings of the EAMT Conference.* Trento..Italy, May

Koehn Philipp. 2009. A process study of computer-aided translation, Philipp Koehn, *Machine Translation Journal, 2009*, volume 23, number 4, pages 241-263

Kudashev Igor S. 2007. Desining Translation *Dictionaris of Special Lexica* /I.S.Kudashev. – Helsinki University Print, – 445 p.

Sharoff, Serge . 2004. What is at stake: a case study of Russian expressions starting with a preposition. *Proceedings of the ACL Workshop on Multiword Expressions: Integrating Processing*, July.

Sheremetyeva, Svetlana. 2009. On Extracting Multiword NP Terminology for MT. *Proceedings of the EAMT Conference.* Barcelona, Spain, May.

Shinmori A., Okumura M., Marukawa Y. Iwayama M. 2003. Patent Claim Processing for Readability - Structure Analysis and Term Explanation, *Workshop on Patent Corpus Processing. conjunction with ACL 2003,* Sapporo. Japan, July.

— Invited Talk —

Translators in the Loop: Understanding How they Work with CAT Tools

Maureen Ehrensberger-Dow
Institute of Translation and Interpreting
Zurich University of Applied Sciences
Switzerland
ehre@zhaw.ch

Abstract

The research that we have been carrying out at translators' workplaces over the past few years has provided indications that some CAT tools are not being used to their full potential or are even being ignored by the users they were (or should have been) designed for. Since by nature humans seem to resist changing habits and procedures that do the job, it is easy to attribute that to the intransigence of older translators and shift the focus to designing new tools for digital natives. However, the cognitive demands of processing complex input in one language while producing and revising and/or assessing and revising output in another add a new dimension to the usual considerations of the human-machine loop of interaction, which may be independent of the translators' age or experience. In fact, the productivity constraints that many professional translators work under means that they might be adjusting more to their tools than adjusting their tools' settings to optimize their (the translators') performance. And if those tools have not been designed to meet their users' cognitive and physical ergonomic needs, their use may actually slow down the translation process and have potentially detrimental effects on quality.

Maureen Ehrensberger-Dow is a Canadian psycholinguist who has been involved in research into multilingualism and translation in Switzerland for the past 15 years. She is Professor of Translation Studies in the Zurich University of Applied Sciences' Institute of Translation and Interpreting and principal investigator of the SNSF-financed research projects *Capturing Translation Processes* and the *Cognitive and Physical Ergonomics of Translation*.

Measuring the Cognitive Effort of Literal Translation Processes

Moritz Schaeffer
Dalgas Have 15
Copenhagen Business School
Denmark
ms.ibc@cbs.dk

Michael Carl
Dalgas Have 15
Copenhagen Business School
Denmark
mc.isv@cbs.dk

Abstract

It has been claimed that human translators rely on some sort of literal translation equivalences to produce translations and to check their validity. More effort would be required if translations are less literal. However, to our knowledge, there is no established metric to measure and quantify this claim. This paper attempts to bridge this gap by introducing a metric for measuring literality of translations and assesses the effort that is observed when translators produce translations which deviate from the introduced literality definition.

1 Introduction

In his seminal paper, Ivir (1981: 58) hypothises that:

"The translator begins his search for translation equivalence from formal correspondence, and it is only when the identical-meaning formal correspondent is either not available or not able to ensure equivalence that he resorts to formal correspondents with not-quite-identical meanings or to structural and semantic shifts which destroy formal correspondence altogether. But even in the latter case he makes use of formal correspondence as a check on meaning - to know what he is doing, so to speak."

Related to this notion of "formal correspondence" is the *law of interference* which accounts for the observation that "in translation, phenomena pertaining to the make-up of the source text tend to be transferred to the target text" (Toury, 1995: 275).

However, context or cross-linguistic differences may make it necessary to abandon formal correspondence: it is often necessary to depart from a one-to-one correspondence between source and target text items, levels or ranks, which is confirmed by the statement "without it [formal correspondence], there would be nothing to shift from" (Malmkjær 2011a: 61).

Tirkkonen-Condit (2005) reformulates Ivir's formal correspondence translation hypothesis into a *monitor model*: "It looks as if literal translation is a default rendering procedure, which goes on until it is interrupted by a monitor that alerts about a problem in the outcome." Tirkkonen-Condit (2005:408)

Thus, the *formal correspondence hypothesis*, the *literal translation default rendering procedure,* the *law of interference* and the *monitor model* are all related concepts which seem to assume that one-to-one literal translation correspondences are easier to produce than translations that formally deviate from the source text, as the latter would require more effort, and hence will take longer for a translator to produce.

While it has been difficult to describe in what exactly consist literal translation (Malmkjær 2011b), we define (ideal) literal translation in this paper by the following criteria:

a) Word order is identical in the source and target languages

b) Source and target text items correspond one-to-one

c) Each source word has only one possible translated form in the given context

Although this definition of literality ignores a wide range of phenomena and kinds of equivalence, it allows for quantification and comparison across multiple languages. Any (voluntary or structural) deviation from these criteria would imply a relaxation from a literal translation and thus lead to greater effort, as measured by e.g. longer production times and more gaze activities.

In this paper we assess this hypothesis by analyzing the gazing behavior of translators. As a basis for our investigation we use the TPR-DB (Carl, 2012), which currently contains more than 940 text production sessions (translation, post-editing, editing and copying) in more than 10 different languages[1]. For each translation and post-editing session keystroke and gaze data was collected and stored, and translations were manually aligned. The TPR-DB is therefore ideally suited for answering aspects of the cognitive processes during translation which are shared across individuals and language combinations.

In section 2 we operationalize *literal translation* from a process point of view. We describe a transducer to measure the similarity of word order in the source and target language strings, to account for criteria (a) and (b). We introduce the notion of *translation choices*, derived from a corpus of alternative translations to account for criterion (c) above. In section 3, we correlate the predictions of the *literal translation default rendering procedure* with observed translators' behavior. Section 4 discusses the results.

2 Operationalizing literal translation

In this section, we first present a quantification of translation choices (literality criterion c) and then describe the computation of alignment cross values which account for literality criterion (b) and (c).

Killer		nurse		receives		four		live		sentences	
11	asesino	7	el_enfermero	15	recibe	28	cuatro	12	perpetuas	13	cadenas
6	el_asesino	5	enfermero_asesino	3	es_condenado			12	cadenas	11	perpetuas
3	el_enfermero	4	enfermero	3	condenado_a					2	asesino
2	enfermero_asesino	4	asesino	2	recibe_a						
		3	un_enfermero								
		2	enfermera								

Figure 1: Translation choices and numbers of occurrences as retrieved from 31 En -> ES translations in the TPR-DB

2.1 Translation Choices

A source word can often be translated in many different ways. In order to quantify such translation choices, Choice Network Analysis has been suggested (Campbell, 2000) as a method to infer cognitive processes from the different choices made by different translators: the more choices and the more complex choices a translator has to consider, the more effortful the translation of this particular item is. Campbell (2000) argues that translations by different translators of the same source text can be used to draw inferences about the cognitive processes during translation.

In line with these considerations, to estimate the translation effort for lexical selection, we count the number of different translation realizations for each word. We use the TPR-DB (Carl, 2012, Carl et al. 2014) which contains (among others) a large number of different translations for the same source text. For instance, Figure 1 shows the number of Spanish translation choices

[1] The figures relate to TPR-DBv1.4 which can be downloaded from: http://bridge.cbs.dk/platform/?q=CRITT_TPR-db

produced by 31 different translators for the same English source sentence. Figure 1 only shows translations which occur at least twice. Figure 2 shows one of the realized translations.

There is a considerable variance in the number of translation variants for different words. In 11 out of 31 translations "Killer" was aligned with "asesino", in 6 cases with "el asesino" etc. while for 28 out of 31 cases "four" was translated as "cuatro". Thus, according to the above hypothesis, the translation production of "Killer" would be more effortful than it would be to translate "live" than the translation of "four".

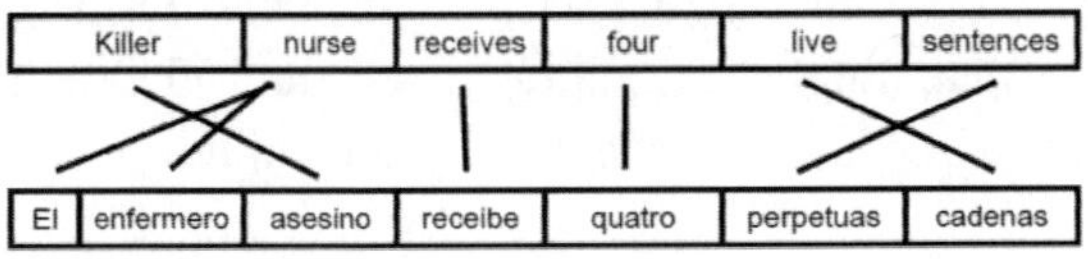

Figure 2: Oracle translation with word alignments

2.2 Alignment crossings

In order to quantify translation locality criterion (a) and (b), we adopt a local metric to quantify the similarity of the source and target language word order, relative to the previous alignment position. The metric is implemented as a transducer which produces translations word by word, writing the correct target language word order into an output buffer, while a reading device successively scans the source text to find the reference word(s) for the next word in the translation.

Given a reference source text (ST), an output oracle translation (TT), and the ST-TT alignments (as in Figure 2), the *CrossT* values indicate the distance between ST reference expressions of successive TT words, in terms of progressions and regressions.

For instance, assume the English source sentence "Killer nurse receives four live sentences" was translated into Spanish with the alignment relations as shown in Figure 2. In order to produce the first Spanish TT word "El", two English words ("Killer" and "nurse") have to be consumed in the reference text, which results in a *Cross* value of 2. Since the second source word ("nurse") emits two adjacent TT words, no further ST word has to be consumed to produce "enfermero", which results in the value *Cross=0.* To produce the third Spanish word, "asesino", one ST word to the left of "nurse" has to be processed, leading to the Cross value -1. The next Spanish word "recibe" is the translation of two words to the right of the current ST cursor position; "cuatro" one ST word ahead etc. with their respective Cross values of 2 and 1. Figure 3 illustrates this process. The inclined reader may continue this example and reconstruct how the *CrossT* values {2,0,-1,2,1,2,-1} are incrementally generated. Thus, *Cross* values indicate the minimum length of the progressions and regressions on the reference text required to generate the output string.

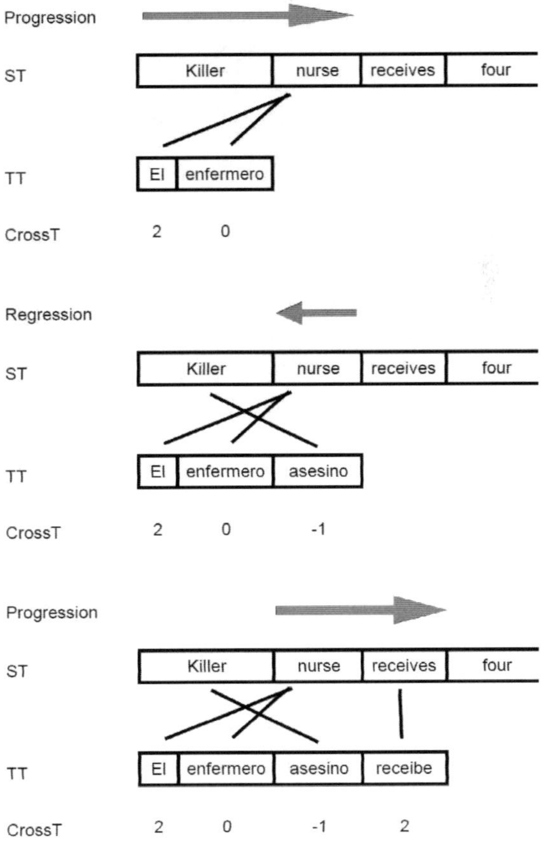

Figure 3: Computation of alignment crossings (CrossT) as length of progressions and regressions in the reference ST.

Cross values can also be computed from the source text. For the *CrossS* values we would then assume the ST text to be the output text and the TT text to be the reference.

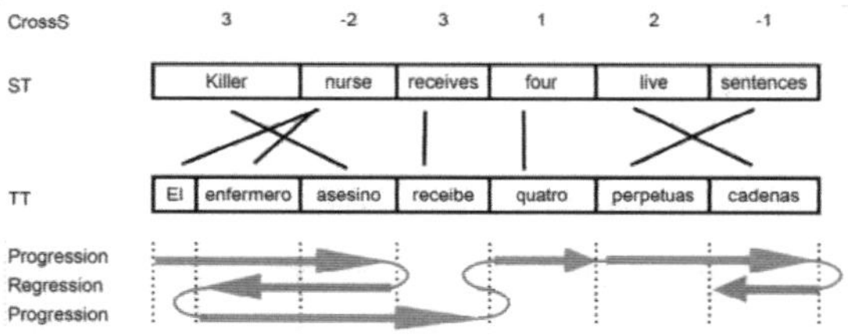

Figure 4: ST alignment crossings (CrossS), as generated when checking the ST against the TT

While *CrossT* values reflect the alignment effort for mapping ST tokens on the TT structure, as is required for translation production, *CrossS* values have a reverse interpretation, as they represent the mapping effort of TT tokens on the ST structure, as is more likely the case during revision. Figure 4 shows the *CrossS* values for the sentence in Figure 2. Note that the sequence of *CrossT* and *CrossS* are not symmetrical: in the given example *CrossS*: {3,-2,3,1,2,-1}. In section 3 we will show that both types of effort occur in translation and in post-editing.

The Cross value is small if source and target languages are (structurally) similar, and consists only of one-to-one token correspondences. The more both languages structurally differ or the less compositional the translations are, the bigger will become the Cross values.

Similarly, we expect to observe a larger number of translation choices as semantic shifts are introduced by the translator or if only "not-quite-identical meanings" are available.

3 Translators behaviour

Different parts of the TPR-DB have been used for the different analysis reported in this section. A set of 313 translations have been investigated to map translation crossings in section 3.1; 86 sessions were used for the post-editing experiment in section 3.2, and 24 translations for translation choices reported in section 3.3.

A simple linear regression was carried, to ascertain the extent to which total reading time (*GazeS* and *GazeT*) can be predicted by *Cross* values in sections 3.1 and 3.2, and by translation choices in section 3.3. The correlation for Cross values in sections 31 and 3.2 was calculated from value 1 to the peak in each distribution in the negative and positive directions. Only Cross values from -8 to 8 are reported because items with higher Cross values are very rare, resulting in vastly unequal numbers of items.

3.1 Alignment Crossing

This section reports an analysis of 313 translation sessions with 17 different source texts into six different languages as contained in the TPR-DB. The target languages were Danish, Spanish, English, Chinese, Hindi and German; the source languages were English and Danish.

Figure 5 depicts gazing time on an ST token with a given *CrossT* value, while Figure 6 depicts gazing time on the TT tokens with a given *CrossS* value. These figures show that higher *CrossT* and *CrossS* values are strongly correlated with *GazeS* and *GazeT* and thus more effortful to process than lower *CrossT* and *CrossS* values.

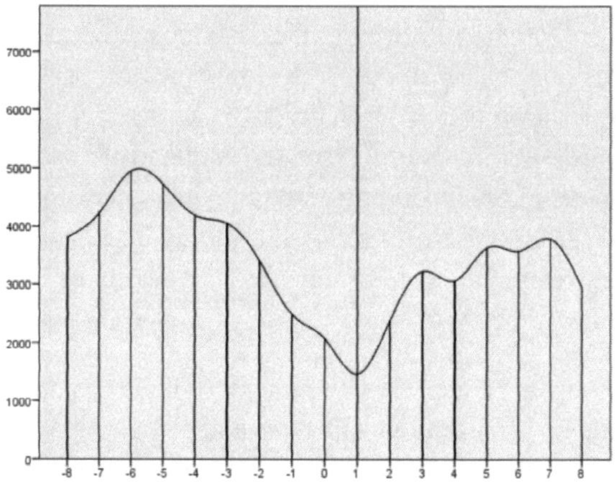

Figure 5: Average gazing time (vertical) on ST token with different CrossT values (horizontal)

Correlation between CrossT values and Total Reading Time on Source Text

As shown in Figure 5, a strong positive correlation was found between *CrossT* values and total reading time on the source text (r=.97 for negative *CrossT* values and r=.91 for positive *CrossT* values). The regression model predicted

97% and 82% of the variance for negative and positive values. The model was a good fit for the data ($F=205.7$, $p<.0005$ and $F=22.89$, $p<.005$, respectively). For every single increase in the negative *CrossT* value, the total reading time on the source text increased by 516ms, for positive *CrossT* value, the total reading time on the source text increased by 347ms.

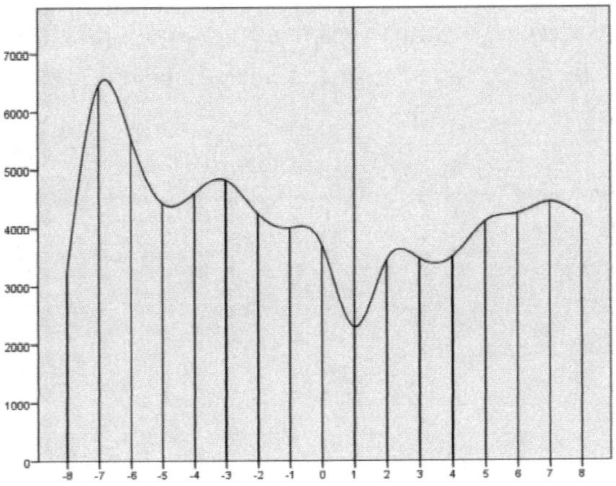

Figure 6: Average gazing time (vertical) on TT tokens for different CrossS values (horizontal)

Correlation between CrossS values and Total Reading Time on Target Text

Also for negative and positive *CrossS* values and total reading time on the TT a strong positive correlation was found ($r=.92$ and $r=.93$, respectively). The regression model predicted 84% and 85% of the variance, and was a good fit for the data ($F=36.97$, $p<.001$, $F=30.69$, $p<.003$). For every single increase in the negative *CrossS* value, the total reading time on the target text increased by 389ms, for positive *CrossS* values the total reading time on the target text increased by 301ms.

3.2 Alignment crossing in post-editing

This section reports an analysis over 86 different post-editing sessions from the TPR-DB of 9 different English source texts which were translated into three different target languages, German, Hindi and Spanish. As in section 3.1 the analysis shows that *CrossT* and *CrossS* values correlate with the total reading time per word (*GazeS* and *GazeT*). Figures 7 and 8 plot gazing times on ST and TT token with different *CrossT* and *CrossS* values during post-editing.

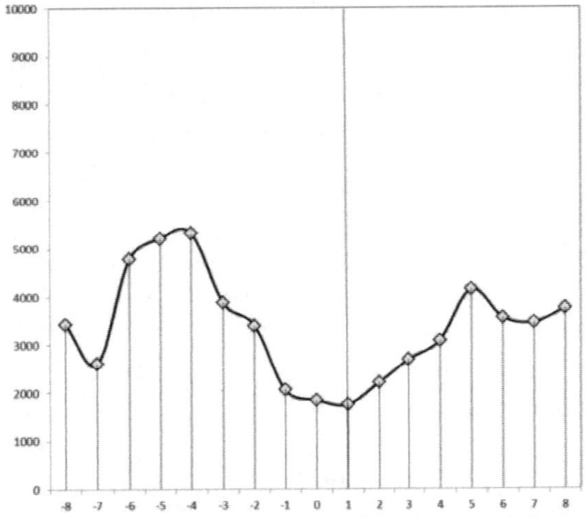

Figure 7: Average gazing time on ST tokens during post-editing for different CrossT values (horizontal)

Correlation between *CrossT* values and total reading time on source text

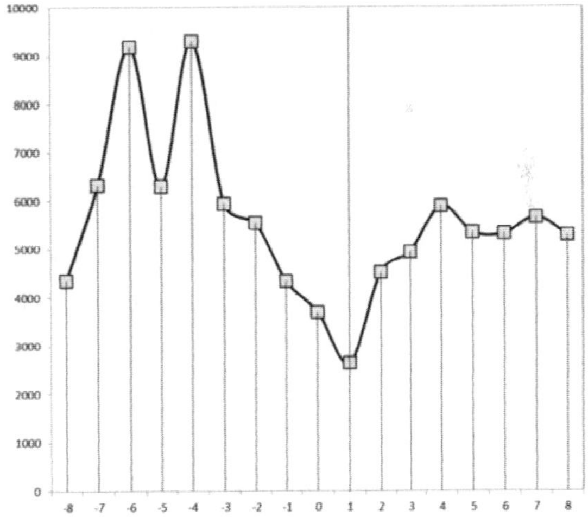

Figure 8: Average gazing time (vertical) on TT tokens during post-editing for different CrossS values (horizontal)

Similarly, a strong positive correlation was found between negative *CrossT* values and total reading time on the source text ($r=.95$ and $r=.98$), and the regression model predicted 88% and 94% of the variance for negative and positive CrossT values. The model was a good fit for the data ($F=38.50$, $p<.003$ and $F=67.56$, $p<.004$). For every single increase of the negative *CrossT* value, the total reading time on the target text increased by 723ms, while for positive CrossT values reading time increased by 566ms.

Correlation between *CrossS* values and total reading time on target text

A strong positive correlation was found between *CrossS* values and total reading time on the target text (r=.95), and the regression model predicted 87% and 89% of the variance for negative and positive CrossS values respective. The model was a good fit for the data (F=35.26, p<.004 and F=38.50, p<.003). For every single increase in the negative CrossS value, the total reading time on the target text increased by 1179ms, while for positive CrossS values reading time increased by 1016ms.

3.3 Translation choices

The data used for translation from scratch used for this purpose are 24 translations of 3 different texts from English into Danish and the data for post-editing used for this purpose are 65 post-edited translations of 9 different source texts involving one source language (English) and two target languages (German and Spanish). The number of alternative translations for every source item of the different source texts were counted. Only words which had up to 9 alternative choices were included in the analysis, partly so that a comparison between translation from scratch and post-editing was possible and partly because there are few items with more than 9 alternative translations.

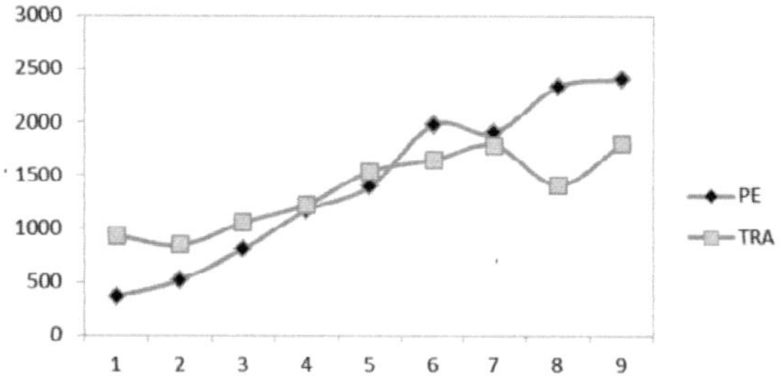

Figure 9: Correlation of alternative translation (horizontal) and average production time (vertical) for translation (TRA) and post-editing (PE).

Correlation between duration and alternatives

As shown in Figure 9, for translation from scratch and for post-editing there was a strong correlation between the time it took participants to produce a target word and the number of alternatives for every source word (r=.89 and r=.99, respectively). With few choices post-editors are quicker than translators, but this distance decreases as the number of translation choices increase. The regression model predicted 76% and 97% of the variance and was a good fit for the data (F=26.14, p<.001) for Translation and (F=269.50, p<.0001) for post-editing. For every increase in the number of alternatives, the production time increased by 117ms, respectively 278ms for translation and post-editing.

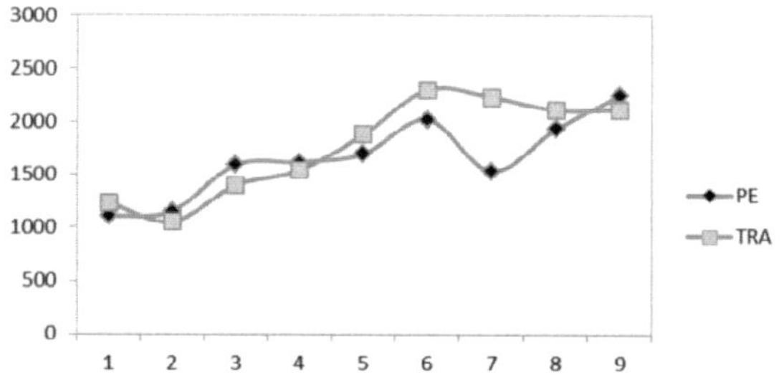

Figure 10: Correlation of alternative translation (horizontal) and average gazing time on TT words (vertical) during translation (TRA) and post-editing (PE).

Correlation between total reading time on the target text and alternatives

Similarly, Figure 10 depicts a strong correlation for translation from scratch and for post-editing between the total reading time on the target text per word and the number of translation choices for every source word (r=.90 and r=.87 respectively). The regression model predicted 77% and 72% of the variance and the model was a good fit for the data; F=28.45, p<.001 and F=21.80, p<.002 for translation and post-editing respectively. For every increase in the number of alternatives, the total reading time on the target text increased by 153ms, and 120ms.

Correlation between total reading time on the target text and alternatives

For translation from scratch, there was a strong correlation between total reading time on the source text per word and he number of alternatives for every source word (r=.76), but the regression model only predicted 52% of the variance. The model was a good fit for the data

($F = 9.74$, $p < .017$). For every increase in the number of alternatives, the total reading time on the source text increased by a modest 47ms.

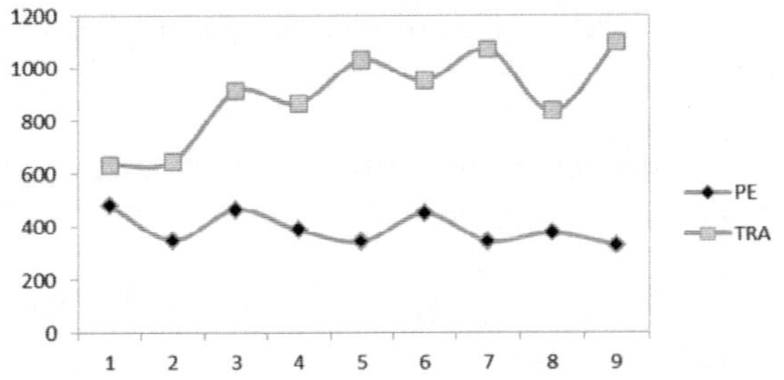

Figure 11 Correlation of alternative translation (horizontal) and average gazing time on ST words (vertical) during translation (TRA) and post-editing (PE).

However, as depicted in Figure 11, for post-editing there was no correlation between total reading time on the source text per word and the number of alternatives for every source word.

4 Discussion

The investigation reported here is not the first of its kind. Dragsted (2012) compared eye movement measures (total reading time and number of fixations) and pauses for words which were translated by 8 participants using the same target word with words for which the eight participants used different words.

She found that the total reading time and the number of fixations on words with many (5-8) alternatives target text items was significantly higher than the number of fixations on words with only one or two different target items. She also found that the pauses prior to critical words were longer for words with many alternatives as compared to words with one or two alternatives.

This seems to confirm the assumption that the more lexical choices a translator has to consider, the more effortful the processing of this item becomes. Campbell (2000: 38) suggests that "the complexity of choices available to the translator to select from" can be taken as a measure of the effort of the related cognitive processes.

Our analysis investigates this suggestion on a larger scale, involving more language pairs and two conditions: translation from scratch and post-editing. It shows similar results to those of Dragsted (2012), but in addition shows that effect of alternatives on *production time* per word was much stronger for post-editing as compared to translation (171ms for translation vs. 278ms for post-editing). This suggests that highly (translation) ambiguous texts should perhaps not be considered for post-editing. In (Carl and Schaeffer, 2014) we look at this effect in more detail by investigating the word translation entropy in human and machine produced translations and propose a translation ambiguity threshold that might be suitable for post-editing.

The effect of translation choices on total *TT reading time* was comparable for translation and post-editing (153ms for translation vs. 120 for post-editing). For total *ST reading time* there was no effect for post-editing, while every additional translation choice increased the total *ST reading time* by 47ms, however modest compared to the effect on TT reading time. This finding suggests that in from scratch translation choices are already processed during ST reading, while during post-editing choices are considered mainly when the gaze is on the TT.

As a second variable we investigate ST-TT crossing values. Higher *Cross* values indicate non-monotonous translation relations such as local distortions of ST-TT alignment, discontinuous, idiomatic or multi-word units, all of which require larger sequences of the source and/or target text to be integrated and related, and thus increased effort when maintaining and processing larger numbers of items in working memory. The large increases of total *ST reading time* for tokens with higher *CrossT* values in translation and post-editing suggests that integrating larger ST chunks is also more effortful during translation and post-editing.

Similar findings are also reported by Jensen et al. (2010) who investigate gazing time for English-Danish verbal translations when they switch their sentence position (SVO → SOV) vs. they remain in both languages in the same sentence position (SVO → SVO). Our investigation generalizes these finding to different language pairs and all kinds of relative ST-TT distortion.

Another observation is related to the large increases in total *TT reading time* for higher *CrossS* values, during translation and post-editing. This observation suggests that translators not only read the ST to generate a TT equivalent, but they also check the produced TT whether it corresponds to the ST. As one could expect, this tendency is very pronounced during post-editing, but appears interestingly also during translation from scratch. The observation is in line with a previous assumption of Carl and Dragsted (2012: 141) who find that source text related processes are "triggered by problems associated with text production rather than" during source text reading.

Note that for all analysis, both translation and post-editing, reading time increased much more with negative *Cross* values than this is the case for positive *Cross* values. This coincides with the finding that regressions - which negative Cross values reflect - are more effortful to process than progressions, since regressions often mirror misunderstanding and imply the integration of already parsed input text (e.g. Reichle et al 2009).

5 Conclusion and outlook

There has been some discussion in the translation process research (TPR) literature on the "tendency of the translating process to proceed literally to a certain extent" Tirkkonen-Condit (2004: 183), where a deviation from the ideal default translation would result in higher effort. However, to our knowledge the literal default translation hypothesis has never been quantified and empirically assessed in a larger context. In this paper we bridge this gap. We provide a quantifiable definition of *literal translation* as a continuous concept involving alternative translation choices and source-target distortions, apply it to a collection of translation and post-editing sessions from the TPR-DB and assess translation effort by measuring gazing and translation time. We find that gaze activity and production time is inversely proportional to the literality of the produced translations. Using linear regression we find in particular:

- More translation choices lead to longer reading and processing time
- Longer relative source-target language distortions increase gaze activity.
- Regressions are more effortful than progressions
- Translators and post-editors map not only the source text against the target, but also the target against the source text

These findings suggest a model in which, paradoxically, translators already know the translations which they produce; they merely refer to the ST - and to the TT for cross-checking - to verify the translation hypothesis which they already have in mind.

A number of issues remain open for further research. For instance, the impact of the target language and the (syntactic) similarity of the source and target languages. According to the hypothesis supported here, closely related languages with similar word order and similar conceptual repository will more likely have more literal translations. They will more often consist of monotonous one-to-one translations, approaching an *ideal literal translation* (Schaeffer, 2013). The more syntactic reordering between source and target text take place the more it will become non-literal.

Another set of questions relates to whether and how the methods discussed here can be used to assess the cognitive effort for translating and/or post-editing entire sentences and texts and the impact on post-editing practice.

Acknowledgments

This project has received funding from the European Union's Seventh Framework Programme for research, technological development and demonstration under grant agreement no 287576. We are grateful to all contributors to the TPR database for allowing us the use of their data.

References

Campbell, Stuart. 2000. "Choice Network Analaysis in Translation Research." In *Intercultural Faultlines. Research Models in Translation Studies I. Textual and Cognitive Aspects*, edited by Maeve Olohan, 29–42. Manchester: St Jerome.

Carl, Michael. 2012. "The CRITT TPR-DB 1.0: A Database for Empirical Human Translation Process Research." In *Proceedings of the AMTA 2012 Workshop on Post-Editing Technology and Practice (WPTP 2012)*, edited by Sharon O'Brien, Michel Simard, and Lucia Specia, 9–18. Stroudsburg, PA: Association for Machine Translation in the Americas (AMTA).

Carl, Michael, Mercedes García Martínez, Bartolomé Mesa-Lao, Nancy Underwood. 2014. "CFT13: A new resource for research into the post-editing process." *Proceedings of LREC*

Carl, Michael, and Barbara Dragsted. 2012. "Inside the Monitor Model : Processes of Default and Challenged Translation Production." *Translation: Computation, Corpora, Cognition* 2 (1): 127–145.

Carl, Michael, and Moritz Schaeffer (2014) "Word Transition Entropy as an Indicator for Expected Machine Translation Quality", Proceedings of LREC

Dragsted, Barbara. 2012. "Indicators of Difficulty in Translation — Correlating Product and Process Data." *Across Languages and Cultures* 13 (1) (June 1): 81–98. doi:10.1556/Acr.13.2012.1.5. http://www.akademiai.com/openurl.asp?genre=article&id=doi:10.1556/Acr.13.2012.1.5.

Ivir, Vladimir. 1981. "Formal Correspondence Vs. Translation Equivalence Revisited." *Poetics Today* 2 (4): 51–59.

Jensen, Kristian T.H., Annette C. Sjørup, and Laura W. Balling. 2010. "Effects of L1 Syntax on L2 Translation." In *Methodology, Technology and Innovation in Translation Process Research: A Tribute to Arnt Lykke Jakobsen*, edited by F. Alves, S. Göpferich, and Mees Inger M., 319–336. Copenhagen: Samfundslitteratur.

Malmkjær, Kirsten. 2011a. "Linguistic Approaches to Translation." In *Oxford Handbook of Translation Studies*, edited by Kirsten Malmkjær and Kevin Windle, 57–70. Oxford: OUP.

Malmkjær, Kirsten. 2011b. "Translation Universals." In *The Oxford Handbook of Translation Studies*, edited by Kirsten Malmkjær and Kevin Windle, 83–94. Oxford: Oxford University Press.

Reichle, Erik D., Tessa Warren, Kerry McConnell. (2009). "Using E-Z Reader to model the effects of higher level language processing on eye movements during reading." *Psychonomic Bulletin & Review*, 16(1), 1–21.

Schaeffer, Moritz. 2013. *The Ideal Literal Translation Hypothesis: The Role of Shared Representations During Translation*. PhD Thesis. University of Leicester.

Tirkkonen-Condit, Sonja. 2004. "Unique Items: Over- or Under-Represented in Translated Language?" In *Translation Universals: Do They Exist?* Amsterdam and Philadelphia: John Benjamins.

Tirkkonen-Condit, Sonja. 2005. "The Monitor Model Revisited: Evidence from Process Research." *Meta: Translators' Journal* 50 (2): 405–414.

Toury, Gideon. 1995. *Descriptive Translation Studies and Beyond. Benjamins Translation Library V4*. Vol. 75. Amsterdam and Philadelphia: John Benjamins.

The Impact of Machine Translation Quality on Human Post-editing

Philipp Koehn[◇⋆]
pkoehn@inf.ed.ac.uk
[◇]Center for Speech and Language Processing
The Johns Hopkins University

Ulrich Germann[⋆]
ugermann@inf.ed.ac.uk
[⋆]School of Informatics
University of Edinburgh

Abstract

We investigate the effect of four different competitive machine translation systems on post-editor productivity and behaviour. The study involves four volunteers post-editing automatic translations of news stories from English to German. We see significant difference in productivity due to the systems (about 20%), and even bigger variance between post-editors.

1 Introduction

Statistical machine translation (SMT) has made considerable progress over the past two decades. Numerous recent studies have shown productivity increases with post-editing of MT output over traditional work practices in human translation (e.g., Guerberof, 2009; Plitt and Masselot, 2010; Garcia, 2011; Pouliquen et al., 2011; Skadiņš et al., 2011; den Bogaert and Sutter, 2013; Vazquez et al., 2013; Green et al., 2013; Läubli et al., 2013).

The advances in statistical machine translation over the past years have been driven to a large extent by frequent (friendly) competitive MT evaluation campaigns, such as the shared tasks at the ACL WMT workshop series (Bojar et al., 2013) and IWSLT (Cettolo et al., 2013), and the NIST Open MT Evaluation.[1] These evaluations usually apply a mix of automatic evaluation metrics, most prominently the BLEU score (Papineni et al., 2001), and more subjective human evaluation criteria such as correctness, accuracy, and fluency.

How the quality increases measured by automatic metrics and subjective evaluation criteria relate to actual increases in the productivity of post-editors is still an open research question. It is also not clear yet if some machine translation approaches — say, syntax-based models — are better suited for post-editing than others. These relationships may very well also depend on the language pair in question and the coarse level of MT quality, from barely good enough for post-editing to almost perfect.

The pilot study presented in this paper investigates the influence of the underlying SMT system on post-editing effort and efficiency. The study focuses on translation of general news text from English into German, with translations created by non-professional post-editors working on output from four different translation systems. The data generated by this study is available for download.[2]

We find that the better systems lead to a productivity gain of roughly 20% and carry out in-depth analysis of editing behavior. A significant finding is the high variance in work styles between the different post-editors, compared to the impact of machine translation systems.

2 Related Work

Koponen (2012) examined the relationship between human assessment of post-editing efforts and objective measures such as post-editing time and number of edit operations. She found that segments that require a lot of reordering are perceived as being more difficult, and that long sentences are considered harder, even if only few words changed. She also reports larger variance between translators in post-editing *time* than in post-editing *operations* — a finding that we confirm here as well.

From a detailed analysis of the types of edits performed in sentences with long versus short post-edit times, Koponen et al. (2012) conclude that the observed differences in edit times can be explained at least in part also by the types of necessary edits and the associated cognitive effort. Deleting superfluous function words, for example, appears to be cognitively simple and takes little time, whereas inserting translations for untranslated words requires more cognitive effort

[1] http://www.nist.gov/itl/iad/mig/openmt.cfm

[2] http://www.casmacat.eu/index.php?n=Main.Downloads

Table 1: News stories used in the study (size is given in number of sentences)

Source	Size	Title
BBC	49	Norway's rakfisk: Is this the world's smelliest fish?
BBC	47	Mexico's Enrique Pena Nieto faces tough start
CNN	45	Bradley Manning didn't complain about mistreatment, prosecutors contend
CNN	63	My Mexican-American identity crisis
Economist	55	Old battles, new Middle East
Guardian	38	Cigarette plain packaging laws come into force in Australia
NY Times	61	In a Constantly Plugged-In World, It's Not All Bad to Be Bored
NY Times	47	In Colorado, No Playbook for New Marijuana Law
Telegraph	95	Petronella Wyatt: I was bullied out of Oxford for being a Tory

and takes longer. They also compare post-editing styles of different post-editors working on identical post-editing tasks.
Another study by Koponen (2013) showed that inter-translator variance is lower in a controlled language setting when translators are given the choice of output from three different machine translation systems.

In the realm of machine translation research, there has been an increasing interest in the use of MT technology by post-editors. A major push are the two EU-funded research projects MATECAT[3] and CASMACAT[4], which are developing an open source translation and post-editing workbench (Federico et al., 2012; Alabau et al., 2013).

At this point, we are not aware of any study that compares directly the impact of different machine translation systems on post-editor productivity and behaviour.

3 Experimental Design

We thus carried out an experiment on an English–German news translation task, using output from four different SMT systems, post-edited by fluent bilingual native speakers of German with no prior experience in professional translation.

3.1 The Translation Task

The Workshop on Statistical Machine Translation (Bojar et al., 2013) organises an annual evaluation campaign for machine translation systems. The subject matter is translation of news stories from sources such as the New York Times or the BBC. We decided to use output from systems submitted to this evaluation campaign, not only because their output is freely available,[5] but also because it comes with automatic metric scores and human judgements of the translation quality.

The translation direction we chose was English–German, partly due to convenience (the authors of this study are fluent in both languages), but also because this language pair poses special challenges to current machine translation technology, due to the syntactic divergence of the two languages.

We selected data from the most recent evaluation campaign. The subset chosen for our post-editing task comprises 9 different news stories, originally written in English, with a total of 500 sentences. Details are shown in Table 1.

3.2 Machine Translation Systems

A total of 15 different machine translation systems participated in the evaluation campaign. We selected four different systems that differ in their architecture and use of training data:

- an anonymized popular online translation system built by a large Internet company (ONLINE-B)
- the syntax-based translation system of the University of Edinburgh (UEDIN-SYNTAX; Nadejde et al., 2013)
- the phrase-based translation system of the University of Edinburgh (UEDIN-PHRASE; Durrani et al., 2013)
- the machine translation system of the University of Uppsala (UU; Stymne et al., 2013)

In the 2013 WMT evaluation campaign, the systems translated a total of 3000 sentences, and their

[3] http://www.matecat.com/
[4] http://www.casmacat.eu/
[5] http://www.statmt.org/wmt13/results.html

Table 2: Machine translation systems used in the study, with quality scores in the WMT 2013 evaluation campaign.

System	BLEU	SUBJECTIVE
ONLINE-B	20.7	0.637
UEDIN-SYNTAX	19.4	0.614
UEDIN-PHRASE	20.1	0.571
UU	16.1	0.361

output was judged with the BLEU score against a professional reference translation and by subjective ranking. The scores obtained for the different systems on the full test set are shown in Table 2. The first three systems are fairly close in quality (although the differences in subjective human judgement scores are statistically significant), whereas the fourth system (UU) clearly lags behind. The best system ONLINE-B was ranked first according to human judgement and thus can be considered state of the art.

From casual observation, the syntax-based system UEDIN-SYNTAX succeeds more frequently in producing grammatically correct translations. The phrase-based system UEDIN-PHRASE, even though trained on the same parallel data, has higher coverage since it does not have the requirement that translation rules have to match syntactic constituents in the target language, which we presume is the main cause behind the lower BLEU score. The two systems use the same language model.

System UU is also a phrase based system, with a decoder that is able to consider the document level context. It was trained on smaller corpora for both the translation model and the language model.

We do not have any insight into the system ONLINE-B, but we conjecture that it is a phrase-based system with syntactic pre-reordering trained on much larger data sets, but not optimised towards the news domain.

Notice the inconsistency between BLEU score and subjective score for the two systems from the University of Edinburgh. Results from other evaluations have also shown (Callison-Burch et al., 2012) that current automatic evaluation metrics do not as much as human judges appreciate the strengths of the syntax-based system, which builds syntactic structures in the target language during translation. Hence, we were particularly interested how the syntax-based system fares with post-editors.

As mentioned above, the nine documents chosen for the post-editing task analysed in this paper (cf. Table 1) were part of the WMT 2013 evaluation data set. All nine documents had English as the original source language.

3.3 Post-Editors

We recruited four English-German bilingual, native German post-editors. Three were students, staff, or faculty at the University of Edinburgh; the fourth had been previously employed on a contractual basis for linguistic annotation work.[6] The post-editors had no professional experience with translation, and differed in language skills.

3.4 Assignment of MT Output

The goal of this study was to investigate how post-editors' behaviour and productivity are influenced by the quality of the underlying machine translation system. Ideally, we would want to present output from different systems to the same post-editor and see how their observable behaviour changes.

However, a post-editor who has seen the output from one MT system for a sentence will be at an advantage when post-editing the output from a second system, by having already spent significant time understanding the source sentence and considering the best translation choices.

Hence we used 4 different post-editors, each to post-edit the output in equal amounts from each of the 4 machine translation systems under investigation, so that each post-editor worked on each sentence once and the entire output from all systems was post-edited once by one of the 4 post-editors.

A concern in this setup is that we never know if we measure differences in post-editors or differences in machine translations systems when comparing the behaviour for any given sentence.

Therefore, each post-editor was assigned a translation for each sentence randomly from any of the machine translation systems. This random assignment allows us to marginalise out the dependence on the post-editor when assessing statistics for the different systems.

[6] The ordering here does not reflect the order of post-editors in the discussion later in this paper.

Table 3: Post-editing speed by editor and system.

System	seconds / word					words / hour				
	1	2	3	4	**mean**	1	2	3	4	**mean**
ONLINE-B	2.95	4.69	9.16	4.98	**5.46**	1,220	768	393	723	**659**
UEDIN-PHRASE	3.04	5.01	9.22	4.70	**5.45**	1,184	719	390	766	**661**
UEDIN-SYNTAX	3.03	4.41	9.20	4.97	**5.38**	1,188	816	391	724	**669**
UU	3.11	5.01	11.59	5.58	**6.35**	1,158	719	311	645	**567**
mean per editor	**3.03**	**4.78**	**9.79**	**5.05**		**1,188**	**753**	**368**	**713**	

4 Productivity

The primary argument for post-editing machine translation output as opposed to more traditional approaches is the potential gain in productivity. If translation professionals can work faster with machine translation, then this has real economic benefits. There are also other considerations, for example that post-editing might be done by professionals that are less skilled in the source language (Koehn, 2010).

We measure productivity by time spent on each sentence. This is not a perfect measure. When working on a news story, post-editors tend to speed up when moving down the story since they have already solved some reoccurring translation problems and get more familiar with the context.

4.1 Productivity by MT System

Our main interests is the average translation speed, broken down by machine translation system. The columns labelled "mean" in Table 3 show the results. While the differences are not big for the top three systems, the syntax-based system comes out on top.

We used bootstrap resampling to test the speed differences for statistical significance. Only system UU is significantly worse than the others (at p-level < 0.01), with about 20% lower productivity.

4.2 Productivity by Post-Editor

Post-editing speed is very strongly influenced by the post-editor's skill and effort. Our post-editors were very diverse, showing large differences in translation speed. See the columns labelled 1 to 4 in Table 3 for details.

In particular, post-editor 3 took more than three times as much time as the fastest (PE 1). According to a post-study interview with Post-Editor 3, there were two reasons for this. First, the post-editor was feeling a bit "under the weather" during the study and found it hard to focus. Second, (s)he found the texts very difficult to translate and struggled with idiomatic expressions and cultural references that (s)he did not understand immediately.

4.3 Productivity by System and Post-Editor

While the large differences between the post-editors are unfortunate when the goal is consistency in results, they provide some data on how post-editors of different skill levels are influenced by the quality of the machine translation systems.

Table 3 breaks down translation speed by machine translation system and post-editor. Interestingly, machine translation quality has hardly any effect on the fast Post-Editor 1, and the lower MT performance of system UU affects only Post-Editors 3 and 4. Post-Editor 2 is noticeably faster with UEDIN-SYNTAX — an effect that cannot be observed for the other post-editors. The differences between the other systems are not large for any of the post-editors.

Statistically significant — as determined by bootstrap resampling — are only the differences in post-editing speed for Post-Editor 3 with system UU versus ONLINE-B and UEDIN-PHRASE at p-level < 0.01, and against UEDIN-SYNTAX at p-level <0.02, and for Post-Editor 4 for UU versus UEDIN-PHRASE at p-level < 0.05. Note that the absence of statistical significance in our data has much to do with the small sample size; more extensive experiments may be necessary to ensure more solid findings.

5 Translation Edit Rate

Given the inherent difficulties in obtaining timing information, we can also measure the impact of machine translation system quality on post-editing effort in terms of how much the post-editors change the machine translation output, as done, for example in Cettolo et al. (2013).

Table 4: Edit rate and types of edits per system

System	HTER	ins	del	sub	shift	wide shift
ONLINE-B	35.7	4.8	7.4	18.9	4.6	5.8
UEDIN-PHRASE	37.9	5.5	7.4	20.0	5.0	6.6
UEDIN-SYNTAX	36.7	4.7	7.6	19.8	4.6	5.7
UU	43.7	4.6	11.4	21.9	5.8	7.2

Table 5: Edit rate and types of edits per post-editor

P-E	HTER	ins	del	sub	shift	wide shift
1	35.2	5.4	6.7	18.7	4.4	5.3
2	43.1	4.1	10.4	23.1	5.4	6.9
3	37.7	5.9	7.9	18.8	5.0	6.6
4	37.5	4.3	8.5	19.6	5.1	6.4

There are two ways to measure how much the machine translation output was edited by the post-editor. One way is to compare the final translation with the original machine translation output. This is what we will do in this section. In Section 6, we will consider which parts of the final translation were actually changed by the post-editor and discuss the difference.

5.1 HTER as Quality Measure

The edit distance between machine translation output and human reference translation can be measured in the number of insertions, deletions, substitutions and (phrasal) moves. A metric that simply counts the minimal number of such edit operations and divides it by the length of the human reference translation is the *translation edit rate*, short TER (Snover et al., 2006).

If the human reference translation is created from the machine translation output to minimise the number of edit operations needed for an acceptable translation, this variant is called *human-mediated* TER, or HTER. Note that in our experiment the post-editors are not strictly trying to minimise the number of edit operations — they may be inclined to make additional changes due to arbitrary considerations of style or perform edits that are faster rather than minimise the number of operations (e.g., deleting whole passages and rewriting them).

5.2 Edits by MT System

Table 4 shows the HTER scores — keep in mind our desiderata above — for the four systems. The scores are similar to the productivity number, with the three leading systems close together and the trailing system UU well behind.

Notably, we draw more statistically significant distinctions here. While as above, UU is significantly worse than all other systems (p-level < 0.01), we also find that ONLINE-B is better than UEDIN-PHRASE (p-level < 0.01).

Hence, HTER is a more sensitive metric than translation speed. This may be due to the fact that the time measurements are noisier than the count of edit operations. But it may also because HTER and productivity (i.e., time) do not measure the exactly the same thing. For instance, edits that require only a few keystrokes may be cognitively demanding (e.g., terminological choices), and thus take more time.

We cannot make any strong claim based on our numbers, but it is worth pointing out that post-editing UEDIN-SYNTAX was slightly faster than ONLINE-B (by 0.08 seconds/word), while the HTER score is lower (by 1 point). A closer look at the edit operations reveals that the post-edit of UEDIN-SYNTAX output required slightly fewer short and long shifts (movements of phrases), but more substitutions. Intuitively, moving a phrase around is a more time-consuming task than replacing a word. The benefit of a syntax-based system that aims to produce correct syntactic structure (including word order), may have real benefits in terms of post-editing time.

5.3 Edits by Post-Editor

Table 5 displays the edit rate broken down by post-editor. There is little correlation between edit rate and post-editor speed. While the fastest Post-Editor 1 produces translations with the smallest edit rate, the difference to two of the others (included the slowest Post-Editor 3) is not large. The

```
+--------+-----------------------------------------------------------------------------------------------------------+
| sec    | current_translation                                                                                       |
+--------+-----------------------------------------------------------------------------------------------------------+
|  0.000 | Norwegen ist es nicht oft auf die globale Agenda - und die meisten Nachrichten, wie es scheint.          |
|  0.508 | Norwegen ist esnicht oft auf die globale Agenda - und die meisten Nachrichten, wie es scheint.           |
|  0.733 | Norwegen ist enicht oft auf die globale Agenda - und die meisten Nachrichten, wie es scheint.            |
|  0.970 | Norwegen ist enicht oft auf die globale Agenda - und die meisten Nachrichten, wie es scheint.            |
|  0.975 | Norwegen ist nicht oft auf die globale Agenda - und die meisten Nachrichten, wie es scheint.             |
|  3.317 | Norwegen ist nicht oft auf di globale Agenda - und die meisten Nachrichten, wie es scheint.              |
|  3.413 | Norwegen ist nicht oft auf d globale Agenda - und die meisten Nachrichten, wie es scheint.               |
|  3.524 | Norwegen ist nicht oft auf de globale Agenda - und die meisten Nachrichten, wie es scheint.              |
|  3.588 | Norwegen ist nicht oft auf der globale Agenda - und die meisten Nachrichten, wie es scheint.             |
|  5.116 | Norwegen ist nicht oft auf der globalen Agenda - und die meisten Nachrichten, wie es scheint.            |
| 17.986 | Norwegen ist nicht oft auf der globalen Agenda - und die meisten , wie es scheint.                       |
| 19.386 | Norwegen ist nicht oft auf der globalen NachrichtenAgenda - und die meisten , wie es scheint.            |
| 20.116 | Norwegen ist nicht oft auf der globalen Nachrichtengenda - und die meisten , wie es scheint.             |
| 20.196 | Norwegen ist nicht oft auf der globalen Nachrichtenagenda - und die meisten , wie es scheint.            |
| 20.298 | Norwegen ist nicht oft auf der globalen Nachrichtenagenda - und die meisten , wie es scheint.            |
| 29.596 | Norwegen ist nicht oft auf der globalen Nachrichtenagenda - und die meisten scheint.                     |
| 31.459 | Norwegen ist nicht oft auf der globalen Nachrichtenagenda - und die meisten schein.                      |
| 31.659 | Norwegen ist nicht oft auf der globalen Nachrichtenagenda - und die meisten scheine.                     |
| 31.796 | Norwegen ist nicht oft auf der globalen Nachrichtenagenda - und die meisten scheinen.                    |
| 32.060 | Norwegen ist nicht oft auf der globalen Nachrichtenagenda - und die meisten scheinen .                   |
| 34.283 | Norwegen ist nicht oft auf der globalen Nachrichtenagenda - und die meisten scheinen d.                  |
| 34.380 | Norwegen ist nicht oft auf der globalen Nachrichtenagenda - und die meisten scheinen da.                 |
| 34.443 | Norwegen ist nicht oft auf der globalen Nachrichtenagenda - und die meisten scheinen das.                |
| 34.636 | Norwegen ist nicht oft auf der globalen Nachrichtenagenda - und die meisten scheinen das .               |
| 35.507 | Norwegen ist nicht oft auf der globalen Nachrichtenagenda - und die meisten scheinen das s.              |
| 35.637 | Norwegen ist nicht oft auf der globalen Nachrichtenagenda - und die meisten scheinen das so.             |
| 35.744 | Norwegen ist nicht oft auf der globalen Nachrichtenagenda - und die meisten scheinen das so .            |
| 35.949 | Norwegen ist nicht oft auf der globalen Nachrichtenagenda - und die meisten scheinen das so z.           |
| 36.053 | Norwegen ist nicht oft auf der globalen Nachrichtenagenda - und die meisten scheinen das so zu.          |
| 36.166 | Norwegen ist nicht oft auf der globalen Nachrichtenagenda - und die meisten scheinen das so zu .         |
| 36.805 | Norwegen ist nicht oft auf der globalen Nachrichtenagenda - und die meisten scheinen das so zu w.        |
| 38.011 | Norwegen ist nicht oft auf der globalen Nachrichtenagenda - und die meisten scheinen das so zu wo.       |
| 38.394 | Norwegen ist nicht oft auf der globalen Nachrichtenagenda - und die meisten scheinen das so zu wol.      |
| 38.699 | Norwegen ist nicht oft auf der globalen Nachrichtenagenda - und die meisten scheinen das so zu woll.     |
| 38.795 | Norwegen ist nicht oft auf der globalen Nachrichtenagenda - und die meisten scheinen das so zu wolle.    |
| 38.947 | Norwegen ist nicht oft auf der globalen Nachrichtenagenda - und die meisten scheinen das so zu wollen.   |
+--------+-----------------------------------------------------------------------------------------------------------+
| char   | mmmmmmmmmmmmmmmmmmmmmmmmmmmmttmmmmmmmmtmppppppppppptmmmmmmmmmmmmmmmmmmmmmmmmmmmmmmtttttttttttttttttttm   |
| word   | m        m   m     m   m   x   x        x                 m m   m   m       x        t   t  t  t     m   |
+--------+-----------------------------------------------------------------------------------------------------------+
```

Figure 1: Analysis of the post-editing process: Most editing actions that result in changes in the translation are adding or deleting of a character by a keystroke. However, notice the cut (17.986 sec) and paste (19.386 sec) action. Each character can be traced either to the original machine translation output (`m`), a typing action of the post-editor (`t`), or a pasting action of the post-editor (`p`). This then allows tokens in the output classified as either original MT (`m`), typed (`t`), pasted (not in figure) or partially edited (`x`).

outlier here is Post-Editor 2, whose output has a much larger edit rate.

6 Editing Actions

The HTER is an analysis of the *product* of post-editing. The final translation is compared to the original machine translation output. In this section, we examine how the *process* of post-editing is influenced by the machine translation system.

Our post-editing workbench provides detailed logging of each HCI interaction (key strokes, mouse clicks, etc.). This allows us to reconstruct how a translation was generated. See Figure 1 for an example how a translated was edited.

Table 6: Character provenance by system

System	MT	typed	pasted
ONLINE-B	68.3	28.0	3.3
UEDIN-PHRASE	62.9	31.3	5.2
UEDIN-SYNTAX	65.9	29.1	4.5
UU	56.1	37.9	5.6

6.1 Character Provenance by System

If we follow the editing actions, we can trace the origin of each letter in the final output: was it part of the original MT output, was it typed in by the user, or moved in a cut and paste action? Table 6 breaks down the characters in the final translations

Table 7: Token provenance by system

System	MT	typed	pasted	edited
ONLINE-B	65.2	21.4	2.3	10.8
UEDIN-PHRASE	60.5	24.7	3.9	10.6
UEDIN-SYNTAX	62.6	22.4	3.4	11.3
UU	53.2	31.0	4.0	11.7

by origin for each system. The numbers correspond to the HTER scores, with a remarkable consistency ranking for typed and pasted characters.

6.2 Token Provenance by System

We perform a similar analysis on the word level, introducing a fourth type of provenance: words whose characters are of mixed origin, i.e., words that were partially edited. Table 7 shows the numbers for each machine translation system. The suspicion from the HTER score that the syntax-based system UEDIN-SYNTAX requires less movement is not confirmed by these numbers. There are significantly more words moved by pasting (3.4%) than for ONLINE-B (2.3%). In general, cutting and pasting is not as common as the HTER score would suggest: the two types of shifts moved 10.3% and 10.2% of phrases, respectively. It seems that most words that could be moved are rather deleted and typed again.

6.3 Behaviour By Post-Editor

The post-editors differ significantly in their behaviour, as the numbers in Table 8 illustrate. Post-Editor 1, who is the fastest, leaves the most characters unchanged (72.9% vs. 57.7–64.4% for the others). Remarkably, this did not result in a dramatically lower HTER score (recall: 35.2 vs. 37.5–43.1 for the others).

Post-Editor 3, while taking the longest time, does not change the most number of characters. However, (s)he uses dramatically more cutting and pasting. Is this activity particularly slow? One way to check is to examine more closely how the post-editors spread out their actions over time.

Table 8: Character provenance by post-editor

Post-Editor	MT	typed	pasted
1	72.9	22.9	3.5
2	57.7	39.4	2.7
3	58.9	29.5	10.7
4	64.4	33.5	1.9

7 Editing Activities

Koehn (2009) suggests to divide up the time spent by translators and post-editors into intervals of the following types:

- initial pauses: the pause at the beginning of the translation, if it exists
- end pause: the pause at the end of the translation, if it exists
- short pause of length 2–6 seconds
- medium pauses of length 6–60 seconds
- big pauses longer than 60 seconds
- various working activities (in our case just typing and mouse actions)

When we break up the time spent on each activity and normalise it by the number of words in the original machine translation output, we get the numbers in Table 9, per machine translation system and post-editor.

The worse quality of the UU system causes mainly more work activity, big medium pauses. Each contributes roughly 0.3 seconds per word. The syntax-based system UEDIN-SYNTAX may pose fewer hard translation problems (showing up in initial and big pauses) than the HTER-preferred ONLINE-B system, but the effect is not strong.

We noted that ONLINE-B has a statistically significant better HTER score than UEDIN-PHRASE. While this is reflected in the additional working activity for the latter (2.41 sec./word vs. 2.26 sec./word), time is made up in the pauses. Our data is not sufficiently conclusive to gain any deeper insight here — it is certainly a question that we want to explore in the future.

The difference in post-editors mirrors some of the earlier findings: The number of characters and words changed leads to longer working activity, but the slow Post-Editor 3 is mainly slowed down by initial, big and medium pauses, indicating difficulties with solving translation problems, and not slow cutting and pasting actions. The faster Post-Editor 1 rarely pauses long and is quick with typing and mouse movements.

8 Conclusion

We compared how four different machine translation systems affect post-editing productivity and behaviour by analysing final translations and user

Table 9: Time spent on different activities, by machine translation system (top) and post-editor (bottom).

System	initial pause	big pause	med. pause	short pause	end pause	working
ONLINE-B	0.37 s/w	0.61 s/w	1.88 s/w	0.30 s/w	0.00 s/w	2.26 s/w
UEDIN-PHRASE	0.32 s/w	0.55 s/w	1.74 s/w	0.32 s/w	0.00 s/w	2.41 s/w
UEDIN-SYNTAX	0.32 s/w	0.50 s/w	1.90 s/w	0.31 s/w	0.00 s/w	2.30 s/w
UU	0.28 s/w	0.74 s/w	2.14 s/w	0.34 s/w	0.00 s/w	2.75 s/w

Post-Editor	initial pause	big pause	med. pause	short pause	end pause	working
1	0.35 s/w	0.01 s/w	0.63 s/w	0.27 s/w	0.00 s/w	1.76 s/w
2	0.04 s/w	0.19 s/w	1.13 s/w	0.35 s/w	0.00 s/w	3.06 s/w
3	0.91 s/w	1.85 s/w	3.99 s/w	0.29 s/w	0.00 s/w	2.53 s/w
4	0.02 s/w	0.36 s/w	1.94 s/w	0.35 s/w	0.00 s/w	2.33 s/w

activity data. The best system under consideration yielded abut 20% better productivity than the worst, although the three systems on top are not statistically significantly different in terms of productivity.

We noted differences in metrics that measure productivity and edit distance metrics. The latter allowed us to draw more statistically significant conclusions, but may measure something distinct. Productivity is the main concern of commercial use of post-editing machine translation, and we find that better machine translation leads to less time spent on editing, but more importantly, less time spent of figuring out harder translation problems (indicated by pauses of more than six seconds).

Finally, an important finding is that the differences between post-editors is much larger than the difference between machine translation systems. This points towards the importance of skilled post-editors, but this finding should be validated with professional post-editors, and not the volunteers used in this study.

Acknowledgements

This work was supported under the CASMACAT project (grant agreement N° 287576) by the European Union 7th Framework Programme (FP7/2007-2013).

References

Alabau, Vicent, Ragnar Bonk, Christian Buck, Michael Carl, Francisco Casacuberta, Mercedes García-Martínez, Jesús González, Philipp Koehn, Luis Leiva, Bartolomé Mesa-Lao, Daniel Ortiz, Herve Saint-Amand, Germán Sanchis, and Chara Tsoukala. 2013. "CASMACAT: An open source workbench for advanced computer aided translation." *The Prague Bulletin of Mathematical Linguistics*, 100:101–112.

Bojar, Ondřej, Christian Buck, Chris Callison-Burch, Christian Federmann, Barry Haddow, Philipp Koehn, Christof Monz, Matt Post, Radu Soricut, and Lucia Specia. 2013. "Findings of the 2013 Workshop on Statistical Machine Translation." *Proceedings of the Eighth Workshop on Statistical Machine Translation*, 1–44. Sofia, Bulgaria.

Callison-Burch, Chris, Philipp Koehn, Christof Monz, Matt Post, Radu Soricut, and Lucia Specia. 2012. "Findings of the 2012 workshop on statistical machine translation." *Proceedings of the Seventh Workshop on Statistical Machine Translation*, 10–48. Montreal, Canada.

Cettolo, Mauro, Jan Niehues, Sebastian Stüker, Luisa Bentivogli, and Marcello Federico. 2013. "Report on the 10th IWSLT evaluation campaign." *Proceedings of the International Workshop on Spoken Language Translation (IWSLT)*.

den Bogaert, Joachim Van and Nathalie De Sutter. 2013. "Productivity or quality? Let's do both." *Machine Translation Summit XIV*, 381–390.

Durrani, Nadir, Barry Haddow, Kenneth Heafield, and Philipp Koehn. 2013. "Edinburgh's machine translation systems for European language pairs." *Proceedings of the Eighth Workshop on Statistical Machine Translation*, 114–121. Sofia, Bulgaria.

Federico, Marcello, Alessandro Cattelan, and Marco Trombetti. 2012. "Measuring user productivity in machine translation enhanced computer assisted translation." *Proceedings of the Tenth Conference of the Association for Machine Translation in the Americas (AMTA)*.

Garcia, Ignacio. 2011. "Translating by post-editing: is it the way forward?" *Machine Translation*, 25(3):217–237.

Green, Spence, Jeffrey Heer, and Christopher D. Manning. 2013. "The efficacy of human post-editing for language translation." *ACM Human Factors in Computing Systems (CHI)*.

Guerberof, Ana. 2009. "Productivity and quality in mt post-editing." *MT Summit Workshop on New Tools for Translators*.

Koehn, Philipp. 2009. "A process study of computer-aided translation." *Machine Translation*, 23(4):241–263.

Koehn, Philipp. 2010. "Enabling monolingual translators: Post-editing vs. options." *Human Language Technologies: The 2010 Annual Conference of the North American Chapter of the Association for Computational Linguistics*, 537–545. Los Angeles, California.

Koponen, Maarit. 2012. "Comparing human perceptions of post-editing effort with post-editing operations." *Pro-*

ceedings of the Seventh Workshop on Statistical Machine Translation, 227–236. Montreal, Canada.

Koponen, Maarit. 2013. "This translation is not too bad: an analysis of post-editor choices in a machine-translation post-editing task." *Proceedings of Workshop on Post-editing Technology and Practice*, 1–9.

Koponen, Maarit, Wilker Aziz, Luciana Ramos, and Lucia Specia. 2012. "Post-editing time as a measure of cognitive effort ." *AMTA 2012 Workshop on Post-Editing Technology and Practice (WPTP 2012)*, 11–20. San Diego, USA.

Läubli, Samuel, Mark Fishel, Gary Massey, Maureen Ehrensberger-Dow, and Martin Volk. 2013. "Assessing post-editing efficiency in a realistic translation environment." *Proceedings of Workshop on Post-editing Technology and Practice*, 83–91.

Nadejde, Maria, Philip Williams, and Philipp Koehn. 2013. "Edinburgh's syntax-based machine translation systems." *Proceedings of the Eighth Workshop on Statistical Machine Translation*, 170–176. Sofia, Bulgaria.

Papineni, Kishore, Salim Roukos, Todd Ward, and Wei-Jing Zhu. 2001. *BLEU: a Method for Automatic Evaluation of Machine Translation*. Tech. Rep. RC22176(W0109-022), IBM Research Report.

Plitt, Mirko and Francois Masselot. 2010. "A productivity test of statistical machine translation post-editing in a typical localisation context." *Prague Bulletin of Mathematical Linguistics*, 93:7–16.

Pouliquen, Bruno, Christophe Mazenc, and Aldo Iorio. 2011. "Tapta: A user-driven translation system for patent documents based on domain-aware statistical machine translation." *Proceedings of th 15th International Conference of the European Association for Machine Translation (EAMT)*, 5–12.

Skadiņš, Raivis, Maris Puriņš, Inguna Skadiņa, and Andrejs Vasiļjevs. 2011. "Evaluation of SMT in localization to under-resourced inflected language." *Proceedings of the 15th International Conference of the European Association for Machine Translation (EAMT)*, 35–40.

Snover, Matthew, Bonnie J. Dorr, Richard Schwartz, Linnea Micciulla, and John Makhoul. 2006. "A study of translation edit rate with targeted human annotation." *5th Conference of the Association for Machine Translation in the Americas (AMTA)*. Boston, Massachusetts.

Stymne, Sara, Christian Hardmeier, Jörg Tiedemann, and Joakim Nivre. 2013. "Tunable distortion limits and corpus cleaning for SMT." *Proceedings of the Eighth Workshop on Statistical Machine Translation*, 225–231. Sofia, Bulgaria.

Vazquez, Lucia Morado, Silvia Rodriguez Vazquez, and Pierrette Bouillon. 2013. "Comparing forum data post-editing performance using translation memory and machine translation output: A pilot study." *Machine Translation Summit XIV*, 249–256.

Beyond Linguistic Equivalence. An Empirical Study of Translation Evaluation in a Translation Learner Corpus

Mihaela Vela **Anne-Kathrin Schumann** **Andrea Wurm**
Department of Applied Linguistics, Translation and Interpreting
Saarland University, Saarbrücken, Germany
{m.vela, anne.schumann, a.wurm}@mx.uni-saarland.de

Abstract

The realisation that fully automatic translation in many settings is still far from producing output that is equal or superior to human translation has lead to an intense interest in translation evaluation in the MT community. However, research in this field, by now, has not only largely ignored the tremendous amount of relevant knowledge available in a closely related discipline, namely translation studies, but also failed to provide a deeper understanding of the nature of "translation errors" and "translation quality". This paper presents an empirical take on the latter concept, translation quality, by comparing human and automatic evaluations of learner translations in the KOPTE corpus. We will show that translation studies provide sophisticated concepts for translation quality estimation and error annotation. Moreover, by applying well-established MT evaluation scores, namely BLEU and Meteor, to KOPTE learner translations that were graded by a human expert, we hope to shed light on properties (and potential shortcomings) of these scores.

1 Translation quality assessment

In recent years, researchers in the field of MT evaluation have proposed a large variety of methods for assessing the quality of automatically produced translations. Approaches range from fully automatic quality scoring to efforts aimed at the development of "human" evaluation scores that try to exploit the (often tacit) linguistic knowledge of human evaluators. The criteria according to which quality is estimated often include *adequacy*, the degree of meaning preservation, and *fluency*, target language correctness (Callison-Burch et al., 2007). The goals of both "human" evaluation and fully automatic quality scoring are manifold and cover system optimisation as well as benchmarking and comparison.

In translation studies, the scientific (and pre-scientific) discussion on how to assess the quality of human translations has been going on for centuries. In recent years, the development of appropriate concepts and tools has become even more vital to the discipline due to the pressing needs of the language industry. However, different from the belief, typical to MT, that the "goodness" of a translation can be scored on the basis of linguistic criteria alone, the notion of "translation quality", in translation studies, has assumed a multi-faceted shape, distancing itself from a simple strive for equivalence and embracing concepts such as functional, stylistic and pragmatic appropriateness as well as textual coherence. In this section, we provide an overview over approaches to translation quality assessment developed in MT and translation studies to specify how "quality" is being defined in both fields and which methods and features are used. Due to the amount of available literature, this overview is necessarily incomplete, but still insightful with respect to differences and commonalities between MT and human translation evaluation.

1.1 Automatic MT quality scores

MT output is usually evaluated by automatic language-independent metrics which can be applied to any language produced by an MT system. The use of automatic metrics for MT evaluation is legitimate, since MT systems deal with large amounts of data, on which manual evaluation would be very time-consuming and expensive.

Automatic metrics typically compute the closeness (adequacy) of a "hypothesis" to a "reference" translation and differ from each other by how this closeness is measured. The most popular MT evaluation metrics are IBM BLEU (Papineni et al., 2002) and NIST (Doddington, 2002) which are used not only for tuning MT systems, but also as evaluation metrics for shared tasks, such as the Workshop on Statistical Machine Translation (Bojar et al., 2013).

IBM BLEU uses n-gram precision by matching machine translation output against one or more reference translations. It accounts for adequacy and fluency by calculating word precision, respectively the n-gram precision. In order to deal with the over generation of common words, precision counts are clipped, meaning that a reference word is exhausted after it is matched. This is then the modified n-gram precision. For N=4 the modified n-gram precision is calculated and the results are combined by using the geometric mean. Instead of recall, the brevity penalty (BP) is used. It penalizes candidate translations which are shorter than the reference translations.

The NIST metric is derived from IBM BLEU. The NIST score is the arithmetic mean of modified n-gram precision for N=5 scaled by BP. Additionally, NIST also considers the information gain of each n-gram, giving more weight to more informative (less frequent) n-grams and less weight to less informative (more frequent) n-grams.

Another often used machine translation evaluation metric is Meteor (Denkowski and Lavie, 2011). Different from IBM BLEU and NIST, Meteor evaluates a candidate translation by calculating precision and recall on the unigram level and combining them into a parametrized harmonic mean. The result from the harmonic mean is then scaled by a fragmentation penalty which penalizes gaps and differences in word order.

Besides these evaluation metrics, several other metrics are sometimes used for the evaluation of MT output. Some of these are the WER (word error-rate) metric based on the Levensthein distance (Levenshtein, 1966), the position-independent error rate metric PER (Tillmann et al., 1997) and the translation edit rate metric TER (Snover et al., 2006) with its newer version TERp (Snover et al., 2009).

1.2 Human MT quality evaluation

Human evaluation of MT output is performed in different ways. The most frequently used evaluation method seems to be a simple ranking of translated sentences by a "reasonable number of evaluators" (Farrús et al., 2010). According to Birch et al. (2013), this form of evaluation was used, among others, during the last STATMT workshops and can thus be considered rather popular. APPRAISE (Federmann, 2012) is a tool that can be used for such as task, since it allows for the manual ranking of sentences, quality estimation, error annotation and post-editing.

Other forms of evaluation, however, exist. For example, Birch et al. (2013) propose HMEANT, an evaluation score based on MEANT (Lo and Wu, 2011), a semi-automatic MT quality score that measures the degree of meaning preservation by comparing verb frames and semantic roles of hypothesis translations to their respective counterparts in the reference translation(s). Unfortunately, Birch et al. (2013) report difficulty in producing coherent role alignments between hypotheses and translations, a problem that affects the final HMEANT score calculation. This, however, seems hardly surprising given the difficulty of the annotation task (although, following the authors' description, some familiarity of the annotators with the linguistic key concepts can be assumed) and the fact that guidelines and training are meant to be minimal.

Another (indirect) human evaluation method for MT that is also employed for error analysis are reading comprehension tests (e.g. Maney et al. (2012), Weiss and Ahrenberg (2012)). Moreover, HTER (Snover et al., 2006) is a TER-based repair-oriented metric which uses human annotators (the only apparent qualificational requirement being fluency in the target language) to generate "targeted" reference translations by post-editing the MT output or the existing reference translations, following the goal to find the shortest path between the hypothesis and a "correct" reference. Snover et al. (2006) report a high correlation between evaluation with HTER and traditional human adequacy and fluency judgements. Last but not least, Somers (2011) mentions other repair-oriented measures such as post-editing effort measured by the amount of key-strokes or time spent on producing a "correct" translation on the basis of MT output.

1.3 The notion of quality in translation studies

Discussions of translation "quality", in translation studies, for a long time focused on *equivalence* which, in its oldest and simplest form, used to echo *adequacy* as understood by today's MT researchers: "good" translation was viewed as an optimal compromise between meaning preservation and target language correctness, which was especially relevant to the translation of religious texts. For example, Kußmaul (2000) emphatically cites Martin Luther's famous Bible translation into German as an example of "good" translation because Luther, according to his own testimony and following his reformative ambition, focused on producing fluent, easily understandable text rather than mimicking the linguistic structures of the Hebrew, Aramaic and Greek originals (see also Windle and Pym (2011) for a further discussion).

More recent work in translation studies has abandoned one-dimensional views of the relation between source and target text and postulates that, depending on the communicative context within and for which a translation is produced, this relation can vary greatly. That is, the degree of linguistic or semantic "fidelity" of a good translation towards the source text depends on functional criteria. This view is echoed in the concepts of "primary vs. secondary", "documentary vs. instrumental" and "covert vs. overt" translation (Hönig, 2003). The consequence of this shift in paradigms is that, since different *translation strategies* may be appropriately adopted in different situations, evaluation criteria become essentially dependent on the *function* that the translation is going to play in the target language and culture. This view is most prominently advocated by the so-called *skopos theory* (cf. Dizdar (2003)). *Translation errors*, then, are not just simple violations of the target language system or outright failures to translate words or segments, but violations of the *translation task* that can manifest themselves on all levels of text production (Nord, 2003). It is important to point out that, in this framework, *linguistic errors* are just one type of error covering not only one of the favourite MT error categories, namely un- and mistranslated words (compare, for example, Stymne and Ahrenberg (2012), Weiss and Ahrenberg (2012), Popović et al. (2013)), but also phraseological, idiomatic, syntactic, grammatical, modal, temporal, stylistic, cohesion and other kinds of errors. Moreover, *translation-specific errors* occur when the translation does not fulfill its function because of pragmatic (e.g. text-type specific forms of address), cultural (e.g. text conventions, proper names, or other conventions) or formal (e. g. layout) defects (Nord, 2003). Depending on the appropriate translation strategy for a given translation task, these error types may be weighted differently. Furthermore, the communicative and functional view on translation also dictates a change in the concept of equivalence which is no longer considered to be adequately described by the notions of "meaning preservation" or "fidelity", but becomes dependent on aesthetic, connotational, textual, communicative, situational, functional and cognitive aspects (for a detailed discussion see Horn-Helf (1999)). In MT evaluation, most of these aspects have not yet or only in part been considered.

Last but not least, the translation industry has developed normative standards and proofreading schemes. For example, the DIN EN 15038:2006-08 (Deutsches Institut für Normung, 2006) discusses translation errors, quality management and qualificational requirements for translators and proofreaders, while the SAE J2450 standard (Society of Automotive Engineers, 2005) presents a weighted "translation quality metric". An application perspective is given by Mertin (2006) who discusses translation quality management procedures in a big automotive company and, among other things, develops a weighted translation error scheme for proofreading.

1.4 Discussion

The above discussion shows that, while the object of evaluation is the same for both MT and translation studies, namely translation, the differences between evaluation approaches developed in both fields are considerable. Most importantly, in translation studies, translation evaluation is considered an *expert task* for which fluency in one or several languages is certainly not enough, but for which *translation-specific expert knowledge* is required. Another important distinction is that evaluation, again in translation studies, is normally not carried out on the sentence level, since sentences are usually split up into several "units of translation" and can certainly contain more than one "translation problem". Consequently, the popular MT practice of ranking whole sentences according to some automatic score, by anonymous evaluators or even users of Amazon Turk (e.g. in the introduction to Bojar et al. (2013)), from a translation studies point of view, is unlikely to provide reasonable evaluations. Last but not least, the MT community's strive for adequacy or meaning preservation does not match the notions of weighting translation errors, of adopting different translation strategies and, consequently, does not fit the complicated source/target text relations that have been acknowledged by translation studies. Evaluation methods that are based on simple measures of linguistic equality such as n-gram overlap (BLEU) or, just slightly more complicated, the preservation of syntactic frames and semantic roles (MEANT) fail to provide straightforward criteria for distinguishing between *legitimate* and *illegitimate* variation. Moreover, semantic and pragmatic criteria as well as the notion of "reference translation" remain, at best, rather unclear.

On the other hand, the MT community has recognised translation evaluation as an unresolved research problem. For example, Birch et al. (2013) state that ranking judgements are difficult to generalise, while Callison-Burch et al. (2007) carry out extensive correlation tests of a whole range of automatic MT evaluation metrics in comparison to human judgements, showing that BLEU does not rank highest, but still remains in the top segment. It still needs to be shown how MT research can benefit from more sophisticated evaluation measures and whether all the parameters that are considered relevant to the evaluation of human translations are relevant for MT usage scenarios, too. In the remainder of this paper, we present a study on how much and possibly for which reasons automatic MT evaluation scores (namely BLEU and Meteor) differ from translation expert quality judgements on extracts of a French-German translation learner corpus.

2 The KOPTE corpus

2.1 General corpus design

The KOPTE project (Wurm, 2013) was designed to enable research on translation evaluation in a university training course (master's level) for translators and to enlighten students' translation problems as well as their problem solving strategies. To achieve this goal, a corpus of student translations was compiled. The corpus consists of several translations of the same source texts produced by student translators in a classroom setting. As a whole, it covers 985 translations of 77 source texts amounting to a total of 318,467 tokens. Source texts were taken from French newspapers and translated into German in class over a span of several years, the translation brief calling for a ready-to-publish text to be printed in a German national newspaper. Consequently, all translation tasks include the use of idiomatic language, explanations of culture-specific items, changes in the explicitness of macrotextual cohesive elements, etc.[1]

2.2 Annotation of translation features and translation evaluation in KOPTE

Student translations were evaluated by one of the authors, an experienced translation teacher, with the aim of giving feedback to students. All translations were graded and *errors* as well as *good solutions* were marked in the text according to a fine-grained evaluation scheme. In this scheme, the weight of evaluated items is indicated through numbers ranging from plus/minus 1 (minor) to plus/minus 8 (major). Based on these evaluations, each translation was assigned a final grade according to the German grading system on a scale ranging from 1 ("very good") to 6 ("highly erroneous") with in-between intervals at the levels of .0, .3 and .7. To calculate this grade, positive and negative evaluations were summed up separately, before the negative score was subtracted from the positive one. A score of around zero corresponds to the grade "good" (=2), to achieve "very good" (=1) the student needs a surplus of positive evaluations.

The evaluation scheme based on which student translations are graded is divided into external and internal factors. *External* characteristics describe the communicative situation given by the source text and the translation brief (author, recipient, medium, location, time). *Internal* factors, on the other hand, comprise eight categories: form, structure, cohesion, stylistics/register, grammar, lexis/semantics, translation-specific problems, function. These categories are containers for more fine-grained criteria which can be applied to segments of the (source or target) text or even to the whole text, depending on the nature of the criterion. Some internal subcriteria of the scheme are summarised in Table 1. A quantitative analysis of error types in KOPTE shows that semantic/lexical errors are by far the most common error in the student translations (Wurm, 2013).

Evaluations in KOPTE were carried out by just

[1] More information about KOPTE is available from http://fr46.uni-saarland.de/index.php?id=3702&L=%2524L.

one evaluator for the reason that, in a classroom setting, multiple evaluations are not feasible. Although multiple evaluations would have been considered highly valuable, the data available from KOPTE was evaluated by an experienced translation scholar with long-standing experience in teaching translation. Moreover, the evaluation scheme is much more detailed than error annotation schemes that are normally described in the literature and it is theoretically well-motivated. An analysis of the median grades in our data sample (compare Tables 2–4) shows that grading varies only slightly between different texts, considering the maximum variation potential ranging from 1 to 6, and thus can be considered consistent.

Criteria	Examples of subcriteria
author, recipients, medium, topic, location, time	—
form	paragraphs, formatting
structure	thematic, progression, macrostructure, illustrations
cohesion	reference, connections
stylistics	style, genre
grammar	determiners, modality, syntax
semantics	textual semantics, idioms, numbers, terminology
translation problems	erroneous source text, proper names, culture-specific items, ideology, math. units, pragmatics, allusions
function	goal dependence

Table 1: Internal evaluation criteria in the KOPTE annotation scheme.

3 Experiments

The goal of our experiments was to study whether the human translation expert judgements in KOPTE can be mimicked using simple automatic quality metrics as used in MT, namely BLEU and Meteor. More specifically, we aim at:

- studying how automatic evaluation scores relate to fine-grained human expert evaluations,
- investigating whether a higher number of references improves the automatic scores and why (or why not),
- examining whether a higher number of references provides more reliable evaluation scores as measured by an improved correlation with the human expert judgments.

In order to study the behaviour of automatic MT evaluation scores, we conducted three experiments by applying IBM BLEU (Papineni et al., 2002) and Meteor 1.4 (Denkowski and Lavie, 2011) to a sample of KOPTE translations that were produced by translation students preparing for their final master's exams. Scores were calculated on the complete texts. To evaluate the overall performance of the automatic evaluation scores on these texts, we calculated Kendall's rank correlation coefficient for each text following the procedure described in Sachs and Hedderich (2009). Correlations were calculated for:

- the human expert grades and BLEU scores for each translation,
- the human expert grades and Meteor scores for each translation,
- BLEU and Meteor scores for each translation.

3.1 Experimental setup and results

In a first experiment, we applied the automatic evaluation scores to the source texts given in Table 2, choosing, for each text, the student translation with the best human grade as reference translation. The median human grades as well as mean BLEU and Meteor and correlation scores obtained for each text (excluding the reference translation) are included in Table 2. In a second experiment, we repeated this procedure, however, using a set of three reference translations. Results are given in Table 3. Finally, in a last experiment we used five reference translations selected according to their human expert grade (Table 4). In both steps, source texts for which less than four hypotheses were available were excluded from the data sets.

3.2 Discussion

The tables show that in the first experiment a set of 152 translations was evaluated, whereas in the second and third experiment these numbers were reduced to 108 and 68 respectively due to the selection of more references. The human expert evaluations rated most of these translations at least as acceptable, as can be seen from the median grade for each experiment which was 2.3 in the first experiment and consecutively decreased to 3.0 for the third experiment, again due to the selection of more "good" translations as references. The

Source text	Human trans./ source text	Median grades	Mean BLEU	Mean Meteor	Correlation Human-BLEU	Correlation Human-Meteor	Correlation BLEU-Meteor
AT001	7	2.7	0.15	0.33	−0.39	−0.73	0.24
AT002	12	2.3	0.15	0.35	−0.20	−0.43	0.49
AT004	12	2.7	0.19	0.37	0.14	0.11	0.63
AT005	12	2.3	0.20	0.36	0.32	0.45	0.45
AT008	10	2.15	0.23	0.38	−0.43	−0.29	0.78
AT010	11	2.7	0.25	0.41	0.06	−0.10	0.56
AT012	9	2.0	0.22	0.40	−0.30	−0.36	0.50
AT015	5	2.0	0.11	0.28	0.36	0.12	0.60
AT017	7	2.3	0.22	0.38	−0.20	0.06	0.71
AT021	4	3.0	0.18	0.39	−0.55	−0.55	1.00
AT023	6	2.3	0.22	0.38	0.50	−0.07	−0.20
AT025	4	2.15	0.13	0.36	0.33	0.0	0.00
AT026	21	3.0	0.12	0.26	−0.19	−0.35	0.67
AT039	13	3.0	0.10	0.29	−0.08	0.03	0.49
AT052	7	2.0	0.17	0.31	−0.32	0.05	0.00
AT053	7	2.3	0.18	0.32	0.62	0.39	0.33
AT059	5	2.0	0.24	0.36	0.00	0.22	0.80

Table 2: Source texts, number of human translations per source text, median of the obtained grade per source text, mean of the BLEU and Meteor scores per source text and Kendall's rank correlation coefficients for the first experiment.

Source text	Human trans./ source text	Median grades	Mean BLEU	Mean Meteor	Correlation Human−BLEU	Correlation Human-Meteor	Correlation BLEU-Meteor
AT001	5	3.0	0.17	0.36	−0.12	0.36	0.60
AT002	10	2.3	0.17	0.36	−0.14	0.05	0.38
AT004	10	2.85	0.20	0.37	0.39	0.16	0.51
AT005	10	2.3	0.20	0.40	−0.10	0.05	0.47
AT008	8	2.5	0.25	0.45	−0.67	−0.15	0.00
AT010	9	2.7	0.23	0.41	−0.10	−0.50	0.28
AT012	7	2.3	0.23	0.43	0.00	0.11	0.52
AT017	5	2.3	0.21	0.43	0.12	0.36	0.60
AT023	4	2.5	0.21	0.38	0.41	0.81	0.67
AT026	19	3.3	0.10	0.26	−0.31	−0.41	0.77
AT039	11	3.0	0.11	0.34	0.06	0.14	0.74
AT052	5	2.0	0.18	0.40	0.12	0.36	0.20
AT053	5	2.3	0.17	0.35	0.36	−0.12	0.40

Table 3: Source texts, number of human translations per source text, median of the obtained grade per source text, mean of the BLEU and Meteor scores per source text and Kendall's rank correlation coefficients for the second experiment.

grades for the best translations selected as references range for the first and second experiment between 1.0 and 2.3, whereas for the third experiment the selected references were evaluated with grades between 1.0 and 2.7. Nevertheless, the median grade for the references in all three experiments is always 1.7. From the overall median grade and the median grade of the selected translations as reference we can notice, that the translations selected as references were indeed "better" than the remaining ones.

The BLEU and Meteor scores given in the tables are mean values over the individual translations' scores for each source text. These scores are very low, reaching a maximum of 0.25 over all three experiments for BLEU and 0.45 for Meteor. However, given the human expert grades the translations cannot be considered unreadable. In fact, the correlation coefficients show that neither BLEU nor Meteor (except a few exceptional cases) correlate with the human quality judgements, however, they show a (weak) tendency to correlate with each other. Moreover, the data shows that the addition of reference translations results neither in significantly higher BLEU or Meteor scores nor in improved correlation.

3.3 Qualitative analysis

Our finding that human quality judgements do not correlate with automatic scores if the object of evaluation is a translation produced by a human (as opposed to a machine) matches earlier results presented by Doddington (2002) within the context of evaluating NIST. Doddington (2002) proposes the explanation that "differences between professional translators are far more subtle [than differences between machine-produced translations, the authors] and thus less well characterized

Source text	Human trans./ source text	Median grades	Mean BLEU	Mean Meteor	Correlation Human-BLEU	Correlation Human-Meteor	Correlation BLEU-Meteor
AT002	8	2. 5	0. 17	0. 36	−0. 08	0. 00	0. 43
AT004	8	3. 0	0. 20	0. 36	0. 00	0. 23	0. 71
AT005	8	2. 3	0. 20	0. 42	0. 00	0. 08	0. 43
AT008	6	2. 85	0. 26	0. 45	−0. 55	−0. 14	0. 33
AT010	7	2. 7	0. 23	0. 41	0. 00	−0. 12	0. 05
AT012	5	2. 3	0. 23	0. 43	0. 22	0. 22	0. 40
AT026	17	3. 3	0. 11	0. 31	−0. 24	−0. 34	0. 62
AT039	9	3. 0	0. 10	0. 37	0. 22	0. 55	0. 22

Table 4: Source texts, number of human translations per source text, median of the obtained grade per source text, mean of the BLEU and Meteor scores per source text and Kendall's rank correlation coefficients for the third experiment.

by N-gram statistics." We conducted a qualitative analysis of some KOPTE translations in order to check whether the differences between individual translations are indeed as subtle as suggested by Doddington and to come up at least with hypotheses that could explain the poor performance of the automatic scores. We selected three source texts used in the second experiment, namely AT008, AT023 and AT053 and compared their respective reference translations to selected hypothesis translations. This analysis was conducted on the lexical level alone, that is, most of the features of KOPTE's elaborated evaluation scheme were not even considered. The analysis, however, shows that the amount of variation that can be found just on the lexical level is almost overwhelming. Some examples are listed in Appendix A.

A common phenomenon is simple variation due to synonyms or the use of phrasal variants or paraphrases. Moreover, the listed examples show that lexical variation can be triggered by different source text elements. The phenomena shown in the tables are well-known translation problems, e.g. proper names, colloquial or figurative speech or numbers. The other categories in the table are less clear-cut, that is, they can overlap. In our analysis, source text elements that cannot be translated literally, but instead call for a creative solution were classified as translation problems. Different translation strategies can be applied to different kinds of problems, most importantly to the translation of culture-specific items, proper names, underspecified source text elements or culture-specific arguments. The respective table and other examples that we analysed show that for this category some translators chose to add additional information, to adapt the perspective to the German target audience (for example, by adapting pronouns or deictic elements) or to adapt the formatting choices to the variant preferred by the target culture (e.g. commas instead of fullstops, different types of quotation marks), whereas other translators chose to translate literally. Both strategies are legitimate under certain circumstances, however, it can be assumed that adaptations require a greater cognitive effort. Source ambiguities, according to our preliminary typology, are source text features that can be interpreted in different ways - at least for a translator translating from a foreign language (as opposed to a native speaker). Obviously, the line between this category and outright translation errors is not very clear.

However, it needs to be stated that also for the other categories - while many variants are correct and legitimate - not all are equally good. Best solutions for given problems are distributed unequally across the translations studied. Beyond the purely lexical level, extensive variation can be witnessed on the syntactic, but also the grammatical level. For example, some translators chose to break the rather complicated syntax of the French original into simpler, easily readable sentences, producing, in some cases, considerable shifts in the information structure of the text - often a legitimate strategy.

With respect to the performance of the automatic scores, our preliminary study - that still calls for larger-scale and in-depth verification - suggests that neither BLEU nor Meteor are able to cope with the amount of variation found in the data. More specifically, they cannot distinguish between legitimate and illegitimate variation or grave and slight errors respectively, but seem to fail to match acceptable variants because of lexical and phrasal variation or divergent grammatical structures resulting in different verb frames, word sequences and text lengths, not to talk even about acceptable variation on higher linguistic levels. Therefore, automatic scores seem to overrate surface differences and thus assign very low scores to many translations that were found to be at least acceptable by a human expert.

Considering the impact of these findings for MT evaluation purposes, it is not straightforward to assume that the differences that we have observed between the human translations are more "subtle" (in the sense of being unimportant) than the ones produced by machine translation systems. On the contrary, our analysis suggests that "good" translations are characterised by creative solutions that are not easily reproducible but that help to achieve target language readability and comprehensibility. This is a fundamental quality aspect of translation independently of its production mode. Moreover, it is difficult to see why some of the variants that we observed in the human translations selected from KOPTE, once the context shifts from human to machine translation, should be found valid in one situation and invalid in another, depending on the training and test data used for developing an MT system: A high amount of the variation found in the human translations goes back to the legitimate use of the creative and constructive powers of natural language, and it is, among others, these powers that should be mimicked by MT output.

4 Conclusion and future work

In this paper, we have studied the performance of two fully automatic MT evaluation metrics, namely BLEU and Meteor, in comparison to human translation expert evaluations on a sample of learner translations from the KOPTE corpus. The automatic scores were tested in three experiments with a varying number of reference translations and their performance was compared to the human evaluations by means of Kendall's rank correlation coefficient. The experiments suggest that both BLEU and Meteor systematically underestimate the quality of the translations tested, that is, they assign scores that, given the human expert evaluations, seem to be by far too low. Moreover, they do not consistently correlate with the human expert evaluations. Coming up with explanations for this failure is not straightforward, however, the results of our qualitative and explorative analysis suggest that lexical similarity scores are not able to cope satisfactorily neither with standard lexical variation (paraphrases etc.) nor with dissimilarities that can be traced back to the specific nature of the translation process, leave alone linguistic levels beyond the lexicon. For Meteor, this shortcoming may partly be alleviated by the provision of richer sets of synonyms and paraphrases, however, the amount of uncovered variation is still immense. In fact, it seems that many more reference translations would be needed in order to cover the whole range of legitimate variants that can be used to translate a given source text - a scenario that seems hardly feasible! So how can BLEU or Meteor scores be interpreted when they are given in MT papers? Based on our analyses, it seems clear that these scores are based on a data-driven notion of translation quality, that is, they measure the degree of compliance of a hypothesis translation with some reference set. This is insofar problematic as studies based on different reference sets cannot be compared, neither can BLEU or Meteor scores be generalised to other domains. Even more importantly, BLEU or Meteor scores cannot be used to measure a data-independent concept of quality or even the usability of a translation for a target audience which, as we have shown, depends on many more factors than just lexical surface overlap.

However, our study also leads to some open research questions. One of these questions is whether automatic evaluation scores can still be used for more coarse-grained distinctions, that is, to distinguish "really bad" translations from "really good" ones. The fine-grained distinctions made by the evaluator of KOPTE on generally rather good translations do not allow us to answer this question. Future work will also deal with a comparison of mistakes made by MT systems as opposed to human translators as well as with the question how (and which) translation-specific aspects can be applied to the evaluation of MT systems.

References

Alexandra Birch, Barry Haddow, Ulrich Germann, Maria Nadejde, Christian Buck, and Philipp Koehn. 2013. The feasibility of HMEANT as a human MT evaluation metric. In *Proceedings of the 8th Workshop on SMT*, pages 52–61.

Ondřej Bojar, Christian Buck, Chris Callison-Burch, Barry Haddow, Philipp Koehn, Christof Monz, Matt Post, Hervé Saint-Amand, Radu Soricut, and Lucia Specia, editors. 2013. *Proceedings of the 8th Workshop on SMT*. ACL.

Chris Callison-Burch, Cameron Fordyce, Philipp Koehn, Christof Monz, and Josh Schroeder. 2007.

(Meta-) evaluation of machine translation. In *Proceedings of the 2nd Workshop on SMT*, pages 136–158.

Michael Denkowski and Alon Lavie. 2011. Meteor 1.3: Automatic metric for reliable optimization and evaluation of machine translation systems. In *Proceedings of the 6th Workshop on SMT*, pages 85–91.

Deutsches Institut für Normung. 2006. *DIN EN 15038:2006-08: Übersetzungsdienstleistungen-Dienstleistungsanforderungen*. Beuth.

Dilek Dizdar. 2003. Skopostheorie. In *Handbuch Translation*, pages 104–107. Stauffenburg.

George Doddington. 2002. Automatic evaluation of machine translation quality using n-gram cooccurrence statistics. In *Proceedings of the 2nd International Conference on HLT*, pages 138–145.

Mireia Farrús, Marta R. Costa-Jussà, José B. Mariño, and José A. R. Fonollosa. 2010. Linguistic-based evaluation criteria to identify statistical machine translation errors. In *Proceedings of the 14th Annual Conference of the EAMT*, pages 167–173.

Christian Federmann. 2012. Appraise: An open-source toolkit for manual evaluation of machine translation output. *PBML*, 98:25–35, 9.

Hans Hönig. 2003. Humanübersetzung (therapeutisch vs. diagnostisch). In *Handbuch Translation*, pages 378–381. Stauffenburg.

Brigitte Horn-Helf. 1999. *Technisches Übersetzen in Theorie und Praxis*. Franke.

Paul Kußmaul. 2000. *Kreatives Übersetzen*. Stauffenburg.

Vladimir Iosifovich Levenshtein. 1966. Binary codes capable of correcting deletions, insertions and reversals. *Soviet Physics Doklady*, 10(8):707–710.

Chi-Kiu Lo and Dekai Wu. 2011. MEANT: An inexpensive, high-accuracy, semi-automatic metric for evaluating translation utility based on semantic roles. In *Proceedings of the 49th Annual Meeting of the ACL*, pages 220–229.

Tucker Maney, Linda Sibert, Dennis Perzanowski, Kalyan Gupta, and Astrid Schmidt-Nielsen. 2012. Toward determining the comprehensibility of machine translations. In *Proceedings of the 1st PITR*, pages 1–7.

Elvira Mertin. 2006. *Prozessorientiertes Qualitätsmanagement im Dienstleistungsbereich Übersetzen*. Peter Lang.

Christiane Nord. 2003. Transparenz der Korrektur. In *Handbuch Translation*, pages 384–387. Stauffenburg.

Kishore Papineni, Salim Roukos, Todd Ward, and Wei-Jing Zhu. 2002. Bleu: a method for automatic evaluation of machine translation. In *Proceedings of the 40th Annual Meeting of the ACL*, pages 311–318.

Maja Popović, Eleftherios Avramidis, Aljoscha Burchardt, Sabine Hunsicker, Sven Schmeier, Cindy Tscherwinka, David Vilar, and Hans Uszkoreit. 2013. Learning from human judgements of machine translation output. In *MT Summit*, pages 231–238.

Lothar Sachs and Jürgen Hedderich. 2009. *Angewandte Statistik. Methodensammlung mit R*. Springer.

Matthew Snover, Bonnie Dorr, Richard Schwartz, Linnea Micciulla, and John Makhoul. 2006. A study of translation edit rate with targeted human annotation. In *Proceedings of AMTA*, pages 223–231.

Matthew Snover, Nitin Madnani, Bonnie Dorr, and Richard Schwartz. 2009. Fluency, adequacy, or HTER? Exploring different human judgments with a tunable MT metric. In *Proceedings of the 4th Workshop on SMT*, pages 259–268.

Society of Automotive Engineers. 2005. *SAE J2450:2005-08: Translation Quality Metric*. SAE.

Harold Somers. 2011. Machine translation: History, development, and limitations. In *The Oxford Handbook of Translation Studies*, pages 427–440. Oxford University Press.

Sara Stymne and Lars Ahrenberg. 2012. On the practice of error analysis for machine translation evaluation. In *Proceedings of the 8th LREC*, pages 1785–1790.

Christoph Tillmann, Stephan Vogel, Hermann Ney, Alexander Zubiaga, and Hassan Sawaf. 1997. Accelerated DP based search for statistical translation. In *Proceedings of the EUROSPEECH*, pages 2667–2670.

Sandra Weiss and Lars Ahrenberg. 2012. Error profiling for evaluation of machine-translated text: a polish-english case study. In *Proceedings of the Eighth LREC*, pages 1764–1770.

Kevin Windle and Anthony Pym. 2011. European thinking on secular translation. In *The Oxford Handbook of Translation Studies*, pages 7–22. Oxford University Press.

Andrea Wurm. 2013. Eigennamen und Realia in einem Korpus studentischer Übersetzungen (KOPTE). *trans-kom*, 6(2):381–419.

A Examples of lexical variation in human translation

In the examples below, bold face indicates the French source.

A.1 Proper names

président gabonais
Präsidenten von Gabon
Präsidenten Gabuns
Präsidenten von Gabun
Präsident des afrikanischen Landes Gabon
gabunesischen Präsidenten

la Commission nationale de l'informatique et des libertés (CNIL)
Commission nationale de l'informatique et des libertés (CNIL)
französische Datenschutzbehörde (CNIL)
französische Datenschutzkommission CNIL
französische Datenschutzbehörde CNIL
französische Kommission für Datenschutz (CNIL)

A.2 Problematic source text elements (translation problems)

pivot de l'influence française
Stützpunkt des Einflusses Frankreichs
zentralen Figur des französischen Einfluss
Stütze für den Einfluss Frankreichs
Schlüsselfigur für den Einfluss Frankreichs
Garant für den französischen Einfluß

"doyen de l'Afrique"
obersten Würdenträgers Afrikas
"Alten Herrn von Afrika"
"Abtes von Afrika"
"Ältesten von Afrika"
"doyen de l'Afrique"

A.3 Paraphrases

sera-t-elle capable
es schaffen
fähig sein
in der Lage sein
sich als fähig erweisen

se tenir à la bonne distance
auf angemessener Distanz zu bleiben
sich nicht einzumischen
sich herauszuhalten
die gebührende Neutralität zu wahren

A.4 Culture-specific elements and underspecified source text items

la "Françafrique"
"Françafrique"
Französisch-Afrika ("Françafrique")
„Franzafrika"
"Frankafrika"
"Françafrique" d.h. der französisch beeinflussten Gebiete Afrikas

les "voitures Google", équipées de caméras à 360 degrés
mit 360-Grad-Kameras ausgestatteten "Google-Kamerawagen"
Kamera-Autos
Street-View-Wagen mit ihren 360°-Kameras
"Google-Autos", die auf dem Dach eine 360-Grad-Kamera montiert haben,
mit 360-Grad-Kameras ausgestatteten "Street View-Autos"

A.5 Source text ambiguities (syntactic and semantic)

la France a soutenu un régime autoritaire et prédateur, sans pitié pour les opposants
autoritären Systems [...], das kein Mitleid mit seinen Gegnern zeigte
hat Frankreich ohne Rücksicht auf Regimekritiker ein autoritäres Gewaltregime unterstützt
autoritäre und ausbeutende Regime [...], welches keine Gnade für seine Gegner kannte
autoritäres und angriffslustiges Regime [...], das kein Mitleid mit seinen Gegnern hatte
hat Frankreich dieses autoritäre und ausbeuterische System, ohne Mitleid mit dessen Gegnern, gestützt

justes paroles
hat die Wahrheit gesagt
hat [...] die richtigen Worte gefunden
hat die richtigen Worte gefunden
Aussage [...] war nichts als Worte
hat genau das Richtige gesagt

A.6 Numbers

une amende de 100 000 euros
Geldstrafe in Höhe von 100 000 Euro
Strafe von 100 000€
Geldstrafe von 100.000,- EUR
Geldstrafe in Höhe von 100.000 Euro
Bußgeld in Höhe von 100 000€

photographe Yann Arthus-Bertrand, 63 ans
63jährigen Fotografen Yann Arthus-Betrand
Fotographen Yann Arthus-Bertrand (63 Jahre)
Fotografen Yann Arthus-Bertrand (63)
63-jährigen Fotografen Y.A.B.
Fotografen Yann Arthus-Bertrand, 63

A.7 Colloquial or figurative speech

Je vais vite
Ich beeile mich
Ich mache es schnell
Ich bewege mich schnell
Ich hab's eilig
Ich beeile mich

résultats des petits frères
Einnahmen der Vorgänger
Verdienste zusätzlicher kleiner Artikel
Einnahmen durch andere Produkte
Erlöse von Merchandising
Einnahmen aus dem Merchandising

A.8 Source text element triggering correct and incorrect translations

65 chaînes de télévision, dont France 2 et 23 chaînes en Afrique
65 Fernsehsendern, darunter auch France 2 und 23 afrikanische Sender
65 Fernsehsendern, unter anderem France 2 und 23 Sender in Afrika
65 Fernsehsender, darunter der französische Sender France 2 und 23 afrikanische Sender
65 Fernsehkanälen, u.a. 2 in Frankreich und 23 in Afrika
65 Fernsehkanälen, darunter France 2 und 23 afrikanische Sender

Black-box integration of heterogeneous bilingual resources into an interactive translation system

Juan Antonio Pérez-Ortiz
`japerez@dlsi.ua.es`

Daniel Torregrosa
`dtr5@alu.ua.es`

Mikel L. Forcada
`mlf@dlsi.ua.es`

Departament de Llenguatges i Sistemes Informàtics
Universitat d'Alacant, Spain

Abstract

The objective of interactive translation prediction (ITP) is to assist human translators in the translation of texts by making context-based computer-generated suggestions as they type. Most of the ITP systems in literature are strongly coupled with a statistical machine translation system that is conveniently adapted to provide the suggestions. In this paper, however, we propose a *resource-agnostic* approach in which the suggestions are obtained from any bilingual resource (a machine translation system, a translation memory, a bilingual dictionary, etc.) that provides target-language equivalents for source-language segments. These bilingual resources are considered to be black boxes and do not need to be adapted to the peculiarities of the ITP system. Our evaluation shows that savings of up to 85% can be theoretically achieved in the number of keystrokes when using our novel approach. Preliminary user trials indicate that these benefits can be partly transferred to real-world computer-assisted translation interfaces.

1 Introduction

Translation technologies are frequently used to assist human translators. Common approaches consider machine translation (MT) (Hutchins and Somers, 1992) or translation memories (Somers, 2003) to be systems that produce a first (and usually incorrect) prototype of the translation which is then edited by the human translator in order to produce a target-language text that is adequate for publishing. In both situations, the suggestion may be considered as a source of inspiration by the human translators, who will assemble the final translation by on some occasions accepting and rearranging parts of the proposal, or on others introducing their own words when an appropriate equivalent is not included or is not found in the suggestion. The whole process may be viewed as a *negotiation* between the wordings that form in the translator's mind and wordings that already appear in the suggestion. In both approaches the suggestion is generated once, usually before starting to manually translate every new sentence.

The approach introduced in this paper, however, follows a different path, which is strongly connected to the field of *interactive translation prediction*[1] (ITP), a research field which explores a kind of computer-assisted translation framework whose aim is to interactively provide users with suggestions at every step during the translation process.[2] Most works in the field of ITP have focused on statistical MT systems as the only source of translations considered to obtain the suggestions, but our study aims to determine how bilingual resources of any kind can be accommodated into an interoperable ITP. To obtain the suggestions, the source-language sentence to be translated is split up into many different (and possibly overlapping) word segments of up to a given length, and a translation for each segment is obtained by using a bilingual resource which is able to deliver one or more target-language equivalents for a particular source-language segment. These equivalents will be the source of the proposals which will be offered to the human translator during the translation process. In principle, the nature of these bilingual resources is not restricted: in

[1] The name *interactive translation prediction* has recently been proposed (Alabau et al., 2013) for this research field, which has historically been referred to as *target-text mediated interactive MT* (Foster et al., 1997) or simply *interactive MT* (Barrachina et al., 2009). Despite the traditional term, we consider the recent one to be more suitable for our approach since it is not exclusively based on MT.

[2] The interaction can be compared to that of word completion mechanisms in input text boxes and word processors.

this paper we shall explore the use of an MT system, but they may also consist of translation memories, dictionaries, catalogues of bilingual phrases, or a combination of heterogeneous resources. As stated above, MT or translation memories cannot usually deliver appropriate translations at the sentence level, but their proposals usually contain acceptable segments that do not cover the whole sentence but which can be accepted by the user to assemble a good translation, thus saving keystrokes, mouse actions[3] and, possibly, time.

The remainder of the paper is organised as follows. After reviewing the state-of-the-art in ITP in Section 2, we outline the main differences between our proposal and those found in literature in Section 3. Our method for generating translation suggestions from bilingual resources is formally presented in Section 4. We then introduce in Section 5 our experimental set-up and show the results of two evaluations: one that is fully automatic and another consisting of a user trial involving human evaluators. Finally, we discuss the results and propose future lines of research in Section 6.

2 Related work

The systems which have most significantly contributed to the field of ITP are those built in the pioneering TransType project (Foster et al., 1997; Langlais et al., 2000), and its continuation, the TransType2 project (Macklovitch, 2006). These systems observe the current partial translation already typed by the user and, by exploiting an embedded statistical MT engine, propose one or more completions that are compatible with the sentence prefix entered by the user. Various models were considered for the underlying MT system, including alignment templates, phrase-based models, and stochastic finite-state transducers (Barrachina et al., 2009). The proposals offered may range from one or several words, to a completion of the remainder of the target sentence. An automatic best-scenario evaluation with training and evaluation corpora belonging to the same domain (Barrachina et al., 2009) showed that it might theoretically be possible to use only 20–25% of the keystrokes in comparison with the unassisted translation for English–Spanish translation (both directions) and around 45% for English–French and English–German. The results of the user trials (Macklovitch, 2006) showed gains in productivity (measured in number of words translated per hour) of around 15–20%, but despite this, the human translators were not satisfied with the system, principally because they had to correct the same errors in the proposals over and over again (the models in the underlying statistical MT system remained unchanged during the translation process).

A number of projects continued the research where TransType2 had left off. Caitra (Koehn, 2009) is an ITP tool which uses both the phrase table and the decoder of a statistical MT system to generate suggestions; although individual results vary, translators are generally fastest with post-editing and obtain the highest translation performance when combining post-editing and ITP in the same interface (Koehn and Haddow, 2009). Researchers at the Universitat Politècnica de València have also made significant improvements to the TransType2 system such as online learning techniques with which to adaptively generate better proposals from user feedback (Ortiz-Martínez et al., 2011), phrase-table smoothing to cope with segments in the partially typed translation which cannot be generated with the phrases collected during training (Ortiz-Martínez, 2011), or multimodal interfaces (Alabau et al., 2010). The objective of the CASMACAT project (Alabau et al., 2013), which is under active development, is to develop new types of assistance along all these lines. Finally, commercial translation memory systems have also recently started to introduce ITP as one of their basic features (see, for example, SDL Trados AutoSuggest[4]).

3 Innovative nature of our proposal

Common to most of the approaches discussed above is the fact that the underlying translation engine needs to be a glass-box resource, that is, a resource whose behaviour is modified to meet the ITP system needs. The approaches rely on a statistical MT (Koehn, 2010) system which is adapted to provide the list of n-best completions for the remainder of the sentence, given the current sentence prefix already introduced by the user; in order to meet the resulting time constraints, the decoder of the statistical MT system cannot be executed after each keystroke and techniques to compute the search graph once and then reuse it have been proposed (Bender et al., 2005). However, it

[3]In the case of touch devices, other means of interaction (such as gestures) may exist.

[4]http://www.translationzone.com/

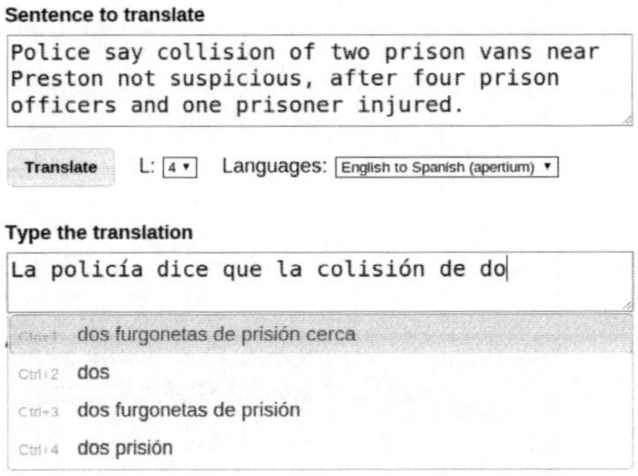

Figure 1: Screenshot of the web interface of our ITP tool showing a translation in progress with some suggestions being offered. The top text box contains the source sentence, whereas users type the translation into the bottom box.

may occur that an ITP system has access to bilingual resources which cannot produce a completion for the rest of the target-language sentence from a given sentence prefix, but are able to supply the translation of a particular source-language segment. This may be owing to either intrinsic reasons inherent to the type of resource being used (for example, a bilingual dictionary can only translate single words or short multi-word units) or extrinsic reasons (for example, an MT system available through a third-party web service cannot be instructed to continue a partial translation).

We propose a black-box treatment of the bilingual resources in contrast to the glass-box approaches found in literature. Unlike them, access to the inner details of the translation system is not necessary; this maintains coupling between the ITP tool and the underlying system to a minimum and provides the opportunity to incorporate additional sources of bilingual information beyond purposely-designed statistical MT systems. Moreover, suggestions are computed once at the start and not after each keystroke, which results in a more effective interaction with the user in execution environments with limited resources.

In this paper, we shall focus on a black-box MT system (Forcada et al., 2011), but we have also begun to explore the integration of other bilingual resources (such as translation memories, dictionaries, catalogues of bilingual phrases, or even a combination of heterogeneous resources). Our system has a web interface similar to that in the projects discussed in Section 2: users freely type the translation of the source sentence, and are offered suggestions *on the fly* in a drop-down list with items based on the current prefix, although this prefix will correspond to the first characters of the word currently being typed and not to the part of the target sentence already entered; users may accept these suggestions (using cursor keys, the mouse or specific hot keys) or ignore them and continue typing. A screenshot of the interface is shown in Figure 1. Despite the cognitive load inherent to any predictive interface, the interface is easy and intuitive to use, even for inexperienced users.

4 Method

Our method starts by splitting the source-language sentence S up into all the (possibly overlapping) segments of length $l \in [1, L]$, where L is the maximum source segment length measured in words. The resulting segments are then translated by means of a bilingual resource (or combinations thereof). The set of *potential proposals* P^S for sentence S is made up of pairs comprising the translation of each segment and the position in the input sentence of the first word of the corresponding source-language segment. See Table 1 for an example of the set P^S obtained in an English to Spanish translation task when using $L = 3$. We shall represent the i-th suggestion as p_i, its target-language segment as $t(p_i)$ and its corresponding source-language word position as $\sigma(p_i)$. Suitable values for L will depend on the bilingual resource: on the one hand, we expect higher values of L to be useful for high-quality MT systems, such as those translating between closely related languages, since adequate translations may stretch to a relatively large number of words; on the other hand, L should be kept small for resources such as dictionaries or low-quality MT systems whose translations quickly deteriorate as the length of the input segment increases.

Let $P_C^S(\hat{w}, j)$ be the subset of P^S including the *compatible suggestions* which can be offered to the user after typing $\hat{w}$ as the prefix of the j-th word in the translated sentence T. The elements of $P_C^S(\hat{w}, j)$ are determined by considering only those suggestions in P^S that have the already-typed word prefix as their own prefix:

$$P_C^S(\hat{w}, j) = \{p_i \in P^S : \hat{w} \in \text{Prefix}(t(p_i))\}$$

For example, in the case of the translation of the English sentence in Table 1, if the user types an *M*, the set of compatible suggestions $P_C^S(\text{“M”}, 1)$

Start position	Source segment	Suggestion
1	My	(Mi,1)
1	My tailor	(Mi sastre,1)
1	My tailor is	(Mi sastre es,1)
2	tailor	(sastre,2)
2	tailor is	(sastre es,2)
2	tailor is healthy	(sastre está sano,2)
3	is	(es,3)
3	is healthy	(está sano,3)
4	healthy	(sano,4)

Table 1: Source-language segments and potential suggestions P^S when translating the sentence $S =$ "My tailor is healthy" into Spanish with $L = 3$.

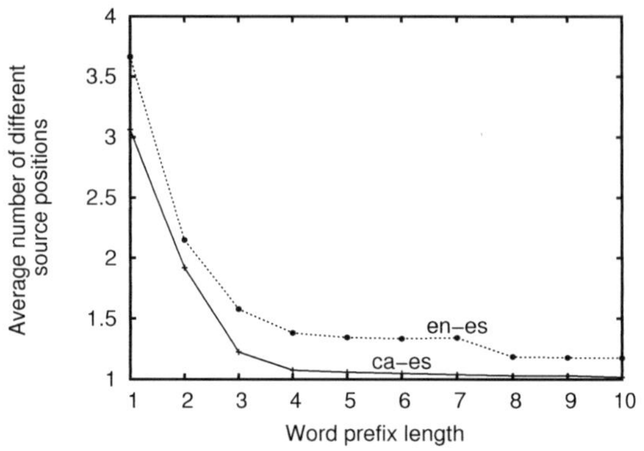

Figure 2: Average number, for all the letters in the alphabet, of different source positions in the source sentence providing compatible suggestions versus length in characters of the typed prefix of the current target word. A system with $L = 4$, $M = \infty$ and no deletion of selected suggestions (see Section 4) was used to obtain the points in this graph. Data is shown for the English–Spanish (*en-es*) and Catalan–Spanish (*es-ca*) corpora used in the automatic experiments (see Section 5).

will contain the suggestions with target-language segments *Mi*, *Mi sastre* and *Mi sastre es*, since they are the only proposals in P^S starting with an *M*. The size of P^S_C is dependent on the value of L, but compatible proposals may also originate from translations of source segments starting at different positions in the input sentence (for example, the set P^S_C after the user types an *s* in the same translation will contain proposals starting with *sastre* and *sano*). More elaborated strategies are consequently necessary to further reduce the number of proposals, since we do not expect users to tolerate lists with more than a few suggestions. In 4.1 we propose the use of a ranking strategy to sort the elements of P^S_C in such a way that it is possible to predict which of them are most suitable to be offered to the user. However, we first elaborate on the issue of compatible suggestions originating from different source positions.

The number of source positions that generate compatible suggestions also depends on the specific word prefix; for example, when users type the letter *d* when translating a long sentence into Spanish, they will probably obtain a significant number of suggestions starting with *de*[5] originating from segments located in different source positions. We measured the number of different positions that provide compatible suggestions when the first characters of the current word are typed during an automatic evaluation of our system (see Section 5); for instance, when translating from English to Spanish, the average is 1.46 after typing *b*, whereas it is 4.73 after typing *d*. Figure 2 shows the average number of different positions for all the letters as users type longer prefixes. Obviously, only suggestions originating from the part of the source sentence currently being translated may be useful, but this position is difficult to determine unambiguously. The degree of success that can be achieved in this task will be explored in greater depth in future work (see Section 6); a simple approximation is presented in the following section.

4.1 Ranking suggestions

In the absence of a strategy with which to rank the suggestions in $P^S_C(\hat{w}, j)$ which we are currently working on, in this paper we explore a naïve distance-based approach which is based solely on the position j: suggestions p_i whose source position $\sigma(p_i)$ is closer[6] to j are prioritised. For example, in the case of the translation in Table 1, if the user types *Mi s*, suggestions starting with *sastre* will be ranked before those starting with *sano*. This linearity assumption can be seen as a rough attempt to determine the part of the input sentence that is currently being translated; more sophisticated approaches will be considered in future work (see Section 6). However, notice that according to Figure 2, the average number of different source positions of the compatible segments quickly becomes closer to 1 when the length of the word prefix is greater than 2; it is therefore expected that the role played by the distance-based ranker will soon decrease as the user continues typing the

[5]The preposition *de* is notably frequent in Spanish texts.

[6]Ties are broken at random.

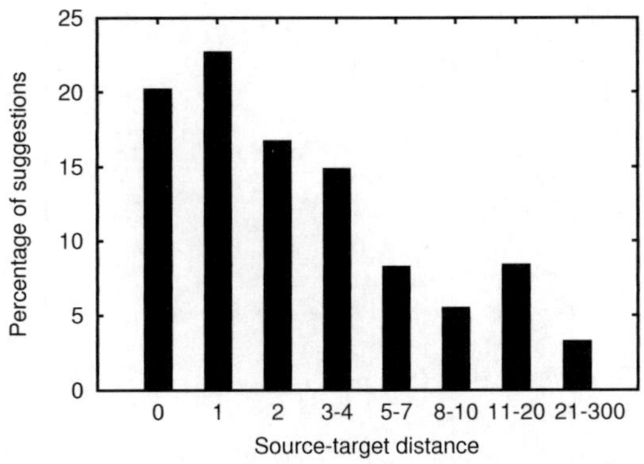

Figure 3: Distribution of the absolute differences (measured in words) between source position of accepted suggestions versus position in the target sentence in which they were selected for the case of Spanish–English translation. $L = 4$, $M = \infty$ and no deletion of selected suggestions (see Section 4) was used to obtain this graph.

current word (although the position of a valid suggestion is far from j, it will probably be the only compatible proposal, and will consequently be selected to be offered).

Translation between closely related languages is often monotonic and most reorderings are local; our distance-based ranking is therefore expected to produce good results for this kind of language pairs. Nevertheless, we cannot in principle expect this ranker to work reasonably well on unrelated languages with different overall grammatical structures (e.g., when translating a language with a verb–subject–object order into another one with a subject–verb–object typology). The graph in Figure 3 represents the distribution of the distances between the source positions of all the accepted suggestions in our automatic Spanish–English evaluation (see Section 5) versus the position in the target sentence of the word for which they were selected. The Pearson correlation coefficient between both positions is very high (0.93), which supports the idea that our naïve distance-based ranking may work reasonably well for the languages used in our experiments.[7]

Let M be the maximum number of suggestions that will eventually be offered to the human translator; the ordered list of *suggestions offered* to the user $P_O^S(\hat{w}, j)$ is made up of a subset of the elements in $P_C^S(\hat{w}, j)$ and restricted so that $|P_O^S(\hat{w}, j)| \leq M$. Note that for the interface to be *friendly*, the value of M should be kept small and, as a result of this, it could easily occur that all the suggestions offered are obtained starting at the same source position (that closest to the current target position) although better suggestions from different positions exist. In order to mitigate the impact of this, in this paper we propose to restrict the number of proposals originating from a particular source position to two (the longest and the shortest, in this order, which are compatible with the typed word prefix) as long as different compatible suggestions originating from a different position exist. The longest is offered in the hope that it will be correct and will contribute towards saving a lot of keystrokes; however, since the quality of machine translations usually degrades with the length of the input segment (see Figure 4), the shortest is also offered. This must, however, be researched in more depth.

4.2 Deleting dispensable suggestions

Suggestions that have been accepted by the user should not be proposed again. In this work, a selected suggestion p_i will be removed from P^S if no other suggestion p_j with the same target-language text $t(p_i)$ and different source position $\sigma(p_j)$ exists in P^S. In this case, those suggestions obtained from the source position $\sigma(p_i)$ are also removed from P^S. Deleting dispensable suggestions allows other useful suggestions to be selected by the ranker in order to be offered.

5 Experimental setup and results

A fully automatic evaluation and a user trial involving human evaluators were conducted. As previously stated in Section 3, the only bilingual resource considered in this paper is an MT system; in particular, the Spanish to Catalan and English to Spanish rule-based MT systems in the free/open-source platform Apertium[8] (Forcada et al., 2011).

5.1 Evaluation metrics

The performance of our system has been measured by using two metrics: *keystroke ratio* (KSR) and *acceptable suggestion ratio* (ASR). On the one hand, the KSR is the ratio between the number of keystrokes and the length of the translated sen-

[7] Although not shown here, similar results are obtained for the Catalan–Spanish pair.

[8] Revision 44632 of the Apertium repository at http://svn.code.sf.net/p/apertium/svn/trunk/ was used for the engine and linguistic data in these experiments.

tence (Langlais et al., 2000). A lower KSR represents a greater saving in keystrokes. In our experiments, selecting a suggestion has the same cost as pressing one key. On the other hand, the ASR measures the percentage of times that at least one of the suggestions in a non-empty P_O^S is selected. If users frequently receive suggestion lists containing no acceptable proposals, they will stop consulting the list and translate without assistance; it is therefore important to measure the number of times the user is needlessly bothered.

5.2 Automatic evaluation

In order to determine optimal values for the different parameters of our system and to obtain an idea of the best results attainable, a number of automatic tests were conducted. The approach followed is identical to that described by Langlais et al. (2000), in which a parallel corpus with pairs of sentences was used, each pair consisting of a sentence S in the source language and a reference translation T in the target language. In the context of our automatic evaluation, S is used as the input sentence to be translated and T is considered as the target output sentence a user is supposed to have in mind and stick to while *typing*. The longest suggestion in P_O^S which concatenated to the already typed text results in a new prefix of T is always used. If P_O^S contains no suggestions at a particular point, then the system continues *typing* according to T. As the algorithm proceeds in a left-to-right longest-match greedy fashion, there is no guarantee that the best possible results will be obtained, but they will be a good approximation.[9] For example, for $T =$ *Mi coche está averiado*, partial output translation *Mi c*, and $P_O^S(\text{“c”}, 2) = \{$*coche*, *coche es*, *coche está roto*$\}$, our automatic evaluation system will proceed as follows: it will first discard *coche está roto*, because *Mi coche está roto* is not a prefix of T; it will then discard *coche es*, because although *Mi coche es* is a prefix of T, it is not a prefix when a blank is added after it; finally, it will select *coche*, because *Mi coche* followed by a blank is a prefix of T and no longer suggestion that also satisfies these conditions exists.

Two different corpora were used for the automatic evaluation: for English–Spanish (*en-es*), a combination of sentences from all the editions of DGT-TM (Steinberger et al., 2012) released in 2004–2011 (15 250 sentences; 163 196 words in English; 190 448 in Spanish) was used; for Catalan–Spanish (*ca-es*), a collection of news items from El Periódico de Catalunya[10] (15 000 sentences; 307 095 words in Catalan; 294 488 in Spanish) was used.

[9]Note that real users could also decide to select suggestions with small errors and fix them, but neither this nor other behaviours are considered in our automatic evaluation.

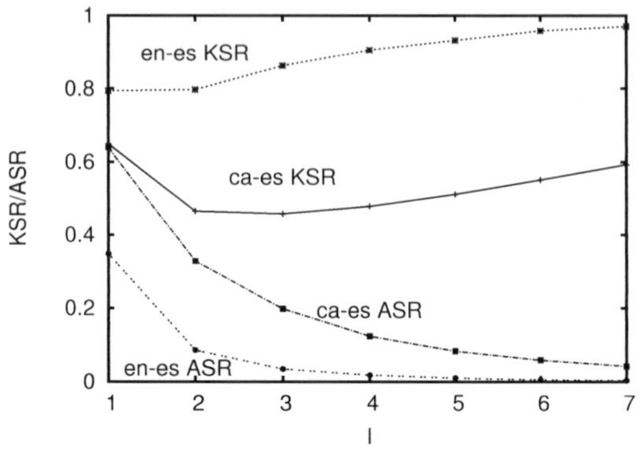

Figure 4: Automatically evaluated KSR versus exact length of the segments l. Longer suggestions are much more useful for Spanish–Catalan (closely related languages) than for English–Spanish: the KSR for $l = 7$ is still a little better than that for $l = 1$ for Catalan–Spanish, but noticeably worse for English–Spanish. ASR quickly degrades as l increases.

5.3 Results of the automatic evaluation

The objective of the automatic evaluation was to estimate the influence of the language pair and the parameters L and M.[11]

Maximum length of segments. We first tested to what extent each different segment length l contributes separately to the KSR. Note that l corresponds in this case to the exact length of the source segments and not to the longest one (as represented by L). $M = \infty$ is used in all the experiments in this section. Figure 4 shows that the KSR becomes worse for greater values of l, which can be explained by the fact that longer machine translations often contain more errors than shorter ones. In the case of Catalan–Spanish, the worst KSR value is for $l = 1$ since adequate suggestions will usually consist of few characters and selecting them will barely contribute to keystroke reduction.

[10]http://www.elperiodico.cat/ca/

[11]95% confidence intervals of the average values presented in this section were calculated using the Student's t-test. The size of the evaluation corpora signifies that the resulting confidence intervals are so small that they would have been imperceptible on the graphs and have therefore been omitted.

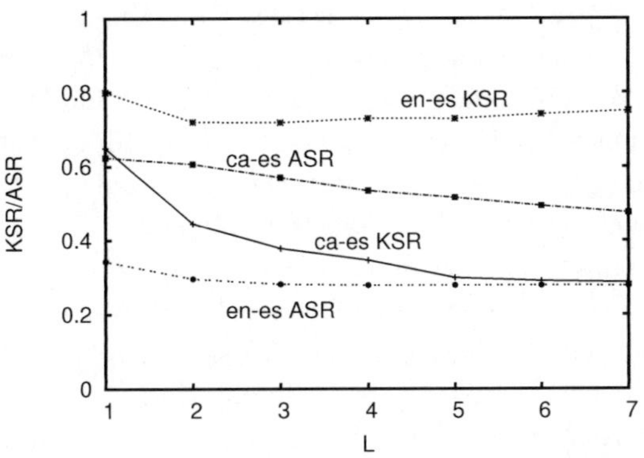

Figure 5: Automatically evaluated KSR/ASR versus maximum length of the segments L. As L increases, the KSR improves, but the ASR is negatively affected.

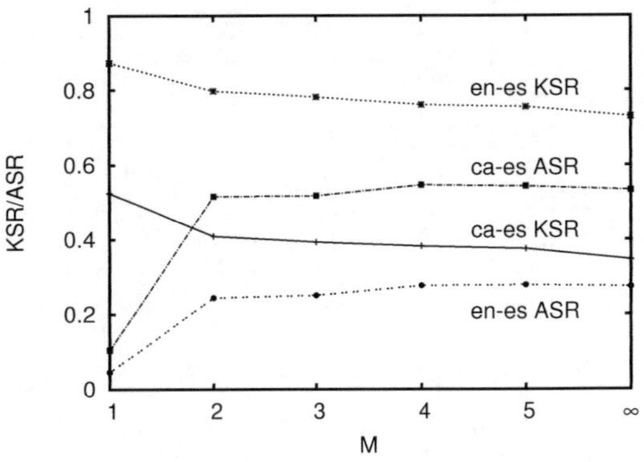

Figure 6: Automatically evaluated KSR/ASR versus maximum number M of suggestions offered. Although the results with $M = 1$ (only one suggestion offered) are considerably worse, for higher values of M they quickly approach the results obtained when no ranker was used and all the compatible suggestions were offered ($M = \infty$).

Combining different segment lengths up to length L provides better values of KSR than using only a fixed value $l = L$ (compare Figures 4 and 5). Figure 5 shows an estimation of the best results our method could attain if all the compatible suggestions in P_C^S were included in P_O^S: values between 0.3 and 0.4 for the Catalan–Spanish KSR and between 0.7 and 0.8 for the English–Spanish KSR. The notable difference may be explained by the fact that Apertium performance is much better (Forcada et al., 2011) for Catalan–Spanish (word error rates of around 15%) than for English–Spanish (word error rates of around 70%).

Maximum number of suggestions offered. We evaluated the influence of the maximum size M of the list of suggestions offered to the user and, hence, the impact of the distance-based ranker. $L = 4$ was used, as this value provides good results for both language pairs (see Figure 5). As expected (see Figure 6), the distance-based ranking strategy works remarkably well (values for KSR and ASR from $M = 4$ are similar to those obtained with $M = \infty$) for closely related languages (Catalan–Spanish), in which translations are usually monotonic and reorderings seldom occur. However, the empirical results also show (see again Figure 6) that it also works well for language pairs (English–Spanish) in which long-distance reorderings exist, at least when compared to the results without ranking ($M = \infty$).

5.4 Human evaluation

A preliminary evaluation of a real use of our system involving 8 human non-professional translators (volunteer computer science students) was also conducted. All the users were Spanish native speakers who understood Catalan, but with no experience with ITP systems. As the results of the automatic evaluation show that the performance of the Apertium English–Spanish MT system negatively affects our ITP system (see Section 5), we decided to focus on the Catalan–Spanish scenario. A set of 10 sentences in Catalan were randomly extracted from the same corpus used in the automatic evaluation. The test was designed to take around 20 minutes. The evaluators were allowed to practise with a couple of sentences before starting the trial. After completing the test, they were surveyed about the usefulness of the system. Our ITP system was used with $L = M = 4$.

5.5 Results of the human evaluation

The users were divided into two groups: users 1–4 translated sentences 1–5 assisted by our ITP tool and sentences 6–10 with no assistance, while users 5–8 translated sentences 1–5 with no assistance and sentences 6–10 assisted by the tool. The KSR and translation times for each user are shown in Table 2. This table also includes KSR$'$, which is the value of KSR obtained by running our automatic evaluator (see Section 5.2) using the sentences entered by each user as the reference translations T; this can be considered as an approximation to the best result achievable with the ITP tool. All users attained KSRs that were notice-

User	Sentences 1–5			Sentences 6–10		
	KSR	Time	KSR′	KSR	Time	KSR′
#1	**0.49**	**136**	**0.22**	1.11	137	0.23
#2	**0.64**	**144**	**0.15**	1.21	86	0.22
#3	**0.63**	**209**	**0.22**	1.09	112	0.21
#4	**0.37**	**189**	**0.22**	1.22	199	0.18
#5	1.10	145	0.28	**0.37**	**102**	**0.15**
#6	1.24	150	0.27	**0.51**	**154**	**0.17**
#7	1.15	178	0.30	**0.64**	**147**	**0.17**
#8	1.18	118	0.39	**0.58**	**93**	**0.15**

Table 2: KSR, translation times (seconds) and KSR′ (see main text) for each of the users in the evaluation. Values in bold correspond to the translations with assistance from our ITP system.

ably lower than 1 for the assisted translations and slightly higher than 1 when translating without the ITP system; the former, however, are often worse than the KSR values obtained in the automatic evaluation which are around 0.4 for $L = M = 4$ (see Figure 6). Moreover, the values for KSR′ show that even better values for KSR could theoretically be attained for these sentences; note, however, that the reference translations in this case were precisely generated by accepting suggestions generated by Apertium.

The users were surveyed to evaluate the following statements in the range from 1 (complete disagreement) to 5 (complete agreement): *the interface is easy to use*; *I would use a tool like this in future translations*; *I have found the suggestions useful*; and *the tool has allowed me to translate faster*. The median of the responses to the first two questions was 5, whereas the median for the two last questions was 4.5. It was evident that the evaluators perceived that the ITP system had helped them to translate faster, although the time values in Table 2 seem to suggest the opposite. Finally, note that this was a small-scale human evaluation and that sounder results will have to be collected under different conditions by increasing the number of users, sentences and languages in the test.

6 Discussion and future work

The automatic evaluation of our ITP system has provided an estimation of its potential for human translators. Note, however, that this evaluation strategy is based on a greedy algorithm which may not adequately reproduce the way in which a human translator might usually perform the task. According to the best results of our automatic experiments, when a maximum of $M = 4$ suggestions are offered and the system selects the longest one that matches the reference translation, 25–65% keystrokes could be saved depending on the language pair. Moreover, 30–55% of the times that a list of suggestions is offered, at least one of the suggestions matches the target sentence.

Our preliminary human tests can be used to discern how well our system could perform, but a more extensive evaluation is needed to explore the influence of parameters, different kinds of users, heterogeneous bilingual resources, new language pairs, particular domains, different interfaces, etc. in greater depth. A comparison with similar tools in literature will also be carried out.

We plan to improve the ranking strategy shown in Section 4.1 by automatically detecting the part of the input sentence being translated at each moment so that segments that originate in those positions are prioritised. We intend to achieve this by combining word alignment and distortion models. The former will be used to determine the alignments between the last words introduced by the user and the words in the input sentence;[12] the latter will predict which source words will be translated next, partly by using information from the alignment model.

The ITP system presented in this paper is implemented in Java, except for the web interface, which is written in HTML and JavaScript. The Java code, however, has been designed in such a way that it can be compiled into JavaScript with the help of the Google Web Toolkit framework;[13] and the same code can therefore be executed either on the browser in JavaScript when human translators interact with the tool, or locally in Java when performing the automatic evaluation. The entire code of the application is available[14] under a free software license (GNU Affero General Public License, version 3); this ensures the reproducibility of the experiments and allows our ITP system to be integrated into professional translation tools.

Acknowledgments. This work has been partly funded by the Spanish Ministerio de Economía y Competitividad through project TIN 2012-32615.

[12] On-the-fly, light alignment models have been proposed which do not require parallel corpora and are based on the translation of all the possible segments of the sentence with the help of black-box bilingual resources (Esplà-Gomis et al., 2012); these models would fit nicely into our ITP method.

[13] http://www.gwtproject.org/

[14] https://github.com/jaspock/forecat

References

Vicent Alabau, Daniel Ortiz-Martínez, Alberto Sanchis, and Francisco Casacuberta. 2010. Multimodal interactive machine translation. In *ICMI-MLMI '10: Proceedings of the 2010 International Conference on Multimodal Interfaces*.

Vicent Alabau, Ragnar Bonk, Christian Buck, Michael Carl, Francisco Casacuberta, Mercedes García-Martínez, Jesús González-Rubio, Philipp Koehn, Luis A. Leiva, Bartolomé Mesa-Lao, Daniel Ortiz, Herve Saint-Amand, Germán Sanchis-Trilles, and Chara Tsoukala. 2013. CASMACAT: An open source workbench for advanced computer aided translation. *Prague Bull. Math. Linguistics*, 100:101–112.

Sergio Barrachina, Oliver Bender, Francisco Casacuberta, Jorge Civera, Elsa Cubel, Shahram Khadivi, Antonio Lagarda, Hermann Ney, Jesús Tomás, Enrique Vidal, and Juan-Miguel Vilar. 2009. Statistical approaches to computer-assisted translation. *Computational Linguistics*, 35(1):3–28.

Oliver Bender, David Vilar, Richard Zens, and Hermann Ney. 2005. Comparison of generation strategies for interactive machine translation. In *Proceedings of EAMT 2005 (10th Annual Conference of the European Association for Machine Translation*, pages 30–40.

Miquel Esplà-Gomis, Felipe Sánchez-Martínez, and Mikel L. Forcada. 2012. Using external sources of bilingual information for on-the-fly word alignment. Technical report, Departament de Llenguatges i Sistemes Informàtics, Universitat d'Alacant.

Mikel L Forcada, Mireia Ginestí-Rosell, Jacob Nordfalk, Jim O'Regan, Sergio Ortiz-Rojas, Juan Antonio Pérez-Ortiz, Felipe Sánchez-Martínez, Gema Ramírez-Sánchez, and Francis M Tyers. 2011. Apertium: a free/open-source platform for rule-based machine translation. *Machine Translation*, 25(2):127–144.

George F. Foster, Pierre Isabelle, and Pierre Plamondon. 1997. Target-text mediated interactive machine translation. *Machine Translation*, 12(1-2):175–194.

W. John Hutchins and Harold L. Somers. 1992. *An introduction to machine translation*. Academic Press.

Philipp Koehn and Barry Haddow. 2009. Interactive assistance to human translators using statistical machine translation methods. *MT Summit XII*.

Philipp Koehn. 2009. A web-based interactive computer aided translation tool. In *Proceedings of the ACL-IJCNLP 2009 Software Demonstrations*, pages 17–20.

Philipp Koehn. 2010. *Statistical Machine Translation*. Cambridge University Press.

Philippe Langlais, Sébastien Sauvé, George Foster, Elliott Macklovitch, and Guy Lapalme. 2000. Evaluation of TransType, a computer-aided translation typing system: a comparison of a theoretical-and a user-oriented evaluation procedures. In *Conference on Language Resources and Evaluation (LREC)*, page 8.

Elliott Macklovitch. 2006. TransType2: The last word. In *Proceedings of the 5th International Conference on Languages Resources and Evaluation (LREC 06)*, pages 167–172.

Daniel Ortiz-Martínez, Luis A. Leiva, Vicent Alabau, Ismael García-Varea, and Francisco Casacuberta. 2011. An interactive machine translation system with online learning. In *Proceedings of the ACL-HLT 2011 System Demonstrations*, pages 68–73.

Daniel Ortiz-Martínez. 2011. *Advances in Fully-Automatic and Interactive Phrase-Based Statistical Machine Translation*. Ph.D. thesis, Universitat Politècnica de València.

Harold L. Somers. 2003. *Computers and Translation: A Translator's Guide*. Benjamins translation library. John Benjamins Publishing Company.

Ralf Steinberger, Andreas Eisele, Szymon Klocek, Spyridon Pilos, and Patrick Schlüter. 2012. DGT-TM: a freely available Translation Memory in 22 languages. In *Language Resources and Evaluation Conference*, pages 454–459.

The ACCEPT Portal: An Online Framework for the Pre-editing and Post-editing of User-Generated Content

Violeta Seretan
FTI/TIM
University of Geneva
Switzerland
Violeta.Seretan@unige.ch

Johann Roturier
Symantec Ltd.
Dublin, Ireland
johann_roturier@symantec.com

David Silva
Symantec Ltd.
Dublin, Ireland
David_Silva@symantec.com

Pierrette Bouillon
FTI/TIM
University of Geneva
Switzerland
Pierrette.Bouillon@unige.ch

Abstract

With the development of Web 2.0, a lot of content is nowadays generated online by users. Due to its characteristics (e.g., use of jargon and abbreviations, typos, grammatical and style errors), the user-generated content poses specific challenges to machine translation. This paper presents an online platform devoted to the pre-editing of user-generated content and its post-editing, two main types of human assistance strategies which are combined with domain adaptation and other techniques in order to improve the translation of this type of content. The platform has recently been released publicly and is being tested by two main types of user communities, namely, technical forum users and volunteer translators.

1 Introduction

User-generated content – i.e., information posted by Internet users in social communication channels like blogs, forum posts, social networks – is one of the main sources of information available today. Huge volumes of such content are created each day, reach a very broad audience instantly.[1]

The democratisation of content creation due to the emergence of the Web 2.0 paradigm also means a diversification of the languages used on the Internet.[2] Despite its availability, the new content is only accessible to the speakers of the language in which it was created. The automatic translation of user-generated content is therefore one of the key issues to be addressed in the field of human language technologies. However, as stated by Jiang et al. (2012), despite the obvious benefits, there are relatively little attempts at translating user-generated content.

The reason may lie in the fact that user-generated content is very challenging for machine translation. As shown, among others, by Nagarajan and Gamon (2011), there are several characteristics of this content that pose new processing challenges with respect to traditional content: informal style, slang, abbreviations, specific terminology, irregular grammar and spelling. Indeed, Internet users are rarely professional writers.[3] They often write in a language which is not their own, and sacrifice quality for speed, not paying attention to spelling, punctuation, or grammar rules.

The ACCEPT project[4] addresses these challenges by developing a technology integrating modules for automatic and manual content pre-editing, statistical machine translation, as well as output evaluation and post-editing. Thus, the project aims to improve the translation of user-generated content by proposing a full workflow, in which the participation of humans is essential.

The application scenario considered in the project are user communities sharing specific information on a given topic. The project focuses, more specifically, on the following use cases:

1. the commercial use case, in which the target community is the user community built around a software company in order for members to help each other with issues related to products;
2. the NGO use case, in which non-governmental organisations such as Doctors Without Borders produce health-care content for distributions in areas of need.

[1] For instance, 58 million tweets are sent on average per day (http://www.statisticbrain.com/twitter-statistics/).

[2] See http://en.wikipedia.org/wiki/Languages_used_on_the_Internet for statistics.

[3] Even when they are, as in the case of government agencies, the type of content produced (e.g., tweets) still poses "multiple challenges" to translation (Gotti et al., 2013).

[4] http://www.accept-project.eu/

The language pairs considered in the project are English to French, German and Japanese, as well as French into English for the first use case (involving technical forum information), and French to and from English for the second use case (involving healthcare information).

Past halfway into its research program, the project has accomplished significant progress in the main areas mentioned above (pre-editing, statistical machine translation, post-editing, and evaluation). The ACCEPT technology has recently been released to the broad public as an online framework, which demonstrates the different modules of the workflow and provides access to associated software components (plug-ins, APIs), as well as to documentation. The pre-editing technology has been deployed on the targeted user forum[5], allowing users to check their messages before posting them. The post-editing technology is being used by a community of translators, which provide pro-bono translation services to the NGOs considered in our second use case.

In this paper, we describe the framework by presenting its architecture and main modules (Section 2). We discuss related work in Section 3 and conclude in Section 4.

2 The Framework

The ACCEPT technology has been made accessible to a broad audience in the form of an online framework, i.e., an integrated environment where registered users can perform pre-editing, post-editing and evaluation work. The framework – henceforth, the ACCEPT Portal – is hosted on a cloud computing infrastructure and is available at `www.accept-portal.eu`.

2.1 Architecture of the Framework

As explained in Section 1, the ACCEPT technology consists of the following main modules:

1. Pre-editing module;
2. Machine translation module,
3. Post-editing module,
4. Evaluation module.

The typical workflow is incremental, but the modules are independent. They can be used both within and outside the portal, as they are built on a REST API facilitating integration.

[5] `https://community.norton.com/`

In the remaining of this section, we introduce each of the framework modules.[6]

2.2 Pre-editing Module

The pre-editing module leverages existing lingware which provides authoring support rules aimed at language professionals, by relying on shallow language processing (Bredenkamp et al., 2000). The existing English checker and the linguistic resources on which it relies have been extended and adapted to suit the type of data generated by community users. In particular, the software extension consisted of designing a number of pre-editing rules aimed at source normalisation, for the purpose of making the input text easier to handle by the SMT systems. In the case of French, the pre-editing rules have been designed from scratch. The pre-editing rules pertain to the levels of spelling, grammar, style and terminology. They are defined using the original lingware's rule formalism and are incorporated into a server dedicated to the project.

The rule development was corpus-driven and was performed on data collected for this purpose. A stable set of pre-edition rules is available in the portal for each of the domains and source languages considered (i.e., technical forum and heathcare data in English and French). The rules are described in detail in the project deliverable D 2.2 (2013).

The rules proposed have been evaluated individually and in combination (Roturier et al., 2012; Gerlach et al., 2013; Seretan et al., 2014). As a general observation, it is important to notice that, for SMT, the improvement of the input text does not go hand in hand with the improvement of translation. For example, in French the rule for correcting verbal forms to the subjunctive tense had a negative impact since the subjunctive is not frequent in the training data. Conversely, it was possible to define lexical reformulations which degraded the quality of the input text, but had a positive impact on translation quality.

The combined impact of the rule application was measured in a variety of settings in a large-scale evaluation campaign involving translation students (Seretan et al., 2014). As the rules are divided into two major groups, those automatically applicable and those requiring human inter-

[6] The MT module will be omitted, as it is not part of the portal. The interested reader is referred to D 4.2 (2013).

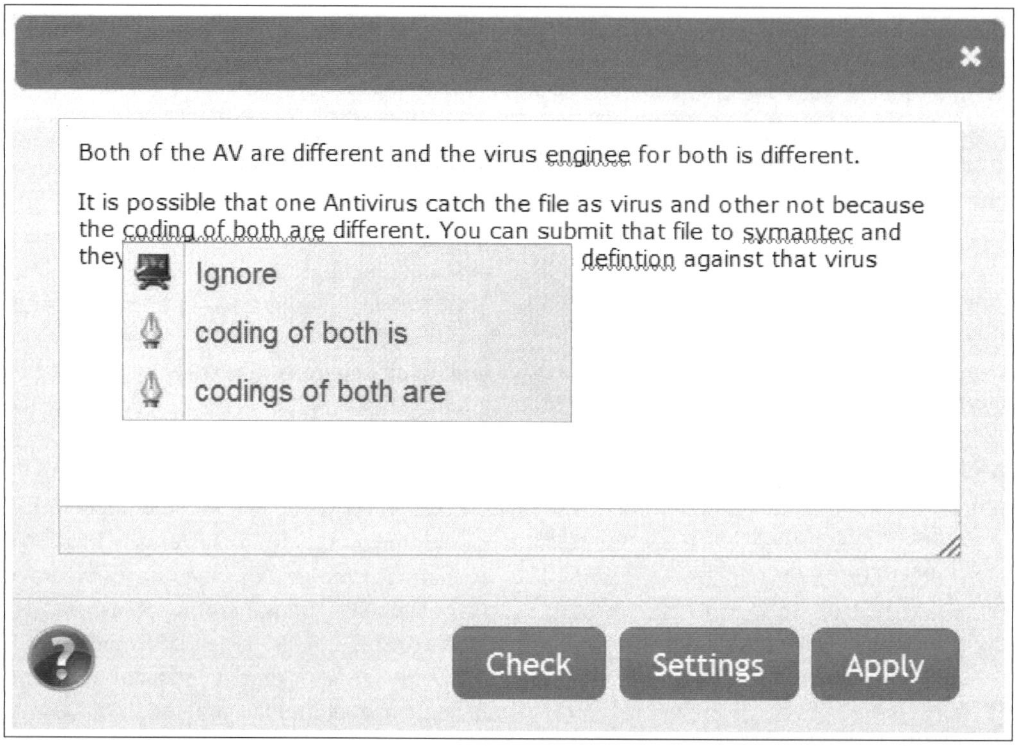

Figure 1: The ACCEPT Pre-edit plug-in in action (screen capture)

vention, the evaluation was carried out for the full set of rules, as well as for the automatic rules only. In addition, the evaluation was performed in both a monolingual and a bilingual setting, i.e., with the evaluators having or not access to the source text, and it involved evaluation scales of different granularities. The evaluation results showed a systematic statistically significant improvement over the baseline when pre-editing is performed on the source content. More details about the evaluation methodology and results can be found in the project deliverable D 9.2.2 (2013).

A data excerpt illustrating the impact of pre-editing on translation quality is presented in Example 1 below. The simple correction of an accented letter, *du* → *dû*, leads to the change of several target words, and to a much better translation of the input sentence.

1. a) Source (original):
   J'ai *du* m'absenter hier après midi.
   b) Source (pre-edited):
   J'ai *dû* m'absenter hier après midi.
   c) Target (original):
   I have the leave me yesterday afternoon.
   d) Target (pre-edited):
   I had to leave yesterday afternoon.

The pre-editing component of the ACCEPT technology is available as a JQuery plug-in, which can be downloaded and installed by Web application owners, so that it can be used with text areas and other text-bearing elements. APIs and accompanying documentation have also been made available, so that the pre-editing rules can be leveraged in automatic steps, without the plug-in, across devices and platforms. A demo site illustrating the use of the plug-in in a TinyMCE environment is available on the portal (see Figure 1).

The latest developments of the pre-editing module include the possibility for users to customise the application of rule sets, in particular, to ignore specific rules and to manage their own dictionary, in order to prevent the activation of checking flags.

2.3 Post-editing Module

The post-editing module of the framework (see also Roturier et al., (2013)) is designed to fulfil the project's objective of collecting post-editing data in order to learn correction rules and, through feedback loops, to integrate them into the SMT engines (with the goal of automating corrections whenever possible). The project relies on the participation of volunteer community members, who are subject matter experts, native speakers of the

Figure 2: The ACCEPT Portal showing the post-editing demo (screen capture)

target language and, possibly, of the source language. Accordingly, the post-editing environment (see Figure 2) provides functionalities for both monolingual and bilingual post-editing.

The post-editing text is organised in tasks belonging to post-editing projects. The latter are created and managed by project administrators, by defining the project settings (e.g., source and target languages, monolingual or bilingual mode, collaborative or non-collaborative type[7]), uploading the text for each task[8], inviting participants by e-mail, and monitoring revision progress.

The post-editors edit the target text in a sentence-by-sentence fashion. They have access to the task guidelines and to help documentation. The interface of the post-editing window displays the whole text, through which they can navigate with next-previous buttons or by clicking on a specific sentence. Users can check the text they are editing by accessing, with a button, the content checking technology described in Section 2.2. Their actions – in terms of keystrokes and usage of translation options – and time spent editing are recorded in the portal.[9] When they are done editing, they can click on a button marking the completion of the task. At any time, they can interrupt their work and save their results for later.

Users can enter a comment on the post-editing task they have performed. The feedback elicited from users include the difficulty of the task and their sentiment (*Was it easy to post-edit? Did you enjoy the post-editing task?*). For systematically collecting user feedback, the project administrators can specify on the project configuration page a link to a post-task survey, which will be sent to users after completing their tasks.

The post-editing module includes a JQuery plug-in for deployment in any Web-based environment; a dedicated section of the portal; APIs enabling the use of the post-editing functionality outside the portal; and sample evaluation projects for several language pairs.

The post-editing technology has been extensively used in specific post-editing campaigns involving translator volunteers and Amazon Mechanical Turk[10] workers. The campaigns, includ-

[7]In a collaborative editing scenario, users may see edits from other users and do not have to repeat them when working on the same project task. Conflicts are avoided by preventing concurrent access.

[8]Currently, the JSON format is used for the input data.

[9]The post-editing data is exported in XLIFF format.

[10]The integration was done via the ACCEPT API.

ing reports on post-task surveys, are documented *inter alia* in deliverable D 8.1.2 (2013). A notable finding was that professional translators, who were reticent towards MT before the task, had a more positive sentiment after post-editing and their motivation to post-edit in the future increased.

2.4 Evaluation Module

The role of the evaluation module is to support the collection of user ratings for assessing the quality of source, machine-translated and post-edited content, and, ultimately, to support the development of the technology created in the project.

This module groups several software components: an evaluation environment available as a section of the portal; APIs enabling the collection of user evaluations in-context; and a third component which is a customisation of the Appraise toolkit for the collaborative collection of human judgements (Federmann, 2012).

As in the case of post-editing module, this module provides functionality for creating and managing projects. Using the evaluation environment/APIs, project creators can define question categories, add questions and possible answers, and upload evaluation data (in JSON format). For traditional evaluation projects, the Appraise system is used instead.

3 Related Work

Transforming the source text in order to better fit the needs of machine translation is a well-investigated area of research. Strategies like source control, source re-ordering, or source simplification at the lexical or structural level have been largely explored; for reviews, see, for instance, Huhn (2013), Kazemi (2013), and Feng (2008), respectively.

User-generated content has been investigated in the context of machine translation in recent work dealing specifically with spelling correction (Bertoldi et al., 2010; Formiga and Fonollosa, 2012); lexical normalisation by substituting ill-formed words with their correct counterpart, e.g., *makn* $\rightarrow$ *making* (Han and Baldwin, 2011); missing word – e.g., zero-pronoun – recovery and punctuation correction (Wang and Ng, 2013).

Rather than focusing on specific phenomena or Web genres (i.e., tweets), we adopt a more general approach in which we address the problem of source normalisation at multiple levels – punctuation, spelling, grammar, and style – for any type of linguistically imperfect text.

Another peculiarity of our approach is that it is rule-based and does not require parallel data for learning corrections. In exchange, a limitation of our pre-editing approach is that it is language-dependent, as the underlying technology is based on shallow analysis and is therefore time-expensive to extend to a new language.

The post-editing technology differs from existing (standalone or Web-based) dedicated tools – e.g., iOmegaT[11] or MateCat[12] – in that it is tailored to community users, and, consequently, it is lighter, it generates more concise reports, and a simpler interface replaces the grid-like format for presenting data. Another specificity is that it is sufficiently flexible to be used in other environments (e.g., Amazon Mechanical Turk, cf. §2.3).

4 Conclusion

The technology outlined in this paper demonstrates a specific case of human-computer interaction, in which, for the first time, several modules are integrated in a full process in which human pre-editors, post-editors and evaluators play a key role for improving the translation of community content. The technology is freely accessible in the online portal, has been deployed on a major user forum, and can be downloaded for integration in other Web-based environments. Since it is built on top of a REST API, it is portable across devices and platforms. The technology would be useful to anyone who needs information instantly and reliably translated, despite linguistic imperfections.

One of the main future developments concerns the further improvement of SMT, by exploring, in particular, the use of text analytics and sentiment detection. In addition, by incorporating post-editing rules and developing techniques to change the phrase table and system parameters dynamically, it will be possible to reduce the amount of error corrections that human post-editors have to perform repeatedly. Another major development (joint work with the CASMACAT European project) will focus on novel types of assistance for translators, aimed specifically at helping translators by identifying problematic parts of the machine translation output and signalling the paraphrases that are more likely to be useful.

[11] `http://try-and-see-mt.org/`
[12] `http://www.matecat.com/`

Acknowledgments

The research leading to these results has received funding from the European Community's Seventh Framework Programme (FP7/2007-2013) under grant agreement n° 288769.

References

Nicola Bertoldi, Mauro Cettolo, and Marcello Federico. 2010. Statistical machine translation of texts with misspelled words. In *Human Language Technologies: The 2010 Annual Conference of the North American Chapter of the Association for Computational Linguistics*, pages 412–419, Los Angeles, California.

Andrew Bredenkamp, Berthold Crysmann, and Mirela Petrea. 2000. Looking for errors: A declarative formalism for resource-adaptive language checking. In *Proceedings of the Second International Conference on Language Resources and Evaluation*, Athens, Greece.

2013. ACCEPT deliverable D 2.2 Definition of pre-editing rules for English and French (final version). `http://www.accept.unige.ch/Products/D2_2_Definition_of_Pre-Editing_Rules_for_English_and_French_with_appendixes.pdf`.

2013. ACCEPT deliverable D 9.2.2: Survey of evaluation results. `http://www.accept.unige.ch/Products/D_9_2_Survey_of_evaluation_results.pdf`.

2013. ACCEPT deliverable D 4.2 Report on robust machine translation: domain adaptation and linguistic back-off. `http://www.accept.unige.ch/Products/D_4_2_Report_on_robust_machine_translation_domain_adaptation_and_linguistic_back-off.pdf`.

2013. ACCEPT deliverable D 8.1.2 Data and report from user studies - Year 2. `http://www.accept.unige.ch/Products/D_8_1_2_Data_and_report_from_user_studies_-_Year_2.pdf`.

Christian Federmann. 2012. Appraise: An open-source toolkit for manual evaluation of machine translation output. *The Prague Bulletin of Mathematical Linguistics (PBML)*, 98:25–35.

Lijun Feng. 2008. Text simplification: A survey. Technical report, CUNY.

Lluís Formiga and José A. R. Fonollosa. 2012. Dealing with input noise in statistical machine translation. In *Proceedings of COLING 2012: Posters*, pages 319–328, Mumbai, India.

Johanna Gerlach, Victoria Porro, Pierrette Bouillon, and Sabine Lehmann. 2013. La préédition avec des règles peu coûteuses, utile pour la TA statistique des forums ? In *Actes de la 20e conférence sur le Traitement Automatique des Langues Naturelles (TALN'2013)*, pages 539–546, Les Sables d'Olonne, France.

Fabrizio Gotti, Philippe Langlais, and Atefeh Farzindar. 2013. Translating government agencies' tweet feeds: Specificities, problems and (a few) solutions. In *Proceedings of the Workshop on Language Analysis in Social Media*, pages 80–89, Atlanta, Georgia.

Bo Han and Timothy Baldwin. 2011. Lexical normalisation of short text messages: Makn sens a #twitter. In *Proceedings of the 49th Annual Meeting of the Association for Computational Linguistics: Human Language Technologies*, pages 368–378, Portland, Oregon.

Jie Jiang, Andy Way, and Rejwanul Haque. 2012. Translating user-generated content in the social networking space. In *Proceedings of the Tenth Biennial Conference of the Association for Machine Translation in the Americas (AMTA-2012)*, San Diego, California.

Arefeh Kazemi, Amirhassan Monadjemi, and Mohammadali Nematbakhsh. 2013. A quick review on reordering approaches in statistical machine translation systems. *IJCER*, 2(4).

Tobias Kuhn. 2013. A survey and classification of controlled natural languages. *Computational Linguistics*.

Meenakshi Nagarajan and Michael Gamon, editors. 2011. *Proceedings of the Workshop on Language in Social Media (LSM 2011)*. Portland, Oregon.

Johann Roturier, Linda Mitchell, Robert Grabowski, and Melanie Siegel. 2012. Using automatic machine translation metrics to analyze the impact of source reformulations. In *Proceedings of the Conference of the Association for Machine Translation in the Americas (AMTA)*, San Diego, California.

Johann Roturier, Linda Mitchell, and David Silva. 2013. The ACCEPT post-editing environment: a flexible and customisable online tool to perform and analyse machine translation post-editing. In *Proceedings of MT Summit XIV Workshop on Post-editing Technology and Practice*, Nice, France.

Violeta Seretan, Pierrette Bouillon, and Johanna Gerlach. 2014. A large-scale evaluation of pre-editing strategies for improving user-generated content translation. In *Proceedings of the 9th Edition of the Language Resources and Evaluation Conference*, Reykjavik, Iceland.

Pidong Wang and Hwee Tou Ng. 2013. A beam-search decoder for normalization of social media text with application to machine translation. In *Proceedings of the 2013 Conference of the North American Chapter of the Association for Computational Linguistics: Human Language Technologies*, pages 471–481, Atlanta, Georgia.

Real Time Adaptive Machine Translation for Post-Editing with cdec and TransCenter

Michael Denkowski **Alon Lavie** **Isabel Lacruz*** **Chris Dyer**
Language Technologies Institute, Carnegie Mellon University, Pittsburgh, PA 15213 USA
*Institute for Applied Linguistics, Kent State University, Kent, OH 44242 USA
{mdenkows,alavie,cdyer}@cs.cmu.edu ilacruz@kent.edu

Abstract

Using machine translation output as a starting point for human translation has recently gained traction in the translation community. This paper describes cdec Realtime, a framework for building adaptive MT systems that learn from post-editor feedback, and TransCenter, a web-based translation interface that connects users to Realtime systems and logs post-editing activity. This combination allows the straightforward deployment of MT systems specifically for post-editing and analysis of human translator productivity when working with these systems. All tools, as well as actual post-editing data collected as part of a validation experiment, are freely available under an open source license.

1 Introduction

This paper describes the end-to-end machine translation post-editing setup provided by cdec Realtime and TransCenter. As the quality of MT systems continues to improve, the idea of using automatic translation as a primary technology in assisting human translators has become increasingly attractive. Recent work has explored the possibilities of integrating MT into human translation workflows by providing MT-generated translations as a starting point for translators to correct, as opposed to translating source sentences from scratch. The motivation for this process is to dramatically reduce human translation effort while improving translator productivity and consistency. This computer-aided approach is directly applicable to the wealth of scenarios that still require precise human-quality translation that MT is currently unable to deliver, including an ever-increasing number of government, commercial, and community-driven projects.

The software described in the following sections enables users to translate documents with the assistance of an adaptive MT system using a web-based interface. The system learns from user feedback, improving translation quality as users work. All user interaction is logged, allowing post-editing sessions to be replayed and analyzed. All software is freely available under an open source license, allowing anyone to easily build, deploy, and evaluate MT systems specifically for post-editing. We first describe the underlying adaptive MT paradigm (§2) and the Realtime implementation (§3). We then describe TransCenter (§4) and the results of an end-to-end post-editing experiment with human translators (§5). All data collected as part of this validation experiment is also publicly available.

2 Adaptive Machine Translation

Traditional machine translation systems operate in batch mode: statistical translation models are estimated from large volumes of sentence-parallel bilingual text and then used to translate new text. Incorporating new data requires a full system rebuild, an expensive operation taking up to days of time. As such, MT systems in production scenarios typically remain static for large periods of time (months or even indefinitely). Recently, an *adaptive* MT paradigm has been introduced specifically for post-editing (Denkowski et al., 2014). Three major MT system components are extended to support online updates, allowing human post-editor feedback to be immediately incorporated:

- An online translation model is updated to include new translations extracted from post-editing data.
- A dynamic language model is updated to include post-edited target language text.
- An online update is made to the system's feature weights after each sentence is post-edited.

These extensions allow the MT system to generate improved translations that require significantly less effort to correct for later sentences in the document. This paradigm is now implemented in the freely available `cdec` (Dyer et al., 2010) machine translation toolkit as Realtime, part of the `pycdec` (Chahuneau et al., 2012) Python API.

Standard MT systems use aggregate statistics from all training text to learn a single large translation grammar (in the case of `cdec`'s hierarchical phrase-based model (Chiang, 2007), a synchronous context-free grammar) consisting of rules annotated with feature scores. As an alternative, the bitext can be *indexed* using a suffix array (Lopez, 2008), a data structure allowing fast source-side lookups. When a new sentence is to be translated, training sentences that share spans of text with the input sentence are *sampled* from the suffix array. Statistics from the sample are used to learn a small, sentence-specific grammar on-the-fly. The adaptive paradigm extends this approach to support online updates by also indexing the new bilingual sentences generated as a post-editor works. When a new sentence is translated, matching sentences are sampled from the post-editing data as well as the suffix array. All feature scores that can be computed on a suffix array sample can be identically computed on the combined sample, allowing uniform handling of all data. An additional "post-edit support" feature is included that indicates whether a grammar rule was extracted from the post-editing data. This allows an optimizer to learn to prefer translations that originate from human feedback. This adaptation approach also serves as a platform for exploring expanded post-editing-aware feature sets; any feature that can be computed from standard text can be added to the model and will automatically include post-editing data. Implementationally, feature scoring is broken out into a single Python source file containing a single function for each feature score. New feature functions can be added easily.

The adaptive paradigm uses two language models. A standard (static) n-gram language model estimated on large monolingual text allows the system to prefer translations more similar to human-generated text in the target language. A (dynamic) Bayesian n-gram language model (Teh, 2006) can be updated with observations of the post-edited output in a straightforward way. This smaller model exactly covers the training bitext and all post-editing data, letting the system up-weight translations with newly learned vocabulary and phrasing absent in the large monolingual text. Finally, the margin-infused relaxed algorithm (MIRA) (Crammer et al., 2006; Eidelman, 2012) is used to make an online parameter update after each sentence is post-edited, minimizing model error. This allows the system to continuously rescale weights for translation and language model features that adapt over time.

Since true post-editing data is infeasible to collect during system development and internal testing, as standard MT pipelines require tens of thousands of sentences to be translated with low latency, a simulated post-editing paradigm (Hardt and Elming, 2010) can be used, wherein pre-generated reference translations act as a stand-in for actual post-editing. This approximation is effective for tuning and internal evaluation when real post-editing data is unavailable. In simulated post-editing tasks, decoding (for both the test corpus and each pass over the development corpus during optimization) begins with baseline models trained on standard bilingual and monolingual text. After each sentence is translated, the following take place in order: First, MIRA uses the new source–reference pair to update weights for the current models. Second, the source is aligned to the reference using word-alignment models learned from the initial data and used to update the translation grammar. Third, the reference is added to the Bayesian language model. As sentences are translated, the models gain valuable context information, allowing them to adapt to the specific target document and translator. Context is reset at the start of each development or test corpus. Systems optimized with simulated post-editing can then be deployed to serve real human translators without further modification.

3 `cdec` Realtime

Now included as part of the free, open source `cdec` machine translation toolkit (Dyer et al., 2010), Realtime[1] provides an efficient implementation of the adaptive MT paradigm that can serve an arbitrary number of unique post-editors concurrently. A full Realtime tutorial, including step-by-step instructions for installing required software and building full adaptive systems, is avail-

[1] `https://github.com/redpony/cdec/tree/master/realtime`

```
import rt

# Start new Realtime translator using a Spanish--English
# system and automatic, language-independent text normalization
# (pre-tokenization and post-detokenization)
translator = rt.RealtimeTranslator('es-en.d', tmpdir='/tmp', cache_size=5,
    norm=True)

# Translate a sentence for user1
translation = translator.translate('Muchas gracias Chris.', ctx_name='user1')

# Learn from user1's post-edited transaltion
translator.learn('Muchas gracias Chris.', 'Thank you so much, Chris.',
    ctx_name='user1')

# Save, free, and reload state for user1
translator.save_state(file_or_stringio='user1.state', ctx_name='user1')
translator.drop_ctx(ctx_name='user1')
translator.load_state(file_or_stringio='user1.state', ctx_name='user1')
```

Figure 1: Sample code using the Realtime Python API to translate and learn from post-editing.

able online.[2] Building an adaptive system begins with the usual MT pipeline steps: word alignment, bitext indexing (for suffix array grammar extraction), and standard n-gram language model estimation. Additionally, the cpyp[3] package, also freely available, is used to estimate a Bayesian n-gram language model on the target side of the bitext. The cdec grammar extractor and dynamic language model implementations both include support for efficient inclusion of incremental data, allowing optimization with simulated post-editing to be parallelized. The resulting system, optimized for post-editing, is then ready for deployment with Realtime.

At runtime, a Realtime system operates as follows. A single instance of the indexed bitext is loaded into memory for grammar extraction. Single instances of the directional word alignment models are loaded into memory for force-aligning post-edited data. When a new user requests a translation, a new *context* is started. The following are loaded into memory: a table of all post-edited data from the user, a user-specific dynamic language model, and a user-specific decoder (in this case an instance of MIRA that has a user-specific decoder and set of weights). Each user also requires an instance of the large static language model, though all users effectively share a single instance through the memory mapped implementation of KenLM (Heafield, 2011). When a new sentence is to be translated, the grammar extractor samples from the shared background data plus the user-specific post-editing data to generate a sentence-specific grammar incorporating data from all prior sentences translated by the same user. The sentence is then decoded using the user and time-specific grammar, current weights, and current dynamic language model. When a post-edited sentence is available as feedback, the following happen in order: (1) the source-reference pair is used to update feature weights with MIRA, (2) the source-reference pair is force-aligned and added to the indexed post-editing data, and (3) the dynamic language model is updated with the reference. User state (current weights and indexed post-edited data for grammars and the language model) can be saved and loaded, allowing models to be loaded and freed from memory as translators start and stop their work. Figure 1 shows a minimal example of the above using the Realtime package. While this paper describes integration with TransCenter, a tool primarily targeting data collection and analysis, the Realtime Python API allows straightforward integration with other computer-assisted translation tools such as full-featured translation workbench environments.

4 TransCenter: Web-Based Translation Research Suite

The TransCenter software (Denkowski and Lavie, 2012) dramatically lowers barriers in post-editing data collection and increases the accuracy and descriptiveness of the collected data. TransCenter

[2] http://www.cs.cmu.edu/~mdenkows/cdec-realtime.html

[3] https://github.com/redpony/cpyp

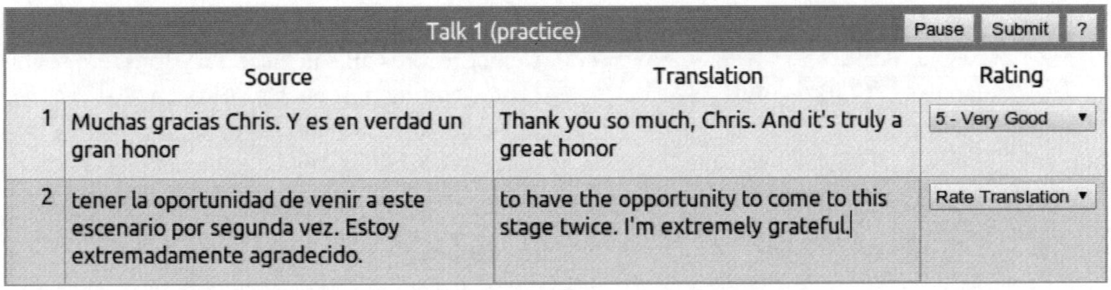

Figure 2: Example of editing and rating machine translations with the TransCenter web interface.

ID	MT	Post-Edited	Rating	Keypress	Mouseclick	Edits	Time
4	because car designers tend to be a little low on the totem,	because car designers tend to be a little low on the totem pole,	4	5	1	5	16677
5	we do not table with only one bottle inside, books	we don't make coffee table books with a single lamp inside,	1	107	1	107	44017
6	and it is thought both cars and product	and cars are thought of so much as a product	2	77	1	77	28907

Figure 3: Example TransCenter summary report for a single user on a document.

provides a web-based translation editing interface that remotely monitors and records user activity. The "live" version[4] now uses `cdec` Realtime to provide on-demand MT that automatically learns from post-editor feedback. Translators use a web browser to access a familiar two-column editing environment (shown in Figure 2) from any computer with an Internet connection. The left column displays the source sentences, while the right column, initially empty, is incrementally populated with translations from the Realtime system as the user works. For each sentence, the translator edits the MT output to be grammatically correct and convey the same information as the source sentence. During editing, all user actions (key presses and mouse clicks) are logged so that the full editing process can be replayed and analyzed. After editing, the final translation is reported to the Realtime system for learning and the next translation is generated. The user is additionally asked to rate the amount of work required to post-edit each sentence immediately after completing it, yielding maximally accurate feedback. The rating scale ranges from 5 (no post-editing required) to 1 (requires total re-translation). TransCenter also records the number of seconds each sentence is focused, allowing for exact timing measurements. A pause button is available if the translator needs to take breaks. TransCenter can generate reports of translator effort as measured by (1) keystroke, (2) exact timing, and (3) actual translator post-assessment. Final translations are also available for calculating edit distance. Millisecond-level timing of all user actions further facilitates time sequence analysis of user actions and pauses. Figure 3 shows an example summary report generated by TransCenter showing a user's activity on each sentence in a document. This information is also output in a simple comma-separated value format for maximum interoperability with other standards-compliant tools.

TransCenter automatically handles resource management with Realtime. When a TransCenter server is started, it loads a Realtime system with zero contexts into memory. As users log in to work on documents, new contexts are created to deliver on-demand translations. As users finish working or take extended breaks, contexts automatically time out and resources are freed. Translator and document-specific state is automatically saved when contexts time out and reloaded when translators resume work with built-in safeguards against missing or duplicating any post-editing data due to timeouts or Internet connectivity issues. This allows any number of translators to work on translation tasks at their convenience.

5 Experiments

In a preliminary experiment to evaluate the impact of adaptive MT in real-world post-editing scenar-

[4]`https://github.com/mjdenkowski/transcenter-live`

	HTER	Rating
Baseline	19.26	4.19
Adaptive	**17.01**	**4.31**

Table 1: Aggregate HTER scores and average translator self-ratings (5 point scale) of post-editing effort for translations of TED talks from Spanish into English.

ios, we compare a static Spanish–English MT system to a comparable adaptive system on a blind out-of-domain test. Competitive with the current state-of-the-art, both systems are trained on the 2012 NAACL WMT (Callison-Burch et al., 2012) constrained resources (2 million bilingual sentences) using the cdec toolkit (Dyer et al., 2010). Blind post-editing evaluation sets are drawn from the Web Inventory of Transcribed and Translated Talks (WIT^3) corpus (Cettolo et al., 2012) that makes transcriptions of TED talks[5] available in several languages, including English and Spanish. We select 4 excerpts from Spanish talk transcripts (totaling 100 sentences) to be translated into English. Five students training to be professional translators post-edit machine translations of these excerpts using TransCenter. Translations are provided by either the static or fully adaptive system. Tasks are divided such that each user translates 2 excerpts with the static system and 2 with the adaptive system and each excerpt is post-edited either 2 or 3 times with each system. Users do not know which system is providing the translations.

Using the data collected by TransCenter, we evaluate post-editing effort with the established human-targeted translation edit rate (HTER) metric (Snover et al., 2006). HTER computes an edit distance score between initial MT outputs and the "targeted" references created by human post-editing, with lower scores being better. Results for the two systems are aggregated over all users and documents. Shown in Table 1, introducing an adaptive MT system results in a significant reduction in editing effort. We additionally average the user post-ratings for each translation by system to evaluate user perception of the adaptive system compared to the static baseline. Also shown in Table 1, we see a slight preference for the adaptive system. This data, as well as precise keystroke, mouse click, and timing information is made freely available for further analysis.[6] TransCenter records all data necessary for more sophisticated editing time analysis (Koehn, 2012) as well as analysis of translator behavior, including pauses (used as an indicator of cognitive effort) (Lacruz et al., 2012).

6 Related Work

There has been a recent push for new computer-aided translation (CAT) tools that leverage adaptive machine translation. The CASMACAT[7] project (Alabau et al., 2013) focuses on building state-of-the-art tools for computer-aided translation. This includes translation predictions backed by machine translation systems that incrementally update model parameters as users edit translations (Martínez-Gómez et al., 2012; López-Salcedo et al., 2012). The MateCat[8] project (Cattelan, 2013) specifically aims to integrate machine translation (including online model adaptation and translation quality estimation) into a web-based CAT tool. Bertoldi et al. (2013) show improvements in translator productivity when using the MateCat tool with an adaptive MT system that uses cache-based translation and language models.

7 Conclusion

This paper describes the free, open source MT post-editing setup provided by `cdec` Realtime and TransCenter. All software and the data collected for a preliminary post-editing experiment are all freely available online. A live demonstration of adaptive MT post-editing powered by Realtime and TransCenter is scheduled for the 2014 EACL Workshop on Humans and Computer-assisted Translation (HaCaT 2014).

Acknowledgements

This work is supported in part by the National Science Foundation under grant IIS-0915327, by the Qatar National Research Fund (a member of the Qatar Foundation) under grant NPRP 09-1140-1-177, and by the NSF-sponsored XSEDE program under grant TG-CCR110017.

[5] http://www.ted.com/talks

[6] www.cs.cmu.edu/~mdenkows/transcenter-round1.tar.gz

[7] http://casmacat.eu/

[8] http://www.matecat.com/

References

Vicent Alabau, Ragnar Bonk, Christian Buck, Michael Carl, Francisco Casacuberta, Mercedes García-Martínez, Jesús González-Rubio, Philipp Koehn, Luis A. Leiva, Bartolomé Mesa-Lao, Daniel Ortiz-Martínez, Hervé Saint-Amand, Germán Sanchis-Trilles, and Chara Tsoukala. 2013. Casmacat: An open source workbench for advanced computer aided translation. In *The Prague Bulletin of Mathematical Linguistics*, pages 101–112.

Nicola Bertoldi, Mauro Cettolo, and Marcello Federico. 2013. Cache-based online adaptation for machine translation enhanced computer assisted translation. In *Proceedings of the XIV Machine Translation Summit*, pages 35–42.

Chris Callison-Burch, Philipp Koehn, Christof Monz, Matt Post, Radu Soricut, and Lucia Specia. 2012. Findings of the 2012 workshop on statistical machine translation. In *Proceedings of the Seventh Workshop on Statistical Machine Translation*, pages 10–51, Montréal, Canada, June. Association for Computational Linguistics.

Alessandro Cattelan. 2013. Second version of MateCat tool. Deliverable 4.2.

Mauro Cettolo, Christian Girardi, and Marcello Federico. 2012. Wit^3: Web inventory of transcribed and translated talks. In *Proceedings of the Sixteenth Annual Conference of the European Association for Machine Translation*.

Victor Chahuneau, Noah A. Smith, and Chris Dyer. 2012. pycdec: A python interface to cdec. *The Prague Bulletin of Mathematical Linguistics*, 98:51–61.

David Chiang. 2007. Hierarchical phrase-based translation. *Computational Linguistics*, 33.

Koby Crammer, Ofer Dekel, Joseph Keshet, Shai Shalev-Shwartz, and Yoram Singer. 2006. Online passive-aggressive algorithms. *Journal of Machine Learning Research*, pages 551–558, March.

Michael Denkowski and Alon Lavie. 2012. TransCenter: Web-based translation research suite. In *AMTA 2012 Workshop on Post-Editing Technology and Practice Demo Session*.

Michael Denkowski, Chris Dyer, and Alon Lavie. 2014. Learning from post-editing: Online model adaptation for statistical machine translation. In *Proceedings of the 14th Conference of the European Chapter of the Association for Computational Linguistics*.

Chris Dyer, Adam Lopez, Juri Ganitkevitch, Jonathan Weese, Ferhan Ture, Phil Blunsom, Hendra Setiawan, Vladimir Eidelman, and Philip Resnik. 2010. cdec: A decoder, alignment, and learning framework for finite-state and context-free translation models. In *Proceedings of the ACL 2010 System Demonstrations*, pages 7–12, Uppsala, Sweden, July. Association for Computational Linguistics.

Vladimir Eidelman. 2012. Optimization strategies for online large-margin learning in machine translation. In *Proceedings of the Seventh Workshop on Statistical Machine Translation*, pages 480–489, Montréal, Canada, June. Association for Computational Linguistics.

Daniel Hardt and Jakob Elming. 2010. Incremental re-training for post-editing smt. In *Proceedings of the Ninth Conference of the Association for Machine Translation in the Americas*.

Kenneth Heafield. 2011. KenLM: faster and smaller language model queries. In *Proceedings of the Sixth Workshop on Statistical Machine Translation*, pages 187–197, Edinburgh, Scotland, United Kingdom, July.

Philipp Koehn. 2012. Computer-aided translation. Machine Translation Marathon.

Isabel Lacruz, Gregory M. Shreve, and Erik Angelone. 2012. Average Pause Ratio as an Indicator of Cognitive Effort in Post-Editing: A Case Study. In *AMTA 2012 Workshop on Post-Editing Technology and Practice (WPTP 2012)*, pages 21–30, San Diego, USA, October. Association for Machine Translation in the Americas (AMTA).

Adam Lopez. 2008. Machine translation by pattern matching. In *Dissertation, University of Maryland*, March.

Francisco-Javier López-Salcedo, Germán Sanchis-Trilles, and Francisco Casacuberta. 2012. Online learning of log-linear weights in interactive machine translation. *Advances in Speech and Language Technologies for Iberian Languages*, pages 277–286.

Pascual Martínez-Gómez, Germán Sanchis-Trilles, and Francisco Casacuberta. 2012. Online adaptation strategies for statistical machine translation in post-editing scenarios. *Pattern Recognition*, 45:3193–3203.

Matthew Snover, Bonnie Dorr, Richard Schwartz, Linnea Micciulla, and John Makhoul. 2006. A study of translation edit rate with targeted human annotation. In *Proceedings of the 7th Conference of the. Association for Machine Translation of the Americas*, pages 223–231.

Yee Whye Teh. 2006. A hierarchical Bayesian language model based on Pitman-Yor processes. In *Proc. of ACL*.

Confidence-based Active Learning Methods for Machine Translation

Varvara Logacheva
University of Sheffield
Sheffield, United Kingdom
v.logacheva@sheffield.ac.uk

Lucia Specia
University of Sheffield
Sheffield, United Kingdom
l.specia@sheffield.ac.uk

Abstract

The paper presents experiments with active learning methods for the acquisition of training data in the context of machine translation. We propose a confidence-based method which is superior to the state-of-the-art method both in terms of quality and complexity. Additionally, we discovered that oracle selection techniques that use real quality scores lead to poor results, making the effectiveness of confidence-driven methods of active learning for machine translation questionable.

1 Introduction

Active learning (AL) is a technique for the automatic selection of data which is most useful for model building. In the context of machine translation (MT), AL is particularly important as the acquisition of data often has a high cost, i.e. new source texts need to be translated manually. Thus it is beneficial to select for manual translation sentences which can lead to better translation quality.

The majority of AL methods for MT is based on the (dis)similarity of sentences with respect to the training data, with particular focus on domain adaptation. Eck et al. (2005) suggest a TF-IDF metric to choose sentences with words absent in the training corpus. Ambati et al. (2010) propose a metric of informativeness relying on unseen n-grams.

Bloodgood and Callison-Burch (2010) use n-gram frequency and coverage of the additional data as selection criteria. Their technique solicits translations for phrases instead of entire sentences, which saves user effort and leads to quality improvements even if the initial dataset is already sizeable.

A recent trend is to select source sentences based on an estimate of the quality of their translation by a baseline MT system. It is assumed that if a sentence has been translated well with the existing data, it will not contribute to improving the translation quality. If however a sentence has been translated erroneously, it might have words or phrases that are absent or incorrectly represented. Haffari et al. (2009) train a classifier to define the sentences to select. The classifier uses a set of features of the source sentences and their automatic translations: n-grams and phrases frequency, MT model score, etc. Ananthakrishnan et al. (2010) build a pairwise classifier that ranks sentences according to the proportion of n-grams they contain that can cause errors. For quality estimation, Banerjee et al. (2013) train language models of well and badly translated sentences. The usefulness of a sentence is measured as the difference of its perplexities in these two language models.

In this research we also explore a quality-based AL technique. Compared to its predecessors, our method is based on a more complex and therefore potentially more reliable quality estimation framework. It uses wider range of features, which go beyond those used in previous work, covering information from both source and target sentences.

Another important novel feature in our work is the addition of real post-editions to the MT training data, as opposed to simulated post-editions (human reference translations) as in previous work on AL for MT. As we show in section 3.2, adding post-editions leads to superior translation quality improvements. Additionally, this is a suitable solution for "human in the loop" settings, as post-editing automatically translated sentences tends to be faster and easier than translation from scratch (Koehn and Haddow, 2009). Also, different from previous work, we do not focus on domain adaptation: our experiments involve only in-domain data.

Compared to previous work on confidence-driven AL, our approach has led to better results, but these proved to be highly dependent on a sentence length bias. However, an oracle-based selection using true quality scores has not been shown to perform well. This indicates that the usefulness of quality scores as AL selection criterion in the context of MT needs to be further investigated.

2 Active selection strategy

Our AL sentence selection strategy relies on quality estimation (QE). QE is aimed at predicting the quality of a translated text (in this case, a sentence) without resorting to reference translations. It considers features of the source and machine translated texts, and an often small number (a few hundreds) of examples of translations labelled for quality by humans to train a machine learning algorithm to predict such quality labels for new data.

We use the open source QE framework QuEst (Specia et al., 2013). In our settings it was trained to predict an HTER score (Snover et al., 2006) for each sentence, i.e., the edit distance between the automatic translation and its human post-edited version. QuEst can extract a wide range of features. In our experiments we use only the 17 so-called *baseline features*, which have been shown to perform well in evaluation campaigns (Bojar et al., 2013): number of tokens in sentences, average token length, language model probabilities for source and target sentences, average number of translations per source word, percentage of higher and lower frequency n-grams in source sentence based on MT training corpus, number of punctuation marks in source and target sentences.

Similarly to Ananthakrishnan et al. (2010), we assume that the most useful sentences are those that lead to larger translation errors. However, instead of looking at the n-grams that caused errors — a very sparse indicator requiring significantly larger amounts of training data, we account for errors in a more general way: the (QuEst predicted) percentage of edits (HTER) that would be necessary to transform the MT output into a correct sentence.

3 Experiments and results

3.1 Datasets and MT settings

For the AL data selection experiment, two datasets are necessary: parallel sentences to train an initial, baseline MT system, and an additional pool of parallel sentences to select from. Our goal was to study potential improvements in the baseline MT system in a realistic "human in the loop" scenario, where source sentences are translated by the baseline system and post-edited by humans before they are added to the system. As it has been shown in (Potet et al., 2012), post-editions tend to be closer to source sentences than freely created translations. One of our research questions was to investigate whether they would be more useful to improve MT quality.

We chose the biggest corpus with machine translations and post-editions available to date: the LIG French–English post-editions corpus (Potet et al., 2012). It contains 10,881 quadruples of the type: *<source sentence, reference translation, automatic translation, post-edited automatic translation>*. Out of these, we selected 9,000 as the pool to be added to be baseline MT system, and the remaining 1,881 to train the QE system for the experiments with AL. For QE training, we use the HTER scores between MT and its post-edited version as computed by the TERp tool.[1]

We use the Moses toolkit with standard settings[2] to build the (baseline) statistical MT systems. As training data, we use the French–English News Commentary corpus released by the WMT13 shared task (Bojar et al., 2013). For the AL experiments, the size of the pool of additional data (10,000) poses a limitation. To examine improvements obtained by adding fractions of up to only 9,000 sentences, we took a small random subset of the WMT13 data for these experiments (Table 1). Although these figures may seem small, the settings are realistic for many language pairs and text domains where larger data sets are simply not available.

We should also note that all the data used in our experiments belongs to the same domain: the LIG SMT system which produced sentences for the post-editions corpus was trained on Europarl and News commentary datasets (Potet et al., 2010), but the post-edited sentences themselves were taken from *news* test sets released for WMT shared tasks in different years. Our baseline system is trained on a fraction of the *news* commentary corpus. Finally, we tune and test all our systems on WMT shared task *news* news datasets (those which do not overlap with the post-editions corpus).

[1] http://www.umiacs.umd.edu/~snover/terp/

[2] http://www.statmt.org/moses/?n=Moses.Baseline

Corpora	Size (sentences)
Initial data (baseline MT system)	
Training - subset of News Commentary corpus	10,000
Tuning - WMT newstest-2012	3,000
Test - WMT newstest-2013	3,000
Additional data (AL data)	
Post-editions corpus:	10,881
- **Training QE** system	1,881
- **AL pool**	9,000

Table 1: Datasets

3.2 Post-editions versus references

In order to compare the impact of post-editions and reference translations on MT quality, we added these two variants of translations to baseline MT systems of different sizes, including the entire News Commentary corpus. The figures for BLEU (Papineni et al., 2002) scores in Table 2 show that adding post-editions results in significantly better quality than adding the same number of reference translations[3]. This effect can be seen even when the additional data corresponds to only a small fraction of the training data.

In addition, it does not seem to matter which MT system produced the translations which were then post-edited in the post-edition corpus. Even if the output of a third-party system was used (as in our case), it improves the quality of machine translations for unseen data. We assume that since post-editions tend to be closer to original sentences than free translations (Potet et al., 2012), they generally help produce better source-target alignments, leading to the extraction of good quality phrases.

Baseline corpus (sentences)	Results (BLEU)		
	Baseline	**Ref**	**PE**
150,000	22.41	22.95	23.21
50,000	20.22	20.91	22.01
10,000	15.09	18.65	20.44

Table 2: Influence of post-edited and reference translations on MT quality. **Ref**: baseline system with added free references, **PE**: baseline system with added post-editions.

[3]These systems use the whole post-editions set (10,881 sentences) as opposed to 9,000-sentence subset which we use further in our AL experiments. Therefore the figures reported in this table are higher than those in subsequent sections.

3.3 AL settings

The experimental settings for all methods are as follows. First, a baseline MT system is trained. Then a batch of 1,000 sentences is selected from the data pool with an AL strategy, and the selected data is removed from the pool. The MT system is rebuilt using a concatenation of the initial training data and the new batch. The process is repeated until the pool is empty, with subsequent steps using the MT system trained on the previous step as a baseline. The performance of each MT system is measured in terms of BLEU scores. We use the following AL strategies:

- **QuEst**: our method described in section 2.
- **Random**: random selection of sentences.
- **HTER**: oracle-based selection based on true HTER scores of sentences in the pool, instead of the QuEst estimated HTER scores.
- **Ranking**: AL strategy described in (Ananthakrishnan et al., 2010) for comparison.

3.4 AL results

Our initial results in Figure 1 show that our selection strategy (**QuEst**) consistently outperforms the **Random** selection baseline.

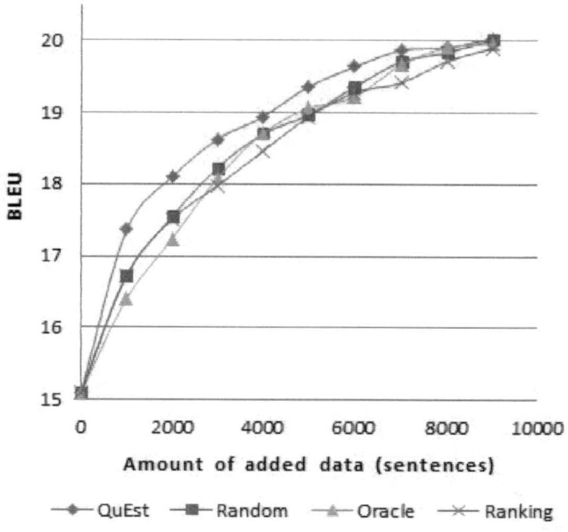

Figure 1: Performance of MT systems enhanced with data selected by different AL strategies

In comparison with previous work, we found that the error-based **Ranking** strategy performs closely to **Random** selection, although (Ananthakrishnan et al., 2010) reports it to be better.

Compared to **QuEst**, we believe the lower figures of the **Ranking** strategy are due to the fact that the latter considers features of only one type (source n-grams), whereas QuEst uses a range of different features of the source and translation sentences.

Interestingly, the **Oracle** method underperforms our QE-based method, although we expected the use of real HTER scores to be more effective. In order to understand the reasons behind such behaviour, we examined the batches selected by **QuEst** and **Oracle** strategies more closely. We found that the distribution of sentence lengths in batches by the two strategies is very different (see Figure 2). While in batches selected by **QuEst** the average sentence length steadily decreases as more data is added, in **Oracle** batches the average length was almost uniform for all batches, except the first one, which contains shorter sentences.

This is explained by HTER formulation: HTER is computed as the number of edits over the sentence length, and therefore in shorter sentences every edit is given more weight. For example, the HTER score of a 5-word sentence with one error is 0.2, whereas a sentence of 20 words with the same single error has a score of 0.05. However, it is doubtful that the former sentence will be more useful for an MT system than the latter. Regarding the nature of length bias in the predictions done by **QuEst** system, sentence length is used there as a feature, and longer sentences tend to be estimated as having higher HTER scores (i.e., lower translation quality).

Therefore, sentences with the highest HTER may not actually be the most useful, which makes the **Oracle** strategy inferior to **QuEst**. Moreover, longer sentences chosen by our strategy simply provide more data, so their addition might be more useful even regardless of the amount of errors.

This seems to indicate that the success of our strategy might not be related to the quality of the translations only, but to their length. Another possibility is that sentences selected by **QuEst** might have more errors, which means that they can contribute more to the MT system.

3.5 Additional experiments

In order to check the two hypotheses put forward in the previous section, we conduct two other sets of AL experiments: (i) a selection strategy that chooses longer sentences first (denoted as **Length**) and (ii) a selection strategy that chooses sentences with larger numbers of errors first (**Errors**).

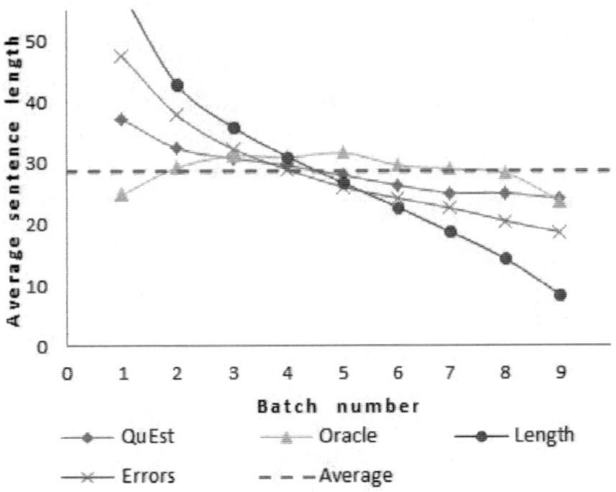

Figure 2: Number of words in batches selected by different AL strategies

Figure 3 shows that a simple length-based strategy yields better results than any of the other tested strategies. Therefore, in cases when the corpus has sufficient variation in sentence length, length-based selection might perform at least as well as other more sophisticated criteria. The experiments with confidence-based selection described in (Ananthakrishnan et al., 2010) were free of this length bias, as sentences much longer or shorter than average were deliberately filtered out.

Interestingly, results for the **Errors** strategy are slightly worse than those for **QuEst**, although the former is guaranteed to choose sentences with the largest number of errors and has even stronger length bias than **QuEst** (see figure 2). Therefore, the reasons hypothesised to be behind the superiority of **QuEst** over **Oracle** (longer sentences and larger number of errors) are actually not the only factors that influence the quality of an AL strategy.

3.6 Length-independent results

Despite the success of the length-based strategy, we do not believe that it is enough for an effective AL technique. First of all, the experiment with the **Errors** strategy demonstrated that more data does not always lead to better results. Furthermore, our aim is to reduce the translator's effort in cases when the additional data needs to be translated or post-edited manually. However, longer sentences usually take more time to translate or edit, so choosing the longest sentences from a pool of sentences will not reduce translator's effort.

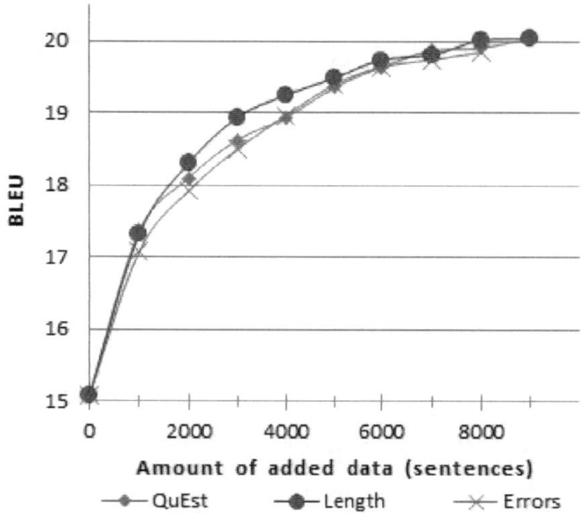

Figure 3: Comparison of our QuEst-based selection with a length-based selection

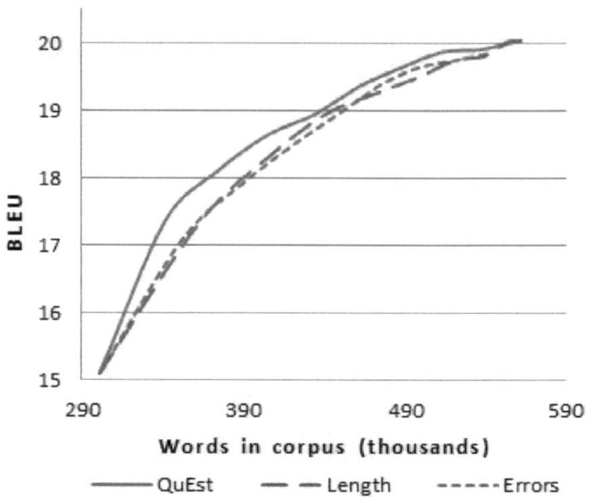

Figure 5: AL quality plotted with respect to data size in words: **QuEst** vs **Length** and **Errors** strategies.

Therefore, we would like to study the effectiveness of our strategy by isolating the sentence length bias. One option is to filter out long sentences, as it was done in (Ananthakrishnan et al., 2010). However, our pool is already too small. Therefore, we plot the performance improvements with respect to training data size in words, instead of sentences. As it was already noted by Bloodgood and Callison-Burch (2010), measuring the amount of added data in sentences can significantly contort the real annotation cost (the cost of acquisition of new translations). So we switch to length-independent representation.

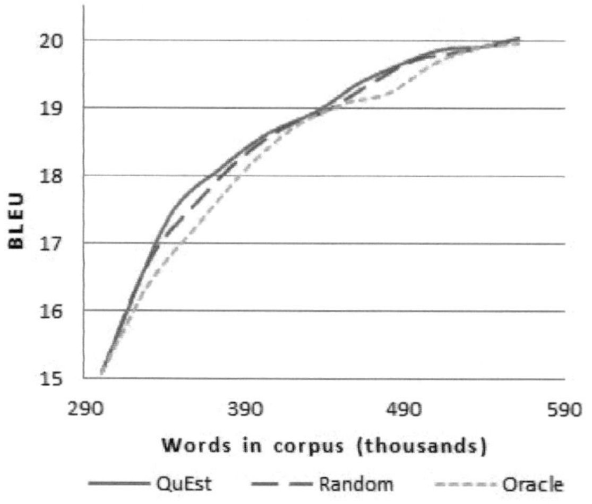

Figure 4: Active learning quality plotted with respect to data size in words: **QuEst** vs **Oracle** strategies.

Figure 4 shows that the **Oracle** strategy in length-independent representation can still be seen to perform worse than both our strategy and random selection. Results of **Length** and **Error** strategies (plotted separately in figure 5 for readability) are very close and both underperform our **QuEst**-based strategy and random selection of data.

Here our experience echoes the results of (Mohit and Hwa, 2007), where the authors propose the idea of *difficult to translate phrases*. It is assumed that extending an MT system with phrases that can cause difficulties during translation is more effective than simply adding new data and re-building the system. Due to the lack of time and human annotators, the authors extracted difficult phrases automatically using a set of features: alignment features, syntactic features, model score, etc. Conversely, we had the human-generated information on what segments have been translated incorrectly. We assumed that the use of this knowledge as part of our AL strategy would give us an upper bound for our AL method results. However, it turned out that prediction based on multiple features is more reliable than precise information on quality, which accounts for only one aspect of data.

4 Conclusions

We presented experiments with an active learning strategy for machine translation based on quality predictions. This strategy performs well compared to another quality-driven strategy and a random baseline. However, we found that it was successful mostly due to its tendency to rate long sentences as having lower quality. Consequently, the AL application that chooses the longest sentences is not less successful when selecting from corpora with large variation in sentence length. A length-independent representation of the results showed that an oracle selection is less effective than our quality-based strategy, which we believe to be due to the nature of corrections and small size of the post-edition corpus. In addition to that, another oracle selection based on the amount of errors and length-based selection show poor results when displayed in length-independent mode.

We believe that the quality estimation strategy benefits from other features that reflect the usefulness of a sentence better than its HTER score and the amount of user corrections. In future work we will examine the influence of individual features of the quality estimation model (such as language model scores) as active learning selection strategy.

References

Vamshi Ambati, Stephan Vogel, and Jaime Carbonell. 2010. Active Learning and Crowd-Sourcing for Machine Translation. *LREC 2010: Proceedings of the seventh international conference on Language Resources and Evaluation, 17-23 May 2010, Valletta, Malta*, pages 2169–2174.

Sankaranarayanan Ananthakrishnan, Rohit Prasad, David Stallard, and Prem Natarajan. 2010. Discriminative Sample Selection for Statistical Machine Translation. *EMNLP-2010: Proceedings of the 2010 Conference on Empirical Methods in Natural Language Processing, October 9-11, 2010, MIT, Massachusetts, USA*, (October):626–635.

Pratyush Banerjee, Raphael Rubino, Johann Roturier, and Josef van Genabith. 2013. Quality Estimation-guided Data Selection for Domain Adaptation of SMT. *MT Summit XIV: proceedings of the fourteenth Machine Translation Summit, September 2-6, 2013, Nice, France*, pages 101–108.

Michael Bloodgood and Chris Callison-Burch. 2010. Bucking the Trend: Large-Scale Cost-Focused Active Learning for Statistical Machine Translation. *ACL 2010: the 48th Annual Meeting of the Association for Computational Linguistics, Uppsala, Sweden, July 11-16, 2010*, pages 854–864.

Ondřej Bojar, Christian Buck, Chris Callison-Burch, Christian Federmann, Barry Haddow, Philipp Koehn, Christof Monz, Matt Post, Radu Soricut, and Lucia Specia. 2013. Findings of the 2013 Workshop on Statistical Machine Translation. In *Proceedings of the Eighth Workshop on Statistical Machine Translation*, pages 1–44, Sofia, Bulgaria, August. Association for Computational Linguistics.

Matthias Eck, Stephan Vogel, and Alex Waibel. 2005. Low Cost Portability for Statistical Machine Translation based on N-gram Frequency and TF-IDF. *IWSLT 2005: Proceedings of the International Workshop on Spoken Language Translation. October 24-25, 2005, Pittsburgh, PA.*

Gholamreza Haffari, Maxim Roy, and Anoop Sarkar. 2009. Active learning for statistical phrase-based machine translation. *Proceedings of Human Language Technologies: The 2009 Annual Conference of the North American Chapter of the Association for Computational Linguistics on - NAACL '09.*

Philipp Koehn and Barry Haddow. 2009. Interactive Assistance to Human Translators using Statistical Machine Translation Methods. *MT Summit XII: proceedings of the twelfth Machine Translation Summit, August 26-30, 2009, Ottawa, Ontario, Canada*, pages 73–80.

Behrang Mohit and Rebecca Hwa. 2007. Localization of Difficult-to-Translate Phrases. *ACL 2007: proceedings of the Second Workshop on Statistical Machine Translation, June 23, 2007, Prague, Czech Republic*, pages 248–255.

Kishore Papineni, Salim Roukos, Todd Ward, and Wei-jing Zhu. 2002. BLEU: a Method for Automatic Evaluation of Machine Translation. *ACL 2002: 40th Annual Meeting of the Association for Computational Linguistics, July 2002, Philadelphia*, pages 311–318.

Marion Potet, Laurent Besacier, and Hervé Blanchon. 2010. The LIG machine translation system for WMT 2010. *ACL 2010: Proceedings of the Joint Fifth Workshop on Statistical Machine Translation and MetricsMATR*, pages 161–166.

Marion Potet, Emmanuelle Esperança-Rodier, Laurent Besacier, and Hervé Blanchon. 2012. Collection of a Large Database of French-English SMT Output Corrections. *LREC 2012: Eighth international conference on Language Resources and Evaluation, 21-27 May 2012, Istanbul, Turkey*, pages 4043–4048.

Matthew Snover, Bonnie Dorr, Richard Schwartz, Linnea Micciulla, and John Makhoul. 2006. A Study of Translation Edit Rate with Targeted Human Annotation. *AMTA 2006: Proceedings of the 7th Conference of the Association for Machine Translation in the Americas, Visions for the Future of Machine Translation, August 8-12, 2006, Cambridge, Massachusetts, USA*, pages 223–231.

Lucia Specia, Kashif Shah, Jose G C de Souza, and Trevor Cohn. 2013. QuEst - A translation quality estimation framework. *ACL 2013: Annual Meeting of the Association for Computational Linguistics, Demo session, August 2013, Sofia, Bulgaria.*

Online Word Alignment for Online Adaptive Machine Translation

M. Amin Farajian
FBK-irst,
University of Trento
Trento, Italy
farajian@fbk.eu

Nicola Bertoldi
FBK-irst
Trento, Italy
bertoldi@fbk.eu

Marcello Federico
FBK-irst
Trento, Italy
federico@fbk.eu

Abstract

A hot task in the Computer Assisted Translation scenario is the integration of Machine Translation (MT) systems that adapt sentence after sentence to the post-edits made by the translators. A main role in the MT online adaptation process is played by the information extracted from source and post-edited sentences, which in turn depends on the quality of the word alignment between them. In fact, this step is particularly crucial when the user corrects the MT output with words for which the system has no prior information. In this paper, we first discuss the application of popular state-of-the-art word aligners to this scenario and reveal their poor performance in aligning unknown words. Then, we propose a fast procedure to refine their outputs and to get more reliable and accurate alignments for unknown words. We evaluate our enhanced word-aligner on three language pairs, namely English-Italian, English-French, and English-Spanish, showing a consistent improvement in aligning unknown words up to 10% absolute F-measure.

1 Introduction

In the adaptive MT the goal is to let the MT system take as soon and as much as possible advantage of user feedback, in order to learn from corrections and to hence avoid repeating the same mistakes in future sentences.

A typical application scenario is the usage by a professional translator of a Computer Assisted Translation (CAT) tool enhanced with a SMT system. For each input sentence, first the translator receives one or more translation suggestions from either a Translation Memory or a SMT system, then (s)he chooses which suggestion is more useful, and finally (s)he creates an approved translation by post-editing. The pair of input sentence and post-edit is a valuable feedback to improve the quality of next suggestions. While the sentence pair is trivially added to the Translation Memory, how to exploit it for improving the SMT system is far to be a solved problem, but rather is a hot and quite recent topic in the MT community.

In online MT adaptation specific issues have to be addressed, which distinguish it from the more standard and investigated task of domain adaptation. First of all, the SMT system should adapt very quickly, because the time between two consecutive requests are usually short, and very precisely, because the translator is annoyed by correcting the same error several time. Then, a crucial point is which and how information is extracted from the feedback, and how it is exploited to update the SMT system. Finally, model updating relies on a little feedback consisting of just one sentence pair.

In this work we focus on the word alignment task which is the first and most important step in extracting information from the given source and its corresponding post-edit. In particular, we are interested in the cases where the given sentence pairs contain new words, for which no prior information is available. This is an important and challenging problem in the online scenario, in which the user interacts with the system and expects that it learns from the previous corrections and does not repeat the same errors again and again.

Unfortunately, state-of-the-art word-aligners show poor generalization capability and are prone to errors when infrequent or new words occur in the sentence pair. Word alignment errors at this stage could cause the extraction of wrong phrase pairs, i.e. wrong translation alternatives, which can lead in producing wrong translations for those words, if they appear in the following sentences.

Our investigation focuses on how to quickly build a highly precise word alignment from a source sentence and its translation. Moreover, we are interested in improving the word alignment of unknown terms, i.e. not present in the training data, because they are one of the most important source of errors in model updating.

Although we are working in the online MT adaptation framework, our proposal is worthwhile per se; indeed, having an improved and fast word aligner can be useful for other interesting tasks, like for instance terminology extraction, translation error detection, and pivot translation.

In Section 2 we report on some recent approaches aiming at improving word alignment. In Section 3, we describe three widely used toolkits, highlight their pros and cons in the online MT adaptation scenario, and compare their performance in aligning unknown terms. In Section 4 we propose a standalone module which refines the word alignment of unknown words; moreover, we present an enhanced faster implementation of the best performing word aligner, to make it usable in the online scenario. In Section 5 we show experimental results of this module on three different languages. Finally, we draw some final comments in Section 6.

2 Related works

Hardt et al. (2010) presented an incremental retraining method which simulates the procedure of learning from post-edited MT outputs (references), in a real time fashion. By dividing the learning task into word alignment and phrase extraction tasks, and replacing the standard word-alignment module, which is a variation of EM algorithm (Och and Ney, 2003), with a greedy search algorithm, they attempt to find a quick approximation of the word alignments of the newly translated sentence. They also use some heuristics to improve the obtained alignments, without supporting it with some proofs or even providing some experimental results. Furthermore, the running time of this approach is not discussed, and it is not clear how effective this approach is in online scenarios.

Blain et al. (2012) have recently studied the problem of incremental learning from post-editing data, with minimum computational complexity and acceptable quality. They use the MT output (hypothesis) as a pivot to find the word alignments between the source sentence and its corresponding reference. Similarly to (Hardt and Elming, 2010), once the word alignment between the source and post-edit sentence pair is generated, they use the standard phrase extraction method to extract the parallel phrase pairs. This work is based on an implicit assumption that MT output is reliable enough to make a bridge between source and reference. However, in the real world this is not always true. The post-editor sometimes makes a lot of changes in the MT output, or even translates the entire sentence from scratch, which makes the post-edit very different from the automatic translation. Moreover, in the presence of new words in the source sentence, the MT system either does not produce any translation for the new word, or directly copies it in the output. Due to the above two reasons, there will be missing alignments between the automatic translation and post-edit, which ultimately results in incomplete paths from source to post-edit. But, the goal here is to accurately align the known words, as well as learning the alignments of the new words, which is not feasible by this approach.

In order to improve the quality of the word alignments McCarley et al. (2011) proposed a trainable correction model which given a sentence pair and their corresponding automatically produced word alignment, it tries to fix the wrong alignment links. Similar to the hill-climbing approach used in IBM models 3-5 (Brown et al., 1993), this approach iteratively performs small modifications in each step, based on the changes of the previous step. However, the use of additional sources of knowledge, such as POS tags of the words and their neighbours, helps the system to take more accurate decisions. But, requiring manual word alignments for learning the alignment moves makes this approach only applicable for a limited number of language pairs for which manual aligned gold references are available.

Tomeh et al. (2010) introduced a supervised discriminative word alignment model for producing higher quality word alignments, which is trained on a manually aligned training corpus. To reduce the search space of the word aligner, they propose to provide the system with a set of automatic word alignments and consider the union of these alignments as the possible search space. This transforms the word alignment process into the alignment refinement task in which given a set of automatic word alignments, the system tries to find the best word alignment points. Similar to (McCarley et al., 2011), this approach relies on the manually annotated training corpora which is not available for most of the language pairs.

3 Word Alignment

Word alignment is the task of finding the correspondence among the words of a sentence pair (Figure 1). From a mathematical point of view, it is a relation among the words, because any word in a sentence can be mapped into zero, one or more words of the other, and vice-versa; in other words, any kind of link is allowed, namely one-to-one, many-to-one, many-to-many, as well as leaving words unaligned. So called IBM models 1-5 (Brown et al., 1993) as well as the HMM-based alignment models (Vogel et al., 1996), and their variations are extensively studied and widely used for this task. They are directional alignment models, because permit only many-to-one links; but often the alignments in the two opposite directions are combined in a so-called symmetrized alignment, which is obtained by intersection, union or other smart combination.

Nowadays, word-aligners are mostly employed in an intermediate step of the training procedure of a SMT system; In this step, the training corpus is word aligned as a side effect of the estimation of the alignment models by means of the Expectation-Maximization algorithm. For this task, they perform sufficiently well, because the training data are often very large, and the limited amount of alignment errors do not have strong impact on the estimation of the translation model.

Instead, the already trained word-aligners are rarely applied for aligning new sentence pairs. In this task their performance are often not satisfactory, due to their poor generalization capability; they are especially prone to errors when infrequent or new words occur in the sentence pair.

This is the actual task to be accomplished in the online adaptive scenario: as soon as a new source and post-edited sentence pair is available, it has to be word aligned quickly and precisely. In this scenario, the sentence pair likely does not belong to the training corpus, hence might contain infrequent or new words, for which the aligner has little or no prior information.

3.1 Evaluation Measures

A word aligner is usually evaluated in terms of *Precision*, *Recall*, and *F-measure* (or shortly F), which are defined as follows (Fraser and Marcu, 2007):

$$Precision = \frac{|A \bigcap P|}{|A|}, \quad Recall = \frac{|A \bigcap S|}{|S|}$$

$$F - measure = \frac{1}{\frac{\alpha}{Precision} + \frac{1-\alpha}{Recall}}$$

where A is the set of automatically computed alignments, and S and P refer to the *sure (unambiguous)* and *possible (ambiguous)* manual alignments; note that $S \subseteq P$. In this paper, α is set to 0.5 for all the experiments, in order to have a balance between Precision and Recall.

In this paper we are mainly interested how the word-aligner performs on the unknown words; hence, we define a version of Precision, Recall, and F metrics focused on the *oov-alignment* only, i.e. the alignments for which either the source or the target word is not included in the training corpus. The subscript all identifies the standard metrics; the subscript oov identifies their oov-based versions.

In Figure 1 we show manual and automatic word alignments between an English-Italian sentence pair. A sure alignment, like *are-sono*, is represented by a solid line, and a possible alignment, like *than-ai*, by a dash line. An oov-alignment, like that linking the unknown English word *deployable* to the Italian word *attivabili*, is identified by a dotted line. According to this example, Precision and Recall will be about 0.85 (=11/13) and 0.91 (=10/11), respectively, and the corresponding F is hence about 0.88. Focusing on the oov-alignment only, Precision_{oov} is 1.00 (=1/1), Recall_{oov} is 0.50 (=1/2), and F_{oov} is 0.67.

3.2 Evaluation Benchmark

In this paper, we compare word-alignment performance of three word-aligners introduced in Section 3.3 on three distinct tasks, namely English-Italian, English-French, and English-Spanish; the training corpora, common to all word-aligners, are subset of the JRC-legal corpus[1] (Steinberger et al.,), of the Europarl corpus V7.0 (Koehn, 2005), and of the Hansard parallel corpus[2], respectively.

[1] `langtech.jrc.it/JRC-Acquis.html`

[2] `www.isi.edu/natural-language/download/hansard/index.html`

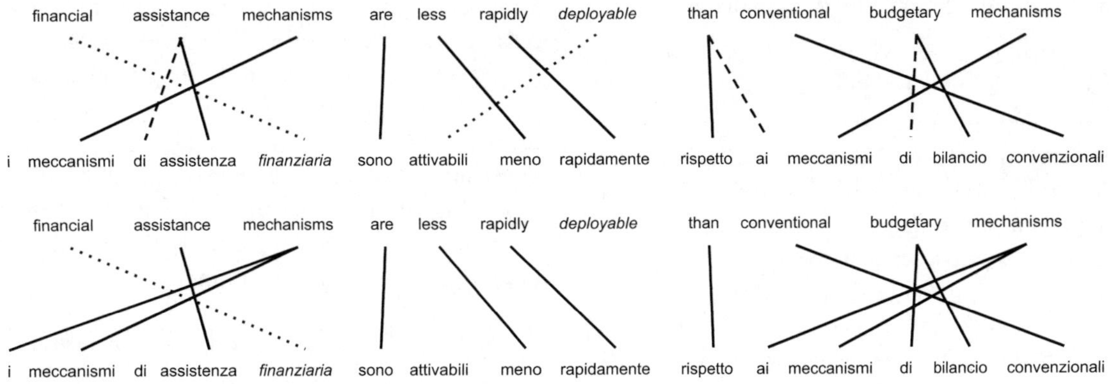

Figure 1: Example of manual (above) and automatic (below) word alignments between an English-Italian sentence pair. Sure and possible alignments are identified by solid and dash lines, respectively, and the oov-alignments by a dotted line. The OOV words, like *deployable* (English) and *finanziaria* (Italian), are printed in italics.

Statistics of the three training corpora are reported in Table 1.

	En-It	En-Fr	En-Es
Segments	940K	1.1M	713K
Tokens_{src}	19.8M	19.8M	19.8M
Tokens_{trg}	20.3M	23.3M	20.4M

Table 1: Statistics of the training corpora for English-Italian, English-French, and English-Spanish tasks.

Three evaluation data sets are also available, which belong to the same domains of the corresponding training corpora. The English-Italian test set was built by two professional translators by correcting an automatically produced word-alignment. The English-French test set is the manually aligned parallel corpus introduced in (Och and Ney, 2000)[3]. The English-Spanish test set was provided by (Lambert et al., 2005)[4]. Statistics of the three test sets are reported in Table 2.

To have a better understanding of the behavior of the word aligners on the unknown words, we created new test sets with an increasing ratio of the unknown words (*oov-rate*), for each task. Starting from each of the original test set, we replaced an increasing portion of randomly chosen words by strings which do not exist in the training corpus; the oov-noise artificially introduced ranges from 1% to 50%. For each value of the artificial oov-noise ($m = 1, ..., 50$), we randomly selected $m\%$ words in both the source and target side independently, and replaced them by artificially created strings. For selecting the words to be replaced by artificially created strings, we do not differentiate between the known and unknown words; hence the actual oov-rate in the test corpus, used in the plots, might be slightly larger.

To further make sure that the random selection of the words does not affect the systems, for each oov-noise we created 10 different test corpora and reported the averaged results. One might think of other approaches for introducing oov-noise, such as replacing singletons or low-frequency words which have more potential to be unknown, instead of randomly selection of the words. But in this paper we decided to follow the random selection of the words.

	En-It	En-Fr	En-Es
Segments	200	484	500
Tokens_{src}	6,773	7,681	14,652
Tokens_{trg}	7,430	8,482	15,516
oov-rate_{src}	0.90	0.27	0.35
oov-rate_{trg}	0.84	0.34	0.32
#alignment	7,380	19,220	21,442

Table 2: Staticts of the test corpora for English-Italian, English-French, and English-Spanish tasks. oov-rate_{src} and oov-rate_{trg} are the ratio of the new words in the source and target side of the test corpus, respectively.

[3] www.cse.unt.edu/~rada/wpt/data/English-French.test.tar.gz

[4] www.computing.dcu.ie/~plambert/data/epps-alignref.html

3.3 State-of-the-art Word Aligners

We consider three widely-used word aligners, namely *berkeley*, *fast-align*, and *mgiza++*. We analyze their performance in aligning an held-out test corpora; in particular, we compare their capability in handling the unknown words. For a fair comparison, all aligners are trained on the same training corpora described in Section 3.2.

berkeley aligner (Liang et al., 2006) applies the co-training approach for training the IBM model 1 and HMM. We trained *berkeley* aligner using 5 iterations of model 1 followed by 5 iterations of HMM. When applied to new sentence pairs, the system produces bi-directional symmetrized alignment.

fast-align is a recently developed unsupervised word aligner that uses a log-linear reparametrization of IBM model 2 for training the word alignment models (Dyer et al., 2013). We exploited the default configuration with 5 iterations for training. As the system is directional, we trained two systems (source-to-target and target-to-source). When applied to new sentence pairs, we first produced the two directional alignments, and then combined them into a symmetrized alignment by using the *grow-diag-final-and* heuristic (Och and Ney, 2003).

mgiza++ (Gao and Vogel, 2008) and its ancestors, i.e. *giza*, and *giza++*, implement all the IBM models and HMM based alignment models. *mgiza++* is a multithreaded version of giza++, which enables an efficient use of multi-core platforms. We trained the system using the following configuration for model iterations: $1^5h^53^34^3$. *mgiza++* also produces directional alignment; hence, we followed the same protocol to create a symmetrize alignment of sentence pairs as we did for *fast-align*.

Differently from *berkeley* and *fast-align*, *mgiza++* somehow adapts its models when applied to new sentence pairs. According to the so-called "forced alignment", it essentially proceeds with the training procedure on these new data starting from pre-trained and pre-loaded models, and produces the alignment as a by-product. In preliminary experiments, we observed that performing 3 iterations of model 4 is the best configuration for *mgiza++* to align the new sentence pairs.

These word aligners are designed to work in offline mode; they load the models and align the whole set of available input data in one shot. However, in the online scenario where a single sentence pair is provided at a time, they need to reload the models every time which is very expensive in terms of I/O operations. In this paper we first were interested in measuring the quality of the word aligners to select the best one. Therefore, we mimic the online modality by forcing them to align one sentence pair at a time.

	Precision		**Recall**		**F-measure**	
	all	*oov*	*all*	*oov*	*all*	*oov*
English-Italian						
fast-align	82.6	33.3	82.8	19.6	82.7	24.7
berkeley	91.9	–	81.0	–	86.1	–
mgiza++	86.2	84.6	89.4	30.8	87.8	45.2
English-French						
fast-align	81.5	47.2	91.8	19.5	86.3	27.6
berkeley	87.9	–	92.9	–	90.3	–
mgiza++	89.0	88.2	96.0	17.2	92.4	28.8
English-Spanish						
fast-align	81.5	31.3	71.8	12.7	76.3	18.1
berkeley	88.7	–	71.2	–	79.0	–
mgiza++	89.2	95.5	80.6	35.6	84.7	51.9

Table 3: Comparison of different widely-used word aligners in terms of precision, recall, and F-measure on English-Italian, English-French, and English-Spanish language pairs. Columns *all* report the evaluation performed on all alignments, while columns *oov* the evaluation performed on the oov-alignments.

The three word aligners were evaluated on the three tasks introduced in Section 3.2. Table 3 shows their performance on the full set of alignments (*all*) and on the subset of oov-alignments (*oov*) in terms of Precision, Recall, and F-measure. The figures show that all aligners perform well on the whole test corpus. *mgiza++* is definitely superior to *fast-align*; it also outperforms *berkeley* in terms of F-measure, but they are comparable in terms of Precision.

Unfortunately, the quality of the word alignments produced for the new words is quite poor for all systems. *mgiza++* outperforms the other aligners in all the language pairs on oov-alignments, and in particular it achieves a very high precision. On the contrary, *berkeley* aligner always fails to detect out-of-vocabulary words; its precision is hence undefined, and consequently its F-measure. To our knowledge of the system, this behavior is expected because of the joint alignment approach used in *berkeley* which produces an alignment between two terms if both the directional models

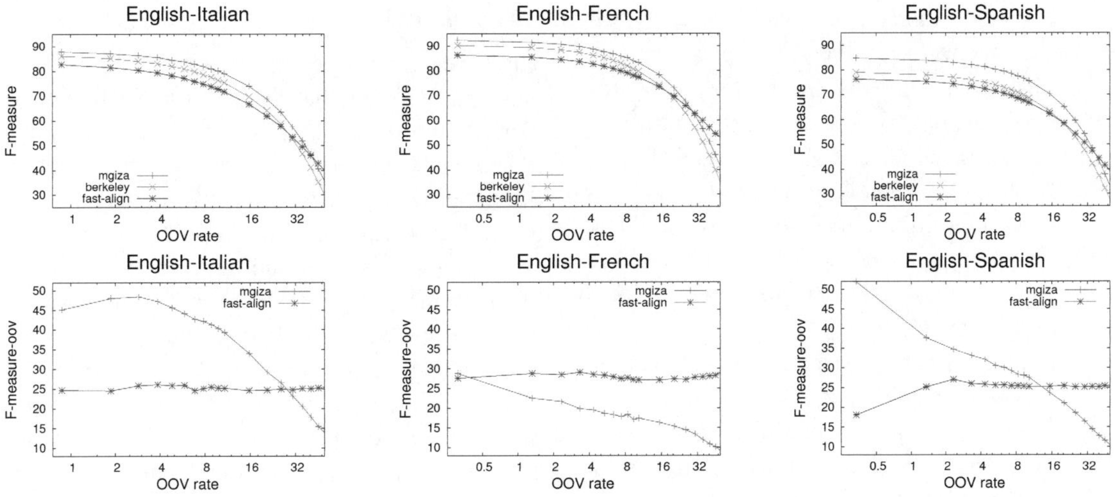

Figure 2: Performance in terms of standard F-measure (above) and oov-based F-measure (below) of the word aligners on test sets with increasing oov-rate, for all language pairs. The oov-based F-measure for *berkeley* is not reported because it is undefined.

agree, and this hardly occurs for unknown words.

To further investigate the behavior of the word aligners on the unknown words, we evaluated their performance on the artificially created test sets, described in Section 3.2. The performance of the word aligners in terms of standard and oov-based F-measure is shown in Figure 2. As expected, the overall F-measure decreases by introducing unknown words. *mgiza++* is more accurate than the other aligners up to oov-rate of 16%.

We observe that *mgiza++* outperforms the others in terms of the oov-based F-measure on the English-Italian and English-Spanish language pairs up to oov-noise of 32% and 16%, respectively. *fast-align* instead performs better in the English-French task. *fast-align* always show a better quality when the oov-rate is very high. oov-based F-measure is not reported for *berkeley* because this aligner is not able to detect oov-alignments as explained above.

4 Enhancement to Word Alignment

4.1 Refinement of oov-alignments

To address the problem of unaligned new words, we present a novel approach, in which the word alignments of the source and target segment pair are induced in two-steps. First, a standard word aligner is applied; most of the words in the source and target sentence pair will be aligned, but most of the unknown words will not. It is worth mentioning that aligning unknown words in this step depends on the quality of the employed word aligner. Once the alignments are computed and symmetrized (if required), phrase extraction procedure is applied to extract all valid phrase-pairs. Note that un-aligned words are included in the extracted phrase pairs, if their surrounding words are aligned.

It has been shown that inclusion of un-aligned words in the phrase-pairs, generally, has negative effects on the translation quality and can produce errors in the translation output (Zhang et al., 2009). Nevertheless, the overlap among phrase-pairs, which contain un-aligned unknown words, can be considered as a valuable source of knowledge for inducing the correct alignment of these words. To get their alignments from the extracted phrase-pairs we follow an approach similar to (Esplá-Gomis et al., 2012) in which the word alignment probabilities are determined by the *alignment strength* measure. Given the source and target segments ($S = \{s_1, \ldots, s_l\}$ and $T = \{t_1, \ldots, s_m\}$), and the set of extracted parallel phrase-pairs (Φ), the alignment strength $\mathcal{A}_{i,j}(S,T,\Phi)$ of the s_i and t_j can be calculated as follows:

$$\mathcal{A}_{i,j}(S,T,\Phi) = \sum_{(\sigma,\tau)\in\Phi} \frac{cover(i,j,\sigma,\tau)}{|\sigma|.|\tau|}$$

$$cover(i,j,\sigma,\tau) = \begin{cases} 1 & \text{if } s_i \in \sigma \text{ and } t_j \in \tau \\ 0 & \text{otherwise} \end{cases}$$

where $|\sigma|$ and $|\tau|$ are the source and target lengths (in words) of the phrase pair (σ, τ).

$cover(i, j, \sigma, \tau)$ simply spots whether the word-pair (s_i, t_j) is covered by the phrase pair (σ, τ).

The alignment strengths are then used to produce the a directional source-to-target word alignments; s_i is aligned to t_j if $\mathcal{A}_{i,j} > 0$ and $\mathcal{A}_{i,j} \geq \mathcal{A}_{i,k}$, $\forall k \in [1, |T|]$. One-to-many alignment is allowed in cases that multiple target words have equal probabilities to be aligned to i-th source word ($\mathcal{A}_{i,j} = \mathcal{A}_{i,k}$). The directional word alignments are then symmetrized.

The new set of symmetrized alignments can be used in different ways: (i) as a replacement of the initial word alignments as in (Esplá-Gomis et al., 2012), or (ii) as additional alignment points to be added to the initial set. According to a preliminary investigation, we choose the latter option: only a subset of the new word alignments is used for updating the initial alignments. More specifically, we add only the alignments of the new words which are not already aligned.

Moreover, our approach differs from that proposed by Esplá-Gomis et al. (2012) in the procedure to collect the original set of phrase pairs from the source and target sentence pair. They rely on the external sources of information such as online machine translation systems (e.g. Google Translate, and Microsoft Translator). Communicating with external MT systems imposes some delays to the pipeline, which is not desired for the online scenario. Furthermore, the words that are not known by the machine translation systems are not covered by any phrase-pair, hence the refinement module is not able to align them.

We instead employ the *phrase-extract* software[5] provided by the Moses toolkit, which relies on the alignment information of the given sentence pair, and allows the inclusion of un-aligned unknown words in the extracted phrase pairs; hence, the refinement module has the potential to find the correct alignment for those words.

Note that there is no constraint on the word alignment and phrase extraction modules used in the first step, hence, any word aligner and phrase extractor can be used for computing the initial alignments and extracting the parallel phrase pairs from the given sentence pairs. But, since the outputs of the first aligner make the ground for obtaining the alignments of the second level, they need to be highly accurate and precise.

[5]The "grow-diag-final-and" heuristic was set for the symmetrization.

4.2 onlineMgiza++

The experiments to compare state-of-the-art word aligners, reported and discussed in Section 3, are carried out offline. This is because the aforementioned word aligners are not designed to work online, and need to load the models every time receives a new sentence pair. Loading the models is very time consuming, and depending on the size of the models might take several minutes, which is not desired for the online scenario.

To overcome this problem, we decided to implement an online version of *mgiza++* which provides the best performance as shown in Section 3.3. This new version, called *onlineMgiza++*, works in client-server mode. It consists of two main modules *mgizaServer* and *mgizaClient*. *mgizaServer* is responsible for computing the alignment of the given sentence pairs. To avoid unnecessary I/O operations, *mgizaServer* loads all the required models once at the beginning of the alignment session, and releases them at the end. *mgizaClient* communicates with the client applications through the standard I/O channel.

In our final experiments we observed some unexpected differences between the results of *mgiza++* and *onlineMgiza++*. Therefore, we do not present the results of *onlineMgiza++* in this paper. However, we expect the two systems produce the same results.

5 Experimental Results

In this section we evaluate the effectiveness of the proposed refinement module. Each considered word aligner was equipped by our refinement module, and compared to its corresponding baseline. Figure 3 shows the oov-based F-measure achieved by the baseline and enhanced word aligners on all test sets and all tasks. We observe that the refinement module consistently improves the F-measure of all aligners on all language pairs;

The improvement for *mgiza++* are big (up to 10%) for very low oov-rates and decreases when the oov-rate increases; the same but smaller behavior is observed for *fast-align*. This is due to the fact that by inserting more oov words into the test sets the systems are able to produce less accurate alignment points, which leads in lower contextual information (i.e. smaller number of overlapping phrase-pairs) for aligning the unknown words. Interestingly, the refinement module applied to the *berkeley* output permits the correct detection of

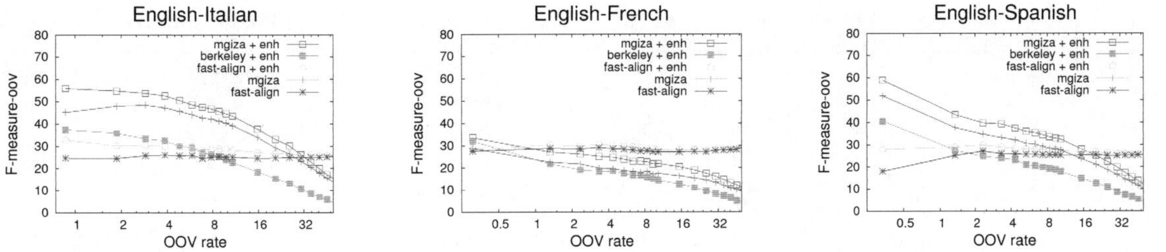

Figure 3: Performance in terms of oov-based F-measure of the baseline and enhanced word aligners on test sets with increasing oov rate, for all language pairs. The oov-based F-measure for *berkeley* is not reported because it is undefined.

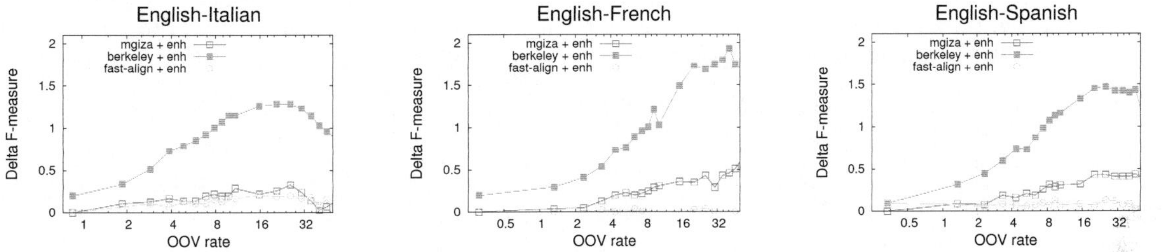

Figure 4: Difference of performance in terms of standard F-measure of the enhanced word aligners from their corresponding baselines on test sets with increasing OOV rate, for all language pairs.

many oov-alignments, which the baseline system can not find most of them.

Furthermore, Figure 4 reports the F-measure differences achieved by the enhanced word-aligners from their corresponding baselines on the full data sets. The refinement module slightly but consistently improves the overall F-measure as well, especially for high oov-rates. The highest improvement is achieved by the enhanced *berkeley* aligner, mainly because its baseline performs worse in this condition.

6 Conclusion

In this paper we discussed the need of having a fast and reliable online word aligner in the online adaptive MT scenario that is able to accurately align the new words. The quality of three state-of-the-art word aligners, namely *berkeley*, *mgiza++*, and *fast-align*, were evaluated on this task in terms of Precision, Recall, and F-measure. For this purpose we created a benchmark in which an increasing amount of the words of the test corpus are randomly replaced by new words in order to augment the oov-rate. The results show that the quality of the aligners on new words is quite low, and suggest that new models are required to effectively address this task. As a first step, we proposed a fast and language independent procedure for aligning the unknown words which refines any given automatic word alignment. The results show that the proposed approach significantly increases the word alignment quality of the new words.

In future we plan to evaluate our approach in an end-to-end evaluation to measure its effect on the final translation. We also plan to investigate the exploitation of additional features such as linguistic and syntactic information in order to further improve the quality of the word alignment models as well as the proposed refinement procedure. However, this requires other policies of introducing new words, rather than just randomly selecting the words and replacing them by artificial strings.

Acknowledgments

This work was supported by the MateCat project, which is funded by the EC under the 7th Framework Programme.

References

F. Blain, H. Schwenk, and J. Senellart. 2012. Incremental adaptation using translation information and post-editing analysis. In *International Workshop on Spoken Language Translation*, pages 234–241, Hong-Kong (China).

Peter F. Brown, Stephen A. Della Pietra, Vincent J. Della Pietra, and Robert L. Mercer. 1993. The mathematics of statistical machine translation: Parameter estimation. *Computational Linguistics*, 19(2):263–312.

Chris Dyer, Victor Chahuneau, and Noah A. Smith. 2013. A simple, fast, and effective reparameterization of ibm model 2. In *Proceedings of the 2013 Conference of the North American Chapter of the Association for Computational Linguistics: Human Language Technologies*, pages 644–648, Atlanta, Georgia, June. Association for Computational Linguistics.

Miquel Esplá-Gomis, Felipe Sánchez-Martínez, and Mikel L. Forcada. 2012. A simple approach to use bilingual information sources for word alignment. *Procesamiento del Lenguaje Natural*, (49):93–100.

Alexander Fraser and Daniel Marcu. 2007. Measuring word alignment quality for statistical machine translation. *Comput. Linguist.*, 33(3):293–303.

Qin Gao and Stephan Vogel. 2008. Parallel implementations of word alignment tool. In *Software Engineering, Testing, and Quality Assurance for Natural Language Processing*, SETQA-NLP '08, pages 49–57, Stroudsburg, PA, USA. Association for Computational Linguistics.

Daniel Hardt and Jakob Elming. 2010. Incremental re-training for post-editing smt. In *9th Conference of the Association for Machine Translation in the Americas (AMTA)*, Denver, United States.

Philipp Koehn. 2005. Europarl: A parallel corpus for statistical machine translation. In *Proceedings of the Tenth Machine Translation Summit (MT Summit X)*, pages 79–86, Phuket, Thailand.

Patrik Lambert, Adrià de Gispert, Rafael E. Banchs, and José B. Mariño. 2005. Guidelines for word alignment evaluation and manual alignment. *Language Resources and Evaluation*, 39(4):267–285.

Percy Liang, Ben Taskar, and Dan Klein. 2006. Alignment by agreent. In *Proceedings of the Human Language Technology Conference of the NAACL, Main Conference*, pages 104–111, New York City, USA, June. Association for Computational Linguistics.

J. Scott McCarley, Abraham Ittycheriah, Salim Roukos, Bing Xiang, and Jian-ming Xu. 2011. A correction model for word alignments. In *Proceedings of the Conference on Empirical Methods in Natural Language Processing*, EMNLP '11, pages 889–898, Stroudsburg, PA, USA. Association for Computational Linguistics.

Franz Josef Och and Hermann Ney. 2000. Improved statistical alignment models. In *Proceedings of the 38th Annual Meeting of the Association of Computational Linguistics (ACL)*.

F.J. Och and H. Ney. 2003. A systematic comparison of various statistical alignment models. *Computational Linguistics*, 29(1):19–51.

Ralf Steinberger, Bruno Pouliquen, Anna Widiger, Camelia Ignat, Tomaž Erjavec, Dan Tufiş, and Dániel Varga. The jrc-acquis: A multilingual aligned parallel corpus with 20+ languages. In *In Proceedings of the 5th International Conference on Language Resources and Evaluation (LREC)*, pages 2142–2147, Genoa, Italy.

Nadi Tomeh, Alexandre Allauzen, Guillaume Wisniewski, and Franois Yvon. 2010. Refining word alignment with discriminative training. In *Proceedings of the ninth Conference of the Association for Machine Translation in the America (AMTA)*.

S. Vogel, H. Ney, and C. Tillmann. 1996. HMM-based word alignment in statistical translation. In *Proceedings of COLING*, pages 836–841, Copenhagen, Denmark.

Yuqi Zhang, Evgeny Matusov, and Hermann Ney. 2009. Are unaligned words important for machine translation? In *Conference of the European Association for Machine Translation*, pages 226–233, Barcelona, Spain.

Quantifying the Influence of MT Output in the Translators' Performance: A Case Study in Technical Translation

Marcos Zampieri
Saarland University
Saarbrücken, Germany
mzampier@uni-koeln.de

Mihaela Vela
Saarland University
Saarbrücken, Germany
m.vela@mx.uni-saarland.de

Abstract

This paper presents experiments on the use of machine translation output for technical translation. MT output was used to produced translation memories that were used with a commercial CAT tool. Our experiments investigate the impact of the use of different translation memories containing MT output in translations' quality and speed compared to the same task without the use of translation memory. We evaluated the performance of 15 novice translators translating technical English texts into German. Results suggest that translators are on average over 28% faster when using TM.

1 Introduction

Professional translators use a number of tools to increase the consistency, quality and speed of their work. Some of these tools include spell checkers, text processing software, terminological databases and others. Among all tools used by professional translators the most important of them nowadays are translation memory (TM) software. TM software use parallel corpora of previously translated examples to serve as models for new translations. Translators then validate or correct previously translated segments and translate new ones increasing the size of the memory after each new translated segment.

One of the great issues in working with TMs is to produce the TM itself. This can be time consuming and the memory should ideally contain a good amount of translated segments to be considered useful and accurate. For this reason, many novice translators do not see the benefits of the use of TM right at the beginning, although it is consensual that on the long run the use of TMs increase the quality and speed of their work. To cope with this limitation, more TM software have provided interface to machine translation (MT) software. MT output can be used to suggest new segments that were not previously translated by a human translator but generated automatically from an MT software. But how helpful are these translations?

To answer this question, the experiments proposed in this paper focus on the translator's performance when using TMs produced by MT output within a commercial CAT tool interface. We evaluate the quality of the translation output as well as the time and effort taken to accomplish each task. The impact of MT and TM in translators' performance has been explored and quantified in different settings (Bowker, 2005; Guerberof, 2009; Guerberof, 2012; Morado Vazquez et al., 2013). We believe this paper constitutes another interesting contribution to the interface between the study of the performance of human translators, CAT tools and machine translation.

2 Related Work

CAT tools have become very popular in the last 20 years. They are used by freelance translators as well as by companies and language service providers to increase translation's quality and speed (Somers and Diaz, 2004; Lagoudaki, 2008). The use of CAT tools is part of the core curriculum of most translation studies degrees and a reasonable level of proficiency in the use of these tools is expected from all graduates. With the improvement of state-of-the-art MT software, a recent trend in CAT research is its integration with machine translation tools as for example the MateCat[1] project (Cettolo et al., 2013).

There is considerable amount of studies on MT post-editing published in the last years (Specia, 2011; Green et al., 2013). Due to the scope of our

[1] www.matecat.com

paper (and space limitation) we will deliberately not discuss the findings of these experiments and instead focus on those that involve the use of translation memories. Post-editing tools are substantially different than commercial CAT tools (such as the one used here) and even though the TMs used in our experiments were produced using MT output, we believe that our experiment setting has more in common with similar studies that investigate TMs than MT post-editing.

The study by Bowker (2005) was one of the first to quantify the influence of TM in translators work. The experiment divided translators in three groups: A, B and C. Translators in Group A did not use a TM, translators in Group B used an unmodified TM and finally translators in group C used a TM that had been deliberately modified with a number of translation errors. The study concluded that when faced with time pressure, translators using TMs tend not to be critical enough about the suggestions presented by the software.

Another similar experiment (Guerberof, 2009) compared productivity and quality of human translations using MT and TM output. The experiment was conducted starting with the hypothesis that the time invested in post-editing one string of machine translated text will correspond to the same time invested in editing a fuzzy matched string located in the 80-90 percent range. This study quantified the performance of 8 translators using a post-editing tool. According to the author, the results indicate that using a TM with 80 to 90 fuzzy matches produces more errors than using MT segments or human translation.

The aforementioned recent work by Morado Vazquez et al. (2013) investigates the performance of twelve human translators (students) using the ACCEPT post-editing tool. Researchers provided MT and TM output and compared time, quality and keystroke effort. Findings of this study indicate that the use of a specific MT has a great impact in the translation activity in all three aspects. In the context of software localization, productivity was also tested by Plitt and Masselot (2010) combining MT output and a post-editing tool. Another study compared the performance of human translators in a scenario using TMs and a commercial CAT tool (Across) with a second scenario using post-editing (Läubli et al., 2013).

As to our study, we used instead of a post-editing tool, a commercial CAT tool, the SDL Trados Studio 2014 version. A similar setting to ours was explored by Federico et al. (2012) using SDL Trados Studio integrating a commercial MT software. We took the decision of working a commercial CAT tool for two reasons: first, because this is the real-world scenario faced by translators in most companies and language service providers[2] and second, because it allows us to explore a different variable that the aforementioned studies did not substantially explore, namely: MT output as TM segments.

3 Setting the Experiment

In our experiments we provided short texts from the domain of software development containing up to 343 tokens each to 15 beginner translators. The average length of these texts ranges between 210 tokens in experiment 1 to 264 tokens in experiment 3 divided in 15 to 17 segments (average) (see table 2). Translators were given English texts and were asked to translate them into German, their mother tongue. One important remark is that all 15 participants were not aware that the TMs we made available were produced using MT output.

The 15 translators who participated in these experiments are all 3rd semester master degree students who have completed a bachelors degree in translation studies and are familiar with CAT tools. All of them attended at least 20 class hours about TM software and related technologies. Translators who participated in this study were all proficient in English and they have studied it as a foreign language at bachelor level.

As previously mentioned, the CAT tool used in these experiments is the most recent version of SDL Trados, the Studio 2014[3] version. Translators were given three different short texts to be translated in three different scenarios:

1. Using no translation memory.
2. Using a translation memory collected with modified MT examples.
3. Using translation memory collected with unmodified MT examples.

In experiment number two we performed a number of modifications in the TM segments. As

[2]Although the use of MT and post-editing software has been growing, commercial TM software is still the most popular alternative.

[3]http://www.sdl.com/campaign/lt/sdl-trados-studio-2014/

can be seen in table 1, these modifications were sufficient to alter the coverage of the TM, but did not introduce translation errors to the memory.[4] The alterations we performed along with an example of each of them can be summarized as follows:

- Deletion: *'To paste the text currently in the clipboard, use the Edit Paste menu item.'* - *'To paste the text, use the Edit Paste menu item.'*

- Modification: *'Persistent Selection is disabled by default.'* - *'Persistent Selection is enabled by default.'*

- Substitution: *'The editor is composed of the following components:'* - *'The editor is composed of the following elements:'*

Three texts were available per scenario, each of them with different TM coverage scores (see table 1). Students were asked to translate the texts at their own pace without time limitation and were allowed to use external linguistic resources such as dictionaries, lexica, parallel concordancers, etc.

3.1 Corpus and TM

The corpus used for these experiments is the KDE corpus obtained from the Opus[5] repository (Tiedemann, 2012). The corpus contains texts from the domain of software engineering, hence the title: 'a case study in technical translation'. We are convinced that technical translation contains a substantial amount of fixed expressions and technical terms different from, for example, news texts. This makes technical translation, to our understanding, an interesting domain for the use of TM by professional translators and for experiments of this kind.

In scenarios 1, 2 and 3 we measured different aspects of translation such as time and edited segments. One known shortcoming of our experiment design is that unlike most post-editing software the reports available in CAT tools are quite poor (e.g. no information about keystrokes is provided). Even so, we stick to our decision of using a TM software and tried to compensate this shortcoming by a careful qualitative and quantitative data analysis after the experiments.

[4]Modifications were carried out in the source and target languages

[5]http://opus.lingfil.uu.se/

Table number 1 presents the coverage scores for the different TMs and texts used in the experiments. Coverage scores were calculated based on the information provided by SDL Trados Studio. We provided 9 different texts to be translated to German (3 for each scenario), the 6 texts provided for experiments 2 and 3 are presented next.

Text	Experiment	TM Coverage
Text D	2	61.23%
Text E	2	78.16%
Text F	2	59.15%
Average	2	66,18%
Text G	3	88.27%
Text H	3	59.92%
Text I	3	65.16%
Average	3	71,12%

Table 1: TM Coverage

We provided different texts and levels of coverage to investigate the impact of this variable. We assured an equal distribution of texts among translators: each text was translated by 5 translators. This allowed us to calculate average results and to consider the average TM coverage difference of 4,93% between experiment 2 and 3.

4 Results

We observed performance gain when using any of the two TMs, which was expectable. The results varied according to the coverage of the TM. In experiment number 3, texts contained on average over 7 segments with 100% matches[6] and experiment number 2 only 2.68. This allowed translators to finish the task faster in experiment number 3. The average results obtained in the different experiments are presented in table number 2.[7]

Criteria	Exp. 1	Exp. 2	Exp. 3
Number of Segments	15.85	15.47	17.29
Number of Tokens	209.86	202.89	264.53
Context Matches		6.58	6.06
Repetitions			0.18
100%		2.68	7.18
95% to 99%		0.42	0.12
85% to 94%		0.21	
75% to 84%		2.11	0.18
50% to 75%			0.19
New Segments	15.86	5.89	3.24
Time Elapsed (mins.)	37m45s	26m3s	19m21s

Table 2: Average Scores

[6]Translators were allowed to modify 100% and context matches.

[7]According to the Trados Studio documentation, a *repetition* occurs every time the tool finds the exact same segment in another (or the same) file the user is translating

As to the time spent per segment, experiments indicate a performance gain of over 52% in experiment number 3 and over 28% in experiment number 2.

Criteria	Exp.1	Exp. 2	Exp. 3
Time Segment (mins.)	2m22s	1m41s	1m07s
Average gain to 1		+28.87%	+52.82%
Average gain to 2			+33.77%

Table 3: Time per Segment

Apart from the expectable performance gain when using TM, we also found a considerable difference between the use of the modified and unmodified TM. Translators completed segments in experiment number 3, on average, 33.77% faster than experiment two. The difference of coverage between the two TMs was 4,93%, which suggests that a few percentage points of TM coverage results on a greater performance boost.

We also have to acknowledge that the experiments were carried out by translators in the same order in which they are presented in this paper. This may, of course, influence performance in all three experiments as translators were more used to the task towards the end of the experiment. One hypothesis is that the poor performance in experiment 1, could be improved if this task was done for last and conversely, the performance boost observed in experiment 3, could be a bit lower if this experiment was done first. This variable was not explored in similar productivity studies such as those presented in section two and, to our understanding, inverting the order of tasks could be an interesting variable to be tested in future experiments.

As a general remark, although all translators had experience with the 2014 version of Trados Studio, we observed a great difficulty in performing simple tasks with Windows for at least half of the group. Simple operations such as copying, renaming and moving files or creating folders in the file system were very time consuming. Trados interface also posed difficulties to translators. For example, the generation of reports through batch tasks in a different window was for most translators confusing. These operations could be simplified as it is in other CAT tools such as memoQ.[8]

[8]http://kilgray.com/products/memoq

4.1 A Glance at Quality Estimation

One of the future directions that this work will take is to investigate the quality of human translations. Our initial hypothesis is that it is possible to apply state-of-the-art metrics such as BLEU (Papineni et al., 2002) or METEOR (Denkowski and Lavie, 2011) to estimate the quality of these translations regardless of how they are produced.

For machine translation output, quality nowadays is measured by automatic evaluation metrics such as the aforementioned IBM BLEU (Papineni et al., 2002), NIST (Doddington, 2002), METEOR (Denkowski and Lavie, 2011), the Levenshtein (1966) distance based WER (word error-rate) metric, the position-independent error rate metric PER (Tillmann et al., 1997) and the translation error rate metric TER (Snover et al., 2006) with its newer version TERp (Snover et al., 2009).

The most frequently used one is IBM BLEU (Papineni et al., 2002). It is easy to use, language-independent, fast and requires only the candidate and reference translation. IBM BLEU is based on the n-gram precision by matching the machine translation output against one or more reference translations. It accounts for adequacy and fluency through word precision, respectively the n-gram precision, by calculating the geometric mean. Instead of recall, in IBM BLEU the brevity penalty (BP) was introduced.

Different from IBM BLEU, METEOR evaluates a candidate translation by calculating the precision and recall on unigram level and combining them in a parametrized harmonic mean. The result from the harmonic mean is than scaled by a fragmentation penalty which penalizes gaps and differences in word order.

For our investigation we applied METEOR on the human translated text. Our intention is to test whether we can reproduce the observations from the experiments: is the experiment setting 3 better than the setting of experiment 2? Therefore, METEOR is used here to investigate whether we can correlate it with our experiments and not to evaluate the produced translations. Table number 4 presents the scores obtained with METEOR.

	Exp. 2	Exp. 3
Average Score (mean)	0.14	0.41
Best Result	0.35	0.58
Worst Result	0.11	0.25

Table 4: METEOR Scores

In experiment number 3 we have previously observed that the translators' performance was significantly better and that translators could translate each segment on average 33.77% faster than experiment 2 and 52.82% faster than experiment 1. By applying METEOR scores we can also observe that experiment 3 achieved higher scores which seems to indicate more suitable translations than experiment number 2. Quality estimation is one of the aspects we would like to explore in future work.

5 Conclusion

This paper is a first step towards the comparison of different TMs produced with MT output and their direct impact in human translation. Our study shows a substantial improvement in performance with the use of translation memories containing MT output used trough commercial CAT software. To our knowledge this experiment setting was not tested in similar studies, which makes our paper a new contribution in the study of translators' performance. Although the performance gain seems intuitive, the quantification of these aspects within a controlled experiment was not substantially explored.

We opted for the use of a state-of-the-art commercial CAT tool as this is the real-world scenario that most translators face everyday. In comparison to translating without TM, translators were on average 28.87% faster using a modified TM and 52.82% using an unmodified one. Between the two TMs we observed that translators were on average 33.77% faster when using the unmodified TM. As previously mentioned, the order in which this tasks were carried out should be also taken into account. The performance boost of 33.77% when using a TM that is only 4,93% better is also an interesting outcome of our experiments that should be looked at in more detail.

Finally, in this paper we used METEOR scores to assess whether it is possible to correlate translations' speed, quality and TM coverage. The average score for experiment number 2 was 0.14 and for experiment number 3 was 0.41. Our initial analysis suggests that a relation between the two variables exists for our dataset. Whether this relation can be found in other scenarios is still an open question and we wish to investigate this variable more carefully in future work.

5.1 Future Work

We consider these experiments as a pilot study that was carried out to provide us a set of variables that we wish to investigate further. There are a number of aspects that we wish to look in more detail in future work.

Future experiments include the aforementioned quality estimation analysis by applying state-of-the-art metrics used in machine translation. Using these metrics we would like to explore the extent to which it is possible to use automatic methods to study the interplay between quality and performance in computer assisted translation. Furthermore, we would like to perform a qualitative analysis of the produced translations using human annotators and inter annotator agreement (Carletta, 1996).

The performance boost observed between scenarios 2 and 3 should be looked in more detail in future experiments. We would like to replicate these experiments using other different TMs and explore this variable more carefully. Another aspect that we would like to explore in the future is the direct impact of the use of different CAT tools. Does the same TM combined with different CAT tools produce different results? When conducting these experiments, we observed that a simplified interface may speed up translators' work considerably.

Other directions that our work will take include controlling other variables not taken into account in this pilot study such as: the use of terminological databases, spelling correctors, etc. How and to which extent do they influence performance and quality? Finally, we would also like to use eye-tracking to analyse the focus of attention of translators as it was done in previous experiments (O'brien, 2006).

Acknowledgments

We thank the students who participated in these experiments for their time. We would also like to thank the detailed feedback provided by the anonymous reviewers who helped us to increase the quality of this paper.

References

Lynne Bowker. 2005. Productivity vs quality? a pilot study on the impact of translation memory systems. *Localisation Reader*, pages 133–140.

Jean Carletta. 1996. Assessing agreement on classification tasks: The kappa statistic. *Computational Linguistics*, 22(2):249–254.

Mauro Cettolo, Christophe Servan, Nicola Bertoldi, Marcello Federico, Loic Barrault, and Holger Schwenk. 2013. Issues in incremental adaptation of statistical mt from human post-edits. In *Proceedings of the MT Summit XIV Workshop on Post-editing Technology and Practice (WPTP-2)*, Nice, France.

Michael Denkowski and Alon Lavie. 2011. Meteor 1.3: Automatic Metric for Reliable Optimization and Evaluation of Machine Translation Systems. In *Proceedings of the EMNLP 2011 Workshop on Statistical Machine Translation*.

George Doddington. 2002. Automatic evaluation of machine translation quality using n-gram co-occurrence statistics. In *Proceedings of the Second International Conference on Human Language Technology Research*, HLT 2002, pages 138–145, San Francisco, CA, USA. Morgan Kaufmann Publishers Inc.

Marcello Federico, Alessandro Cattelan, and Marco Trombetti. 2012. Measuring user productivity in machine translation enhanced computer assisted translation. In *Proceedings of Conference of the Association for Machine Translation in the Americas (AMTA)*.

Spence Green, Jeffrey Heer, and Christopher D Manning. 2013. The efficacy of human post-editing for language translation. In *Proceedings of the SIGCHI Conference on Human Factors in Computing Systems*.

Ana Guerberof. 2009. Productivity and quality in the post-editing of outputs from translation memories and machine translation. *Localisation Focus*, 7(1):133–140.

Ana Guerberof. 2012. *Productivity and Quality in the Post-Edition of Outputs from Translation Memories and Machine Translation*. Ph.D. thesis, Rovira and Virgili University Tarragona.

Elina Lagoudaki. 2008. The value of machine translation for the professional translator. In *Proceedings of the 8th Conference of the Association for Machine Translation in the Americas*, pages 262–269, Waikiki, Hawaii.

Samuel Läubli, Mark Fishel, Gary Massey, Maureen Ehrensberger-Dow, and Martin Volk. 2013. Assessing post-editing efficiency in a realistic translation environment. In *Proceedings of MT Summit XIV Workshop on Post-editing Technology and Practice*.

Vladimir Iosifovich Levenshtein. 1966. Binary codes capable of correcting deletions, insertions and reversals. *Soviet Physics Doklady*, (8):707–710, February.

Lucia Morado Vazquez, Silvia Rodriguez Vazquez, and Pierrette Bouillon. 2013. Comparing forum data post-editing performance using translation memory and machine translation output: a pilot study. In *Proceedings of the Machine Translation Summit XIV)*, Nice, France.

Sharon O'brien. 2006. Eye-tracking and translation memory matches. *Perspectives: Studies in Translatology*, 14:185–204.

Kishore Papineni, Salim Roukos, Todd Ward, and Wei-Jing Zhu. 2002. Bleu: A method for automatic evaluation of machine translation. In *Proceedings of the 40th Annual Meeting on Association for Computational Linguistics*, ACL '02, pages 311–318, Stroudsburg, PA, USA. Association for Computational Linguistics.

Mirko Plitt and François Masselot. 2010. A productivity test of statistical machine translation post-editing in a typical localisation context. *The Prague Bulletin of Mathematical Linguistics*, 93:7–16.

Matthew Snover, Bonnie Dorr, Richard Schwartz, Linnea Micciulla, and John Makhoul. 2006. A study of translation edit rate with targeted human annotation. In *Proceedings of Association for Machine Translation in the Americas*, AMTA.

Matthew Snover, Nitin Madnani, Bonnie Dorr, and Richard Schwartz. 2009. Fluency, adequacy, or hter? exploring different human judgments with a tunable mt metric. In *Proceedings of the Fourth Workshop on Statistical Machine Translation at the 12th Meeting of the European Chapter of the Association for Computational Linguistics*, EACL 2009.

Harold Somers and Gabriela Fernandez Diaz. 2004. Translation memory vs. example-based mt: What is the difference? *International Journal of Translation*, 16(2):5–33.

Lucia Specia. 2011. Exploiting objective annotations for measuring translation post-editing effort. In *Proceedings of the 15th Conference of the European Association for Machine Translation*, pages 73–80, Leuven, Belgium.

Jörg Tiedemann. 2012. Parallel data, tools and interfaces in opus. In *Proceedings of the Eight International Conference on Language Resources and Evaluation (LREC'12)*, Istanbul, Turkey. European Language Resources Association (ELRA).

Christoph Tillmann, Stephan Vogel, Hermann Ney, Alexander Zubiaga, and Hassan Sawaf. 1997. Accelerated dp based search for statistical translation. In *European Conference on Speech Communication and Technology*, EUROSPEECH 1977, pages 2667–2670.

Speech-Enabled Computer-Aided Translation: A Satisfaction Survey with Post-Editor Trainees

Bartolomé Mesa-Lao
Center for Research and Innovation in Translation and Translation Technology
Department of International Business Communication
Copenhagen Business School, Denmark
bm.ibc@cbs.dk

Abstract

The present study has surveyed post-editor trainees' views and attitudes before and after the introduction of speech technology as a front end to a computer-aided translation workbench. The aim of the survey was (i) to identify attitudes and perceptions among post-editor trainees before performing a post-editing task using automatic speech recognition (ASR); and (ii) to assess the degree to which post-editors' attitudes and expectations to the use of speech technology changed after actually using it. The survey was based on two questionnaires: the first one administered before the participants performed with the ASR system and the second one at the end of the session, once they have actually used ASR while post-editing machine translation outputs. Overall, the results suggest that the surveyed post-editor trainees tended to report a positive view of ASR in the context of post-editing and they would consider adopting ASR as an input method for future post-editing tasks.

1 Introduction

In recent years, significant progress has been made in advancing automatic speech recognition (ASR) technology. Nowadays it can be found at the other end of customer-support hotlines, it is built into operating systems and it is offered as an alternative text-input method in many mobile devices. This technology is not only improving at a steady pace, but is also becoming increasingly usable and useful.

At the same time, the translation industry is going through a societal and technological change in its evolution. In less than ten years, the industry is considering new tools, workflows and solutions to service a steadily growing market. Given the significant improvements in machine translation (MT) quality and the increasing demand for translations, post-editing of MT is becoming a well-accepted practice in the translation industry, since it has been shown to allow for larger volumes of translations to be produced saving time and costs.

Against this background, it seems reasonable to envisage an era of converge in the future years where speech technology can make a difference in the field of translation technologies. As post-editing services are becoming a common practice among language service providers and ASR is gaining momentum, it seems reasonable to explore the interplay between both fields to create new business solutions and workflows.

In the context of machine-aided human translation and human-aided machine translation, different scenarios have been investigated where human translators are brought into the loop interacting with a computer through a variety of input modalities to improve the efficiency and accuracy of the translation process (e.g., Dragsted et al. 2011, Toselli et al. 2011, Vidal 2006). ASR systems have the potential to improve the productivity and comfort of performing computer-based tasks for a wide variety of users, allowing them to enter both text and commands into the computer using just their voice. However, further studies need to be conducted to build up new knowledge about the way in which state-of-the-art ASR software can be applied to one of the most common tasks translators face nowadays, i.e. post-editing of MT outputs.

The present study has two related objectives: First, to report on a satisfaction survey with post-editor trainees after showing them how to use ASR in post-editing tasks. Second, based on the feedback provided by the participants, to assess the change in users' expectations and acceptance of ASR technology as an alternative input method for their daily work.

2 Method

In this study, we explore the potential of combining one of the most popular computer-aided translation workbenches in the market (i.e. memoQ) with one of the most well-known ASR packages (i.e. Dragon Naturally Speaking from Nuance).

2.1 Overview

Two questionnaires were developed and deployed as a survey. The survey was divided into two phases, a prospective phase in which we surveyed post-editor trainees' views and expectations toward ASR and a subsequent retrospective phase in which actual post-editor's experiences and satisfaction with the technology were surveyed. Participants had to answer a 10-item questionnaire in the prospective phase and a 7-item questionnaire in the retrospective phase. These two questionnaires partially overlapped, allowing us to compare, for each participant, the answers given before and after the introduction and use of the target technology.

2.2 Participants profile

Participants were recruited through the Universitat Autònoma de Barcelona (Spain). The group included 11 females and 4 males, ranging in age from 22 to 35. All 15 participants had a full degree in Translation and Interpreting Studies and were regular users of computer-aided translation software (mainly memoQ and SDL Trados Studio). All of them had already performed MT post-editing tasks as part of their previous training as translators and, at the moment of the data collection, they were also taking a 12-hour course on post-editing as part of their master's degree in Translation. None of the participants had ever user Dragon Naturally Speaking, but four participants declared to have tried the speech input options in their mobile phones to dictate text messages.

2.3 Procedure

Individual sessions occurred at a university office. In the first part of the session, each participant had to complete an on-line questionnaire. This initial survey covered the following topics:

1. General information about their profile as translators; including education, years of experience and employment status.
2. Background in computer-aided translation software in their daily life as professional translators.
3. Experience in the field of post-editing MT outputs and training received.
4. Information about their usage of ASR as compared to other input methods and, if applicable, likes and dislike about it.

In the second part of the session, after the initial questionnaire was completed, all participants performed two post-editing tasks under the following two input conditions (one each):

- Condition 1: non-ASR input modality, i.e. keyboard and mouse.
- Condition 2: ASR input modality combined with other non-ASR modalities, i.e. keyboard and mouse.

The language pair involved in the tasks was Spanish to English[1]. Two different texts from the domain of mobile phone marketing were used to perform the post-editing tasks under condition 1 and 2. These two texts were imported to a memoQ project and then fully pre-translated using MT coming from the Google API plug-in in memoQ. The order of the two input conditions and the two texts in each condition were counterbalanced across participants.

In an attempt to unify post-editing criteria among participants, all of them were instructed to follow the same post-editing guidelines aiming at a final high-quality target text[2]. In the ASR input condition, participants also read in hard copy the most frequent commands in Dragon Naturally Speaking v.10 that they could use to post-edit using ASR (*Select <w>, Scratch that, Cut that*, etc.). All of them had to do the basic training tutorial included in the software (5 minutes training on average per participant) in order to improve the recognition accuracy. Following the training, participants also had the chance to practice the dictation of text and commands before actually performing the two post-editing tasks.

[1] Participants performed from L1 to L2.

[2] The post-editing guidelines distributed in hard copy were: i) Retain as much raw MT as possible; ii) Do not introduce stylistic changes; iii) Make corrections only where absolutely necessary, i.e. correct words and phrases that are clearly wrong, inadequate or ambiguous according to English grammar; iv) Make sure there are no mistranslations with regard to the Spanish source text; v) Publishable quality is expected.

In the third part of the session, participants completed a 7-item post-session questionnaire regarding their opinions about ASR while post-editing.

2.4 Data collection and analysis

Survey data

For questionnaires' data, responses to quantitative items were entered into a spreadsheet and mean responses were calculated across participants. For a comparison of responses to different survey items, paired statistics were used: paired t-test for items coded as ordinal variables, and chi-square test for items coded as categorical variables. The questionnaires did not include open-ended questions or comments.

Task log files

For task performance data (which is not going to be elaborated in this paper), computer screen including audio was recorded using BB FlashBack Recorder Pro v. 2.8 from Blueberry Software. With the use of the video recordings, a time-stamped log of user actions and ASR system responses was produced for each participant. Each user action was coded for the following: (i) input method involved; (ii) for the post-editing task involving ASR, text entry rate in the form of text or commands, and (iii), for the same task, which method of error correction was used.

Satisfaction data

Responses to the post-session questionnaire were entered and averaged. We computed an overall ASR "satisfaction score" for each participant by summing the responses to the seven items that related to satisfaction with ASR. We computed a 95 percent confidence interval (CI) for the mean of the satisfaction score to create bounded estimated for the satisfaction score.

3 Survey results

3.1 Usage of speech input method

To determine why participants would decide to use ASR in the future to post-edit, we asked them to rate the importance of eight different reasons, on a scale of 1 to 7, with 7 being the highest in importance. The top reason for deciding to use ASR was that it would involve less fatigue (Table 1).

Reasons for using speech input method	Mean	95% CI
Less fatigue	5.6*	4.9, 6.4
Speed	5.5*	4.8, 6.3
Ease of use	4.9*	4.7, 5.3
Cool technology	4.7*	4.0, 4.8
Limited alternatives	3.1	2.9, 3.3
Accuracy	2.9	2.1, 3.2
Personal preference	2.7	2.3, 2.9
Others	1	1, 1.2

* Reasons with importance significantly greater than neutral rating of 4.0 ($p < 0.05$)

Table **1**: Importance of reasons for using automatic speech recognition (ASR), rated on a scale from 1 to 7.

3.2 Usage of non-speech input methods

Since none of the participants had ever used ASR to perform any of their translation or post-editing assignments before, and in order to understand the relative usage data, we also asked participants about their reasons for choosing non-speech input methods (i.e. keyboard and mouse). For this end, they rated the importance of six reasons on a scale of 1 to 7, with 7 being most important. In the introductory questionnaire, most participants believed that keyboard short-cuts would be quicker and easier than using spoken commands (Table 2).

Reasons for using non-speech input methods	Mean	95% CI
They are easier	6.5*	5.7, 6.8
Less setup involved	6.1*	5.5, 6.3
Frustration with speech	5.9*	5.2, 6.1
They are faster	3.1	2.7, 3.8
Just for variety	2.0	1.3, 2.8
To rest my voice	1.3	1.1, 2.3

* Reasons with importance significantly greater than neutral rating of 4.0 ($p < 0.05$)

Table **2**: Importance of reasons for choosing non-speech input methods instead of automatic speech recognition, rated on a scale from 1 to 7.

Having to train the system (setup involved) in order to improve recognition accuracy or donning a headset for dictating was initially perceived as a barrier for using ASR as the preferred input method. According to the survey, participants would also choose other input methods when ASR performed poorly or not at all, either in general or for dictating particular commands (e.g., for some participants the command *Cut that* was consistently recognized as *Cap that*). Less important reasons were the need to rest one's voice or to switch methods just for variety.

3.3 Opinions about speech and non-speech input methods

Participants rated their satisfaction with 10 usability indicators for both ASR and non-ASR alternatives (Tables 3 and 4).

Likes	% responding *yes*	
	ASR	Non-ASR
Ease	85.3	91.9
Speed	74.9	88.6
Less effort	73.9	75.3
Fun	62.3	23.6
Accuracy	52.7	85.3
Trendy	39.5	23.1

Table **3**: Percentage of participants who liked particular aspects of the automatic speech recognition (ASR) system and non-speech input methods.

Dislikes	% responding *yes*	
	ASR	Non-ASR
Fixing recognition mistakes	74.5	–
Disturbs colleagues	45.9	–
Setup involved	36.8	–
Fatigue	17.3	12.7

Table **4**: Percentage of participants who disliked particular aspects of the automatic speech recognition (ASR) system and non-speech input methods.

ASR for translator-computer interaction succeeds at easing the task (its most-liked benefit). Almost 75% liked the speed they archived with ASR, despite being slower when compared against non-ASR input methods. Almost 74% liked the effort required to use ASR, and only 17.3% found it fatiguing. Participant's largest complaint with ASR was related to recognition accuracy. Only 52.7% liked the recognition accuracy they achieved and fixing recognition mistakes ranked as the top dislike at 74.5%. The second most frequent dislike was potential work environment dissonance or loss of privacy during use of ASR at 45.9% of participants.

Ratings show significant differences between ASR and non-speech input methods, particularly with regard to accuracy and amusement involved (*Fun* item in the questionnaire).

3.4 Post-session questionnaire results

To further examine subjective opinions of ASR in post-editing compared to non-speech input methods, we asked participants to rate their agreement to several statements regarding learnability, ease of use, reliability and fun after performing the post-editing tasks under the two conditions. Agreement was rated on a scale of 1 to 7, from "strongly disagree" to "strongly agree". Table 5 shows participants' level of agreement with the seven statements in the post-session questionnaire.

Statement	Level of agreement	
	Mean	95% CI
1. I expected using ASR in post-editing to be more difficult than it actually is.	6.6*	6.5, 6.8
2. My performance with the selection of ASR commands improved by the end of the session.	6.5*	5.4, 6.9
3. The system correctly recognizes almost every command I dictate.	5.9*	5.5, 6.4
4. It is difficult to correct errors made by the ASR software.	2.9	2.3, 4.1
5. Using ASR in the context of post-editing can be a frustrating experience.	2.4	1.9, 3.8
6. I can enter text more accurately with ASR than with any other method.	2.1	1.7, 2.9
7. I was tired by the end of the session.	1.7	1.2, 2.9

* Agreement significantly greater than neutral rating of 4.0 ($p < 0.05$)

Table **5**: Participants' level of agreement to statements about ASR input method in post-editing tasks. Ratings are on scale 1 to 7, from "strong disagree" to "strongly agree", with 4.0 representing neutral rating.

The results of the post-session questionnaire show that participants had significantly greater than neutral agreement (positively) about ASR in the context of post-editing. Overall they agreed that it is easier to use ASR for post-editing purposes than they actually thought. They also positively agreed that the ASR software was able to recognize almost every command they dictated (i.e. *Select <w>*, *Scratch that*, etc.) and acknowledged that their performance when dictating commands was better as they became more familiar with the task.

When scores were combined for the seven statements into an overall satisfaction score, the average was 73.5 [66.3, 87.4], on a scale of 0 to

100[3]. Thus, this average is significantly more positive than neutral. 12 out of the 15 surveyed participants stated that they will definitely consider adopting ASR in combination with non-speech input modalities in their daily practice as professional translators.

4 Discussion

The results of the present study show that the surveyed post-editor trainees tended to report a very positive view on the use of ASR in the context of post-editing. In general, findings suggest that human translators would not regret the integration of ASR as one of the possible input methods for performing post-editing tasks.

While many questions regarding effective use of ASR remain, this study provides some basis for further efforts to better integrate ASR in the context of computer-aided translation. Some specific insights supported by the collected data are:

- Expectations about ASR were definitely more positive after having performed with speech as an input method. Participants positively agreed that it is easier and more effective than previously thought.
- Most of the challenges (dislikes) of ASR when compared to other non-input methods can be tacked if the user is provided with both ASR and non-ASR input methods for them to be used at their convenience. Participants' views seem to indicate that they would use ASR as a complement rather than a substitute for non-speech input methods.

5 Conclusions

Post-editor trainees have a positive view of ASR when combining traditional non-speech input methods (i.e. keyboard and mouse) with the use of speech. Acknowledging this up front, an interesting field for future work is to introduce proper training on correction strategies. Studies in this direction could help to investigate how training post-editors to apply optimal correction strategies can help them to increase performance and, consequently, user satisfaction.

[3] A score of 100 represents a strong agreement with all positive statements and a strong disagreement with all negative statements, while a score of 50 represents a neutral response to all statements.

Acknowledgments

We would like to thank all the participants in this study for their generous contributions of time, effort and insights.

References

Dragsted, B., Mees, I. M., Gorm Hansen, I. 2011. Speaking your translation: students' first encounter with speech recognition technology, *Translation & Interpreting*, Vol 3(1).

Dymetman,M., Brousseau, J., Foster, G., Isabelle, P., Normandin, Y., & Plamondon, P. 1994. Towards an automatic dictation system for translators: the TransTalk project. *Proceedings of the international conference on spoken language processing* (ICSLP 94), 691–694.

Koester, HH. 2004. Usage, performance, and satisfaction outcomes for experienced users of automatic speech recognition. *Journal of Rehabilitation Research & Development.* Vol 41(5): 739-754.

O'Brien, S. 2012. Translation as human-computer interaction. *Translation Spaces*, 1(1), 101-122.

Toselli, A., Vidal, E., Casacuberta, F. 2011. *Multimodal Interactive Pattern Recognition and Applications*. Springer.

Vidal, E., Casacuberta, F., Rodríguez, L., Civera, J., Martínez-Hinarejos. C.D. 2006. *Computer-Assisted Translation Using Speech Recognition. IEEE Transactions on Audio, Speech, and Language Processing*, 14(3): 941-951.

Author Index